KING
OBAMA

America's
Greatest
Danger

BY

WILL CLARK

KING
OBAMA

America's
Greatest
Danger

ISBN 13: 978-1491231708
ISBN 10: 149123170X

Published by
Motivation Basics
P.O. Box 6327
Diamondhead, MS 39525
Will01@aol.com

For more information about the author
visit
AuthorsDen.com

CONTENTS

INTRODUCTION

How does a country fail? What allows tyranny to prevail? Consider this comment in a local 'Letter to the Editor' that appeared May 27, 2013:

"Now that President Obama is in his second term, legislators are again trying to undermine his objectives for the country. At every opportunity -- Benghazi and the IRS, for examples -- legislators direct our focus away from the important issues confronting us."

Many American citizens have this same attitude about Obama. They believe his government bullying is make believe, and these Gestapo actions by our government are unimportant. Should we ignore these early warning signs of government tyranny and social, cultural, and moral decline? Consider this story from Investors Business Daily:

"The inexplicable raid nearly two years ago on a guitar maker for using allegedly illegal wood that its competitors also used was another targeting by this administration of its political enemies. On Aug. 24, 2011, federal agents executed four search warrants on Gibson Guitar Corp. facilities in Nashville and Memphis, Tenn., and seized several pallets of wood, electronic files and guitars. One of the top makers of acoustic and electric guitars, including the iconic Les Paul introduced in 1952, Gibson was accused of using wood illegally obtained in violation of the century-old Lacey Act, which outlaws trafficking in flora and fauna the harvesting of which had broken foreign laws.

In one raid, the feds hauled away ebony fingerboards, alleging they violated Madagascar law. (Not U.S. law) Gibson responded by obtaining the sworn word of the African island's government that no law had been broken. In another raid, the feds found materials imported from India, claiming they too moved across the globe in violation of Indian law. (Not U.S. law) Gibson's response was that the feds had simply misinterpreted Indian law.

Interestingly, one of Gibson's leading competitors is C.F. Martin & Amp; Co. According to C.F. Martin's catalog, several of their guitars contain "East Indian Rosewood," which is the exact same wood in at least 10 of Gibson's guitars. So why were they not also raided and their inventory of foreign wood seized? (Over 95 percent of this wood goes to China to make expensive $800,000 beds.)

Grossly under-reported at the time was the fact that Gibson's chief executive, Henry Juszkiewicz, contributed to Republican politicians. Recent donations have included $2,000 to Rep. Marsha Blackburn, R-Tenn., and $1,500 to Sen. Lamar Alexander, R-Tenn. By contrast, Chris Martin IV, the Martin & Amp; Co. CEO, is a long-time Democratic supporter, with $35,400 in contributions to Democratic candidates and the Democratic National Committee over the past couple of election cycles.

Gibson described "two hostile raids on its factories by agents (over 30 agents as reported later) carrying weapons and attired in SWAT gear where employees were forced out of the premises, production was shut down, goods were seized as contraband and threats were made that would have forced the business to close." Gibson, fearing a bankrupting legal battle, settled and agreed to pay a $300,000 penalty to the

U.S. Government. It also agreed to make a "community service payment" of $50,000 to the National Fish and Wildlife Foundation to be used on research projects or tree-conservation activities. The feds in return agreed to let Gibson resume importing wood while they sought "clarification" from India.

The Gibson Guitar raid, the IRS intimidation of Tea Party groups, and the fraudulently obtained warrant naming Fox News reporter James Rosen as an "aider, abettor, co-conspirator" in stealing government secrets are but a few examples of the abuse of power by the Obama administration to intimidate those on its enemies list."

Can anyone deny that this raid described above is anything less than the atrocities that began the Gestapo raids? It represents the singling out of an organization based on its political leaning. Is it any different than how tyranny and takeover of a nation began in any other autocratic movement that developed into total tyranny and trampling on Constitutional rights? Although this is a clear example of a growing pattern, it's not the most obvious sign of government danger looming on the near horizon. Everything the Obama administration does moves the acceptance and promotion of tyranny even closer to the brink.

And, here's another clear example of government overreach by Obama and his forces of evil. It's from a Michael Reagan comment, reported by Newsmax.com on August 4, 2012:

"It's taken more than 200 years, two world wars, an industrial revolution, and the dawn of the Internet, but the United States once again finds itself at the mercy of an intolerant king. Instead of a tax on tea, King Barack Obama and his Democrat Knights of the Fast Food Table seem intent on imposing a penalty on chicken — but not all chicken. They are only targeting poultry prepared by Chick-fil-A.

And it's not because King Obama has decreed that Chick-fil-A makes a product that is any way unsuitable for the American people. It's because Chick-fil-A President Dan Cathy had the audacity to make comments supporting the "biblical definition" of marriage as between a man and a woman — comments that directly conflict with the King's recent pronouncement on gay marriage.

Cathy's comments have undoubtedly infuriated the petulant king and his court, so much so that King Obama's mayors in Boston and Chicago issued proclamations of their own aimed at stopping further expansion of Chick-fil-A restaurants in their cities. This is nothing short of outrageous behavior by a king who is obviously out of touch with the rest of us peasants.

King Obama's rule is so egregious in fact that the traditionally left ACLU has weighed in on the side of Chick-fil-A. A senior attorney for the ACLU of Illinois reportedly told an interviewer that any government that can exclude a business for being against same-sex marriage, can also exclude a business for being in support of same-sex marriage. It shows you how far to the left that the Democrat Party has gotten when the ACLU can't support its positions.

Unfortunately, the King's bad behavior doesn't stop with the food we eat. Part of King Obama's healthcare law also took effect this week. It will essentially force most employer-based insurance systems to provide contraceptive services. The implementation of the healthcare mandate comes less than a week after a federal judge in Colorado temporarily blocked the government from enforcing its contraception requirement on the Denver-based Hercules Industry, a private manufacturer of heating, ventilation, and air conditioning equipment, which is run by a Catholic family.

This is a case where King Obama's Justice Department offered the head of Hercules a choice: Either give your employees free contraception or surrender your company to the crown. Put another way, give up your company, or give up your religion.

King Obama

Not only is my father probably rolling over in his grave right now, but I would be so bold to say that FDR and John F. Kennedy are too. We have a president who thinks he's a king. And America cannot afford four more years of a king who can so cavalierly discard the U.S. Constitution when it doesn't suit his political agenda.

I find it somewhat ironic that while the Justice Department is asking people to surrender their religion and their companies, some wealthy Democrats are giving up their passports to escape the tyranny of King Obama."

Should half our population continue to ignore these clear signs of growing government tyranny and support this Obama administration - as began the rise of other dangerous autocratic governments? Should Obama zealots continue to support the Obama mission - to harass and intimidate anyone who disagrees with his plans for our country? As I have reported in previous writings, Obama will not give up the presidency at the end of his current term. His actions suggest he wants a throne - an undisputed throne here in America; the America that once was 'the land of the free.'

But, how could this happen here in America? It's not possible; our system of government is designed to prevent this - isn't it? Perhaps our system of government is designed to encourage liberty and personal freedom, however there are no established safeguards to prevent a planned tyrannical takeover of our government. Who would take the first step to stop a devious tyrant who had set all the stages before he made the final bold despotic move?

Certainly it would not be the military. They are too autocratically controlled and cautious to make any overt action that could be interpreted as a coup against the established government. Any bold military leader opposing even a tyrannical president would be charged with treason and probably shot before a large following could be developed. With the military having to support him, who could initiate any other defensive action to defend our Constitution? No other organization possesses the assets or the organizational structure to stop a United States president who decides to become the unchallenged ruler. The first important question, however, must be how could we arrive at a critical position that would allow this to happen?

Perhaps the inception of the idea of a humanistic government evolving into authoritarianism began with George Orwell's book, '1984' published in 1949. This is the book that introduced the concept of 'Big Brother.' Although the concept of Big Brother has been glibly scoffed at for many years, the idea has never totally disappeared. It's lingered as a threat possibility of the future, but always as one of those impossible probabilities. Perhaps the idea of someone taking over total control of a modern nation is not an idea as alien as first believed. Many signs suggest that near possibility. But, what could create an environment that would support that foreign possibility?

Perhaps Orwell gave the answer to this question when he wrote that book. Under a section of the book titled, 'Ignorance is Strength' he described how some people use the 'ignorant' to support their own aims. He wrote:

"Throughout recorded time, and probably since the end of the Neolithic Age, there have been three kinds of people in the world, the High, the Middle, and the Low. They have been subdivided in many ways, they have borne countless different names, and their relative numbers, as well as their attitude toward one another, have varied from age to age; but the essential structure of society has never altered. Even after enormous upheavals and seemingly irrevocable changes, the same pattern has always reasserted itself, just as a gyroscope will always return to equilibrium however far it is pushed one way or the other." After a change in his story, he continues:

"The aims of these three groups are entirely irreconcilable. The aim of the High is to remain where they are. The aim of the Middle is to change places with the High. The aim of the Low, when they have an aim - for it is an abiding characteristic of the Low that they are too much crushed by drudgery to be more than intermittently conscious of anything outside their daily lives - is to abolish all distinctions and create a society in which all men shall be equal. Thus throughout history a struggle which is the same in its main outlines recurs over and over again. For long periods the High seem to be securely in power, but sooner or later there always comes a moment when they lose either their belief in themselves, or their capacity to govern efficiently, or both. They are then overthrown by the Middle, who enlist the Low on their side by pretending to them that they are fighting for liberty and justice. As soon as they have reached their objective, the Middle thrust the Low back into their old position of servitude, and themselves become the High. Presently a new Middle group splits off from one of the other groups, or from both of them, and the struggle begins over again. Of the three groups, only the Low are never even temporarily successful in achieving their aims."

So, how is Orwell's quote above applicable to events happening today? Is there any relationship? This is a continuing part of that 'Letter to the Editor' I quoted above:

"Legislators attempt to turn back time to the days when women had no rights to their own health and welfare. To the days before unions and the middle-class they helped to create. To those times when the elderly had no Social Security or Medicare to cushion them from life's hardships --- To the "Wild West," in which everyone could tote a gun anywhere."

Many letters and blogs similar to the ideas expressed in this letter appear every day that demonstrate the continuing blind allegiance to Barack Obama, the man who promised many things to many people who consider themselves the forgotten - the disenfranchised of society. These are the people George Orwell identified as the 'Low.' They are the same gullible people who believe a savior will appear to give them fairness, justice, and equality. They believe Barack Obama is that savior - because he promised them exactly what Orwell said the Middle would promise the Low for their support to overthrow the High. In the end, when the real Barack Obama shows himself, they will have less than they had before his promises. They will wait and hope for their next true savior - with even more hate in their hearts for those considered High.

My first inclination is to ask: How stupid and gullible can these people be? They should understand that too much power corrupts even one with the best intentions - if that person is allowed to wield that total power. That's the purpose for our protective Constitution - to dilute and prevent that total power from developing.

Our Constitution is not perfect in design, but it's the best and most protective ever devised by man. Who has openly expressed disdain of our Constitution? Barack Obama. He said it keeps him from doing some things he would like to do for more of the unfortunate in our society. The 'Low' believe those promises mean he plans to make society more equal for them. In reality that means he wants more of the Lows to support him so he can gain even more total control.

Why don't those 'gullible Lows' understand this? Actually, from personal experiences, I understand why they feel the way they do. I understand how they can be duped to expect free 'manna' from the sky with a leader who promises them what he knows he should promise. I had my moments. I do understand. I will explain that next.

1

HOPING FOR THE SAVIOR

To demonstrate and explain how I totally understand the feelings, the hopes, and the aspirations of those whom George Orwell's writing classified as the Low, I'll give a brief history of my background. It began as with many - my father had abandoned us, or was in jail. I don't know where he was.

My mother struggled day-to-day supporting two small children. While I was age two to five, we lived in a 25-foot trailer in a trailer compound near Ingalls Shipbuilding Company in Pascagoula, Mississippi, where my mother was a welder at the shipyard. The trailer park was a small government compound on Mantou Street, just off the Gulf of Mexico beach. None of the green government trailers had plumbing; and community bathroom and cleaning facilities were located in the center of the compound. My mother had to walk a mile every morning and evening going to and from the nursery. Of course, at my age at that time, I really wasn't aware of social or economic differences. I just knew we had less. I thought everybody ate bologna sandwiches at most meals - a slice of bologna and two pieces of dry bread.

The welding job ended in 1945 when the war ended. We had no other place to go, so we migrated back to central Mississippi which is where I was born, and lived awhile with relatives. Vaguely, I remember we lived with relatives on my father's side before we moved to Pascagoula where my mother got her job. When we moved back, I didn't see them again, and we lived with relatives on her side of the family.

She remarried when I was six, but she was still the primary family provider. She worked at a shirt factory in Union for a short time before she was laid off for awhile. During that time, she went to New Orleans and bagged groceries for tips at a large supermarket. About a month later she was reinstated at the shirt factory where she worked for many years. The shirt factory was operating under a supportive state program called: Balancing Agriculture with Industry. Many local women supported their families for many years working at that shirt factory. It closed years ago when that local production process could not compete with foreign manufacturers.

I haven't a clue how she did it, but she bought a fifteen-acre scrub, red-hilly farm, earning only fifty cents an hour at the shirt factory. It included a dilapidated old house that we repaired enough to live in, then upgraded it more several years later when asbestos shingles became popular. Now, those asbestos shingles are banned for health reasons. Six years later we even got indoor plumbing with real running water and a bathtub. The old outhouse deteriorated and collapsed a few years later. Those outhouses would have been useless without a free supply of Montgomery Ward and Sears and Roebuck catalogs.

Today, one might ask how would you take a bath without a bathtub or a shower. Without those conveniences, the way one does things is normal. It was normal to draw several buckets of water from the well, heat some of it on the wood-burning stove or the large black wash pot outside to mix and make the bath water warm, then stand up in the wash tub and bath yourself from the top down. It was simple - it was cumbersome and time-consuming, but it was simple. There were no computers, cell phones, or electronic games to distract one from the time needed to take a bath. We didn't even have a regular old-fashioned telephone like the ones you see in old movies.

I was probably about twelve when we got water and electricity. I remember we had to remove the fireplace and chimney to make room to build a bathroom in that location. In the wintertime the fireplace was a convenient place to read and study. It was also more comfortable than smelling the fumes from the kerosene lamp when we couldn't use the fireplace. Of course, you had to turn often when reading at the fireplace to keep from burning one side of your body.

A new electric lightbulb dangling from the center of the ceiling was like a bright sun. It was almost blinding, and you didn't have to place a book next to it to actually read the words. A bright new day had dawned - we actually had some of the things the 'rich' people in town had. My understanding of the differences in social and economic classes was beginning to creep into my consciousness.

Early on when we moved to the fifteen acres of scrub land, the farm, we got a cow named, Bossy. When I was old enough, maybe nine or ten, I had to milk Bossy twice a day - regardless of the weather or the temperature. Washing the cow parts with cold water, before milking, in the winter time was an interesting experience for both of us. It was an uncomfortable shock for Bossy, and it took forever to warm my hands after I finished. For those who are unaware, once a cow is programmed for milking, the milking must continue or it causes an uncomfortable problem for the cow. I don't remember how long Bossy lasted, maybe seven or eight years, but I do remember the unhappy ending. Anyway, it was sad for a fifteen or sixteen-year-old boy.

Even just one cow was valuable in those days. It was just after WWII ended and certain food commodities still were not available, especially butter and sugar. We usually had extra butter which we traded for sugar and other food items we couldn't find or afford. Most of the basic food items had been diverted to the war effort, therefore certain items, especially sugar, were rationed and required ration coupons. This was the time a new product to replace butter was created. It was called, 'margarine.' At that time, margarine was a block of white substance that had to be mixed with a colored liquid that came in a little capsule, to give it the yellow color. Until it was mixed, the margarine was a pure bright white block. It looked like a block of lard. Maybe it was lard.

During the last few months of Bossy's life, she had arthritis and couldn't stand up by herself early in the morning. Also, the milk she produced was unusable because it was cloudy and had lumps in it. But, I still had to milk her twice a day. She could usually get to her front legs by herself, but I would have to struggle with her to lift her rump off the ground.

Thinking back over sixty years, I vaguely remember we fed that milk to the pigs and cats. Anyway, it was a relief for both of us when, one night, Bossy finally died. The next morning I found her near the barn. Doing what was normal for poor farmers to do at that time, I hitched the mule to the slide, rolled Bossy's body onto the slide and buried her body on the hill across the gully-wash. We didn't replace Bossy because at that time buying milk was cheaper than caring for a cow.

A slide was a wooden sled without wheels that slid on two wood beams held in place with planks creating a floor. It was pulled along the ground with a horse or mule. The normal use for a slide was to transport feed or fertilizer to the fields - too far to hand-carry the hundred-pound bags. I still remember, as I threw the last shovel of dirt on Bossy, if that was the right way to dispose of a cow whose life had worn out helping support a family. I still don't know the answer to that question. Regardless, since I didn't bury Bossy deep, I'm sure the buzzards eventually feasted on the carcass.

King Obama

I was the older of two boys, so I had most of the farm responsibility. My mother still worked at the shirt factory, and my step-father was crippled, and operated a pool hall in town to keep himself occupied. He was a good guy, but wasn't able to do physical things, especially farm tasks.

When I was ten or twelve I started helping in the garden and a nine-acre field on the level land on the other side of the low area, the gully-wash. Ordinarily the garden was an acre, the corn field about five acres, and the cotton field about four acres. Often the corn field and cotton field were different acreage because the government had allocations for growing cotton. When our allocation was only three acres, we grew more corn. I often took some of the corn to the grist mill, about half a mile away to make cornmeal. Sometimes I would use the slide and sometimes the larger wagon. The remainder of the corn was used for the farm animals - when we produced enough corn.

In the dry years we didn't produce much corn. Also, corn was often attacked by mold before the ears developed. Often, we had to buy our cornmeal. In the spring and summer, my mother spent most of her evenings and weekends canning vegetables from the garden. We usually had plenty of food to eat, but not always what was preferred. Eventually, canned squash got pretty boring. Squash grew anywhere.

King cotton has an untold story that most people, today, could never even imagine. In those days, the 1950s, every farmer who called himself a farmer grew cotton. Even in the red clay hills of central Mississippi, where making anything grow - except squash - was tedious, cotton was still the status symbol. Most of my farming effort was spent in the cotton field. School time was even scheduled around the cotton season. Our school year was only eight months, from September to April. April was not too late to plant cotton, and if the weather was right, it would be ready to pick in August. And, even in September there was still enough daylight left to finish the field work after school.

(Even with only an 8-month school year, all 43 classmates graduated high school, most went to college, and all had successful careers. Not one of my classmates was ever on any welfare program, or ever asked the government for aid of any kind. This was in Mississippi, traditionally the most economically depressed and less educated state in the nation.

What was the difference? We were a proud class that understood we had opportunity - not a free ride with a fair share. We challenged and supported each other. We were born as WWII was ending, and were guided by the pride of our nation. We knew our country didn't owe us anything for just existing as a citizen. Furthermore, the prior generation had suffered a great economic disaster and had struggled through two world wars and the Korean conflict. Our parents wanted us to have something better.

Even with working a full-time job, and struggling with home life such as cooking without a modern stove and washing without a washing machine, they still took time to help their children with homework each night. They understood - and we trusted them. My mother got no further than the fourth grade, but she helped with my homework as long as she could. It was enough to set a study pattern.)

Some families had tractors, but most small farmers at that time still had a mule or a work horse. Until the last year I farmed, a mule pulled my plows: the middle-buster, the turning plow, the sweep, and the side-harrow. Each plow was for a different purpose. The laying-by plow was the side-harrow, which loosened the dirt near the plant to help finish growing. How profitable was a small cotton farm? It was similar to buying expensive fishing equipment - and catching only minnows.

During the three years I remember being the 'main worker' on the farm I did all the plowing. My brother helped with most of the hoeing 'chopping' cotton; during the rainy season and until it was 'laid by' it was a constant process because the grass kept growing. Then, the fall was 'cotton picking' time. This was a critical time, because when the cotton was 'ready' it had to be picked before it was damaged by rain. Rain damage decreased the quality of the fibre which decreased the price of the cotton. The highest price was for long and smooth fibre. It was always sold by 'grade.' To rush that picking process, my stepfather always hired four or five black people to help. Now, we can discuss prejudice and discrimination.

Cotton pickers, black or white, were customarily paid five cents a pound. A good picker, in an average cotton row, could pick a hundred to two-hundred pounds a day. I could never get beyond fifty pounds because I kept getting distracted by having to stop and weigh the others' bags when their bags were full. Anyway, that's my excuse. Those who picked a hundred pounds were paid five dollars. I never got paid for any I picked. Furthermore, during my off time, when I helped dairy farmers gather their bales of hay I was paid only three dollars a day. I was very proud of that three dollars, but I still felt there was some unfairness somewhere in that process. Was it discrimination; was it unfair; or was it just another dairy farmer trying to make a living?

When the cotton harvesting was completed, we usually produced two bales each season. I don't remember exactly, but I vaguely remember a bale of cotton began with about twelve hundred pounds of raw picked cotton. That produced a cotton fibre bale of about five hundred pounds. The rest of the raw weight, about seven hundred pounds, was cotton seed and debris. Two years I delivered the cotton to the gin, about two miles away, in a wagon pulled by two mules. The third year, I had the tractor to make the trip.

I never new exactly how much my stepfather was paid by the cotton dealer, but for the cotton and the cotton seed I think it was about two hundred dollar a bale; at least that's what I overheard, occasionally. Apparently, our income for the year, for cotton, was about four hundred dollars. Considering the cost of cotton seed, fertilizer, animal feed and cotton picking, there couldn't have been much profit in the cotton farming venture. It was zero - or less - and much hard work. And, although I'm a white Caucasian, I never got paid for the fifty pounds I picked. Perhaps the idea of discrimination is based on the view from one's position and expectations, not necessarily on the reality of what is.

So went the life of a small cotton farmer in the red clay hills of central Mississippi. The final death knell to the small cotton farmer was the boll weevil attack - and government's restriction against effective insecticides. Thank God for the boll weevil. It freed many small farmers and their families from King Cotton.

This is the basis of my understanding by many people of their feeling that government should be more attentive to their needs, that government should give them more help when they need it. Many times throughout that three or four years I followed behind that mule or horse pulling a plow, I would stop to rest on the flat high ground overlooking a mile or so on the horizon. I imagined there were many people out there, even within my view, who had more money than they really needed; that there were many people who inherited money without having to work or even do anything for it, and many people who cheated other people to get it.

Unaware of the dangers and destructiveness of socialist and communist concepts, I imagined how wonderful it would be if the government had all the money and would spread it evenly, share it, with all citizens. I imagined that would make everyone equal, and I wouldn't have to be embarrassed about the way I lived and the things I had to do. Even with that idea nagging me, I also knew that if I ever got a good job, even a regular low-paying job, that I could do something for myself.

Still, at that time, I felt that life wasn't fair to those of us who had nothing, not even a view of how to be different. Yes, while I toiled without a clear view of what my future would be or could be, I thought the government should more equally distribute the assets of our country. After all, it was the country for all of us. I was young and didn't realize the destructive force of that concept. I was cannon fodder for the

Democratic philosophy.

It was April, 1957, when I graduated from high school, and jobs were scarce. The military people who returned from Korea had filled most of the few jobs that were available after the conflict ended, and war production had halted. Most of my classmates either started college or moved to the larger cities to find jobs. Of course, I had no way to move anywhere to find a job. And, college wasn't even in my realm of consideration. I also had another problem competing for a job. I was a severe stutterer. I couldn't even walk into a business or a factory and complete a sentence to ask for a job. Who would hire someone who couldn't even communicate effectively when so many other more competent applicants were looking for jobs?

Understanding and accepting that, just before I graduated from high school I walked the almost two miles to town to visit the Air Force recruiter's office. The recruiter wasn't there, so I walked back home. About two hours later, while I was working in the field on the other hill across the gully-wash, I saw a blue car pull into our dirt driveway. The driver got out and waved at me across the way, about three hundred yards. After I ran bare-foot across the bottom and to the hill where our house was located, it was the Air Force recruiter waiting in our yard. He said someone had seen me near his office. (It was a small town - population 1600.) Two days after I graduated high school, I was in basic training at Lackland Air Force Base in San Antonio, Texas.

Basic training had many surprises. I imagined the physical training part would be difficult. I kept waiting for the hard parts, but they never came. I guess my hard farm life had prepared me for whatever physical challenges that were faced in basic training. Anyway, after the first few days, I never gave the physical challenges much thought.

The other major surprise was academics. There were more academic classes than I had imagined, including one in particular that I remember very well - speed reading followed by comprehensive tests. Being from a central Mississippi school, I imagined I should have been the least prepared for those academics. To my shock, the least prepared for those classes were trainees from Chicago and Los Angeles. Ordinarily, I was in the top ten percent of all graded academics. It made me reflect back to all my wonderful teachers. In all my classes at Union, Mississippi, every teacher loved their students, and every student totally respected their teachers. There was such respect among everyone. But, this was a new environment, where new and unexpected challenges appeared, especially for a stutterer.

One night while I was taking my turn at 'barracks guard' the duty sergeant called over the intercom system for a report. I don't remember what the question was, but I couldn't get any words from my mouth to answer the sergeant. He expected an instant reply, and when I couldn't say anything immediately, he appeared a few minutes later and charged me with 'sleeping while on duty.' He escorted me to the 'officer of the day' in the orderly room and filed his report. Even though the officer was only a second lieutenant, he understood what had happened and refused to process the sergeant's charge. I don't think the sergeant ever believed I had that stuttering problem, because he still wanted to press the issue - after all, can't everybody talk right?

That was probably the most embarrassing and humiliating thing that's ever happened to me. I couldn't even speak well enough to make a good case for myself. I wondered what would happen to me; should I be content to return to that cotton patch, and come what may?

Anyway, thanks to that astute second lieutenant I wasn't kicked out of the Air Force to return to the cotton field. Many military people jest about the ineptness of second lieutenants but my experience with the first one I ever met left me with great respect for them. He saved my future - and I didn't even know I had a good future planned for myself.

At the end of my eight weeks basic training, there was an urgent need for hospital corpsmen. I was one of the top ten percent in my class to be selected for that career. We remained at Lackland Air Force Base another eight weeks for basic medic (Navy-corpsman) training while we waited for the next Navy Corpsman School class to begin at Great Lakes Naval Training Center in North Chicago, Illinois. I don't remember the exact numbers, but I think it was about twenty of us from the Air Force who were mixed with about eighty or so Navy trainees. We were mixed in the ranks and in the barracks together as if we were one military unit - which we were at that time. I learned many strange new words from those Navy people.

Since I graduated number four in my corpsman school graduating class, I was the fourth to choose from as list of available Air Force bases with openings for enlisted medics. Keesler AFB was on the list when I had my choice, so of course I chose to return to my home state. Keesler was only 180 miles from my hometown, Union.

I arrived at Keesler during the Christmas-New Year holidays. While I was waiting for a hospital duty assignment the first sergeant assigned myself and three others to random details. One of those details was picking up pine cones and debris around the squadron area, which included an old WWII ramp-style hospital which had just been replaced by a new multi-story modern hospital. It snowed while we picked up pine cones. Finally, after another hour I gained enough courage, being the senior detail airman, to ask the first sergeant if we should continue working in the snow. He was surprised we were still out there doing our duty. I don't know if it's ever snowed more than two inches on the Mississippi coast since then, 1957.

After the holidays, I got my hospital duty assignment. Recognizing that I was a stutterer, I was offered a job in what was called 'central supply' at that time - the least desirable job in a hospital. That was before disposal items were available. My job was to gather and wash those soiled items such as rubber gloves, needles and syringes, bedpans, catheters, and all the surgical instruments. After they were washed, they were then sterilized in giant roll-in autoclaves.

Needles were washed by hand before they were sterilized. Then, I was too young to know about things such as hepatitis and other diseases transferred through a prick with a dirty needle. I got pricked hundreds of times.

Occasionally, I had to take equipment orders over the phone, but other than that I wasn't involved with patient or other staff communication. During that time, the only interesting deviation was having to prepare extra items while we were experiencing the Cuban Missile crisis. The Mississippi coast is not far from Cuba.

My life perceptions were changed about a year after that. I had anticipated remaining in the Air Force long enough to retire as a sergeant, and then have enough livelihood to live in a little house trailer somewhere near a river, or maybe just working at menial jobs forever just to survive, or maybe have another large garden. I still felt life was unfair and favored the rich - those who obviously had been endowed with wealthy families when they were born. I felt they never had to work hard and sacrifice for what they had. Otherwise, I was happy just surviving.

But, when I was the honor graduate at the end of a month-long first aid refresher course conducted by a nurse, named Major Constance Ziemba, she changed my life. She kept me in the classroom after the others had left to tell me something she said was 'important.' She said I must immediately enroll in college courses through the base education center. I didn't even know there was such a thing as the 'base education center' and I certainly was aware that I was incapable of passing any college courses. But, she was a major and I was an airman third class (one stripe) so what could I say? It was like God had given me an order. I couldn't look at that officer a week later and say I had not done what she said I must do.

I was late enrolling, and of all the amazing coincidences, the only class not already filled was the one I feared most - Speech 101. I'm not joking and I'm not exaggerating; it really happened. But, what could I say to God if I met her in the hall or in her clinic? I had no choice. I enrolled and paid my fifteen dollars.

The first few classes were on the basics of choosing an appropriate topic, coordinating the elements, arranging and organizing: introduction, body and conclusion. I think I made my first stand-up presentation on the fourth class night. The classes were two hours in the evening beginning at seven, twice a week.

What a surprise when I began my 5-minute speech. I was in a new and different environment with alien feelings and attitudes. I wasn't struggling for mere existence in an everyday setting. I was the center of attention, someone special, a college student who had the same presence as my classmates. I was more focused on the organizational structure and diction than on 'could I do it?' I just did it. I had never felt such awe.

That was the time my freedom was born. That didn't eliminate my normal stuttering in normal situations, but it did demonstrate that there was hope to overcome it. I had never had that feeling before. Perhaps Major Ziemba was a real angel after all - sent by God.

I enrolled in two courses for the next semester. That was four nights a week, for a total of eight hours a week. I still had my regular job in the hospital, and had to study in the spare time I could find. I didn't have time to participate on the squadron sports teams - which, at that time was the spawning ground for promotions. The lower ranks were nominated for promotion by a panel of sergeants within the unit, and approved by the unit commander. Understandably, those who played on the sports teams together were friends and more familiar with each other.

The popular young airmen were the first to get the few promotions that were available at that time. After the third cycle of being neglected for promotion in favor of airmen of much less time-in-grade and time-in-service, I felt I couldn't just keep watching it happen. Perhaps I was less qualified, but I thought it was time someone should prove I was less qualified if that were the case. This was not just about what's fair and right. It was also about money. A promotion would have been about another five dollars a month. Then five dollars was enough for a full tank of gas. I was also paying for my college classes.

Ordinarily, the 'proper' action to take in a case such as this was to use the 'chain of command' to ask the question. I had been in the military long enough to understand that the 'proper' way was not always the effective way. Having the writing skills I had gained through the college courses, I decided to write my congressman asking for an inquiry. I was cautioned not to do it by many superiors because it would be the 'kiss of death' to my military career. I wondered if it had ever been done before - and what had happened. I had to find out. I sent the letter to Congressman Authur Winstead, who was the representative for my old home location. He sent a reply saying he would look into it.

No official ever said anything to me about it, but about two weeks later I could detect different attitudes and glances from the squadron officers and senior NCOs. For whatever reason, I was the first person promoted at the next promotion cycle. A senior sergeant later told me that the letters 'P.I.' had been stamped on my personnel file. He explained that designated 'political influence,' and that my promotion was never in question. I was promoted to airman second class - two stripes, ordinarily identified as an E-3.

After another two years and the same situation with promotions, I wrote another letter expressing the same 'favoritism' concern. This time it was to Senator James Eastland. Again, I was the first to be promoted at the next promotion cycle. I assumed the squadron leaders could not explain why others with less qualifications than myself were being promoted ahead of me. Not long afterward, those promotion boards were removed from the squadron level. Now, formal tests play a major part in selection for promotions. I've always wondered if my two letters had any impact on removing the unfair promotion situation. I will never know.

During that time I was also completing more college courses. Some were during night school, and some were through a challenge test program through the USAFI system. I think that was an acronym for 'United States Armed Forces Institute.' After I had accumulated two years of college through those sources and Air Force training equivalents, I applied to test for Air Force Officer Candidate School (OCS.) Even if I didn't pass the test, or get selected for OCS, I knew it would help me finally get promoted to sergeant. That was my real goal.

After three attempts to pass the OCS test, a year apart, I finally passed it. While I was attending an NCO preparatory school on Keesler AFB, I got a letter announcing I had been selected for OCS at Lackland AFB, Texas. No spaces were open for the next class, so I was scheduled to attend the following class which would begin three months later, January, 1963. The most amazing coincidence is that it was the last class of Air Force OCS. I would attend the very last class. It had been replaced by OTS, Officer Training School, which required a college degree to qualify.

This was a bold step for a young man who just wanted to achieve the rank of sergeant - a young man who only a few years before had been jumping bare-foot over baby cottonmouth snakes from a snake bed unearthed by a plow - usually a middle-buster. How did I never step on one? Great peripheral vision, young reflexes, and familiarity with many snakes. The first time it happened I thought it was earthworms, until I looked closer. It was baby snakes, armed with potent poison when they are born.

During that three months waiting for the OCS class to begin, I took another college course, American Government. This was a new enlightenment about myself and what I believed. I thought I was a Democrat. While studying that book on American Government, I realized I was not a Democrat - I was one of those 'darn Republicans.'

It was that turning point when I realized I wasn't one of

those people standing on the sidelines waiting for big government to take care of them. I didn't need big government watching over my shoulder, telling me everything I had to do to get something from them. I wanted the freedom to do it myself - to make my own choices.

Suddenly, with a new and broader vision opened in my life I realized there were things more important than security. Perhaps freedom and liberty were at least a little more important for someone with a vision of doing something for himself or herself. Where was the pride and feeling of accomplishment if government gives everything to you? Suddenly I realized that when someone offers to care for you, you must give them part of your soul, part of your intellect, and all of your aspirations.

After all, what is the purpose for being a human? Is it to exist to have things; for the government to buy your soul by promising to take care of you? Or is the purpose for being a human to fulfill God's plan - to develop one's abilities as placed here on earth to represent life and presence?

Certainly God must have placed humans on earth to in some way represent his Glory in achievement. Certainly, He didn't put us here to watch us squirm and complain about survival and what we could get from a 'Big Brother.' When it all comes down to the basics, that's the fundamental difference in the philosophies between Democrats and Republicans.

Republicans say 'Let me have the freedom and the self-presence to honor God and His purpose for my existence. Dogmatic Democrats abhor and ridicule that idea. Their ideology is that one's success and achievement must be determined and manipulated within a controlled hierarchy.

I realized that a bloodsucking big government can only get bigger. When it gets too big, we are no longer citizens. We become sheep who provide food for those power-hungry zealots who use us for power food. In George Orwell's book, he calls those sheep 'Proles.' Proles must be a word puzzle he planted, but I haven't been able to decipher it.

I voted for John F. Kennedy for president, but at that time I felt he was the best choice for America. I voted for my feelings about the man, not for his party. I don't know what would have happened if he had lived longer. His successor, Lyndon Johnson, pushed the 'Big Brother' agenda into fast forward with his introduction of the 'Great Society' which sped us faster into the grips of a more controlling big government. Even some Republican leaders have been forced by public pressure to continue that destructive process.

My reality check from that U.S. Government class solidified my urges toward success from within my own instincts as I grew older and more worldly. I no longer rest, propped on a plow in the cotton field and wonder why I didn't get an equal share of my country's wealth. I emboldened the knowledge within myself that God's plan for me was more about effort and achievement than about physical things and wealth - certainly not a 'fair share' of anything. Obama's drive is to suck the blood from his flock of American sheep, those proles, so he can perch peacefully upon his well-deserved throne. But, which throne is his final goal? Could it be the one reserved for another in Jerusalem?

Anyway, before I let myself become distracted expressing my disappointment of my fellow citizens who raise the 'beast' to his prophesied throne, I was discussing my transitional understanding. Once I realized the concept of God placing us here on earth - to do something, not have something - I reinvigorated my actions toward that goal. At that time I was to face that question as an officer, which would give me more opportunities to contribute even more.

During the next fifteen years my assignments included Japan, the Philippines, Vietnam, and Turkey. Also during that time, my service was recognized with awards of The Bronze Star, the Meritorious Service Medal (with an oak leaf cluster, representing two awards) a Joint Services Commendation Medal, and an Air Force Commendation Medal. I put all my effort into serving my country - and the mission I felt God had assigned to me. Now, I see many of my fellow citizens trying to destroy all those things I worked hard and sacrificed for. During that time, my family also shared in many of those sacrifices of separation and uncertainty. My wife and children often had a 'fatherless' home.

So, to answer the questions: Do I know the feelings of a Democrat, or anyone else, who feels our government should give them more consideration and a share of America's bounty? Yes. Do I understand that personal responsibility is more important to one's development and purpose in life than begging on the sidelines or simply waiting for more? Yes.

In summary, a dedicated and die-hard Democrat cannot explain any feelings to me that I've not already experienced. I know - I understand. And I understand what makes the difference in waiting for the government to 'do something,' and the God-given responsibility to do something for yourself and others. We are not put here on earth to take; we are put here to contribute and share our great blessings with others.

No, Barack Obama, I do not want you to give me a fair share so you can own my soul. I want to accept the responsibility to serve God within His purpose, and to share my blessings with all those around me - those who respect those blessing. I will not help you create more Proles.

2

OBAMA'S HATRED OF AMERICA

Any leader of any country should always express his or her pride and confidence in that country. A president should be the image-maker and the promoter. Others do not have the forum to do that. It's a responsibility that should not be toyed with. Barack Obama, however, demeans America by expressing only his disdain of our country and our history. Consider the following examples expressed in his own words. These are only a few, but are representative:

1. Apology to the Muslim World. President Obama, interview with Al Arabiya, January 27, 2009.

"My job to the Muslim world is to communicate that the Americans are not your enemy. We sometimes make mistakes. We have not been perfect. But if you look at the track record, as you say, America was not born as a colonial power, and that the same respect and partnership that America had with the Muslim world as recently as 20 or 30 years ago, there's no reason why we can't restore that."

2. Apology at the G-20 Summit of World Leaders. News conference by President Obama, ExCel Center, London, United Kingdom, April 2, 2009.

"I would like to think that with my election and the early decisions that we've made, that you're starting to see some restoration of America's standing in the world. And although, as you know, I always mistrust polls, international polls seem to indicate that you're seeing people more hopeful about America's leadership.

I just think in a world that is as complex as it is, that it is very important for us to be able to forge partnerships as opposed to simply dictating solutions. Just to try to crystallize the example, there's been a lot of comparison here about Bretton Woods. "Oh, well, last time you saw the entire international architecture being remade." Well, if there's just Roosevelt and Churchill sitting in a room with a brandy, that's an easier negotiation. But that's not the world we live in, and it shouldn't be the world that we live in."

3. Apology to France and Europe. Speech by President Obama, Rhenus Sports Arena, Strasbourg, France, April 3, 2009:

"We must be honest with ourselves. In recent years we've allowed our alliance to drift. I know that there have been honest disagreements over policy, but we also know that there's something more that has crept into our relationship. In America, there's a failure to appreciate Europe's leading role in the world. Instead of celebrating your dynamic union and seeking to partner with you to meet common challenges, there have been times where America has shown arrogance and been dismissive, even derisive."

4. Apology before the Turkish Parliament. Speech by President Obama to the Turkish Parliament, Ankara, Turkey, April 6, 2009.

"Every challenge that we face is more easily met if we tend to our own democratic foundation. This work is never over. That's why, in the United States, we recently ordered the prison at Guantanamo Bay closed. That's why we prohibited--without exception or equivocation--the use of torture. All of us have to change. And sometimes change is hard.

Another issue that confronts all democracies as they move to the future is how we deal with the past. The United States is still working through some of our own darker periods in our history. Facing the Washington Monument that I spoke of is a memorial of Abraham Lincoln, the man who freed those who were enslaved even after Washington led our Revolution. Our country still struggles with the legacies of slavery and segregation, the past treatment of Native Americans.

Human endeavor is by its nature imperfect. History is often tragic, but unresolved, it can be a heavy weight. Each country must work through its past. And reckoning with the past can help us seize a better future."

5. Apology for U.S. Policy toward the Americas. Opinion editorial by President Obama: "Choosing a Better Future in the Americas," April 16, 2009.

"Too often, the United States has not pursued and sustained engagement with our neighbors. We have been too easily distracted by other priorities, and have failed to see that our own progress is tied directly to progress throughout the Americas. My Administration is committed to the promise of a new day. We will renew and sustain a broader partnership between the United States and the hemisphere on behalf of our common prosperity and our common security."

6. Apology to the Summit of the Americas. President Obama, address to the Summit of the Americas opening ceremony, Hyatt Regency, Port of Spain, Trinidad and Tobago, April 17, 2009.

"All of us must now renew the common stake that we have in one another. I know that promises of partnership have gone unfulfilled in the past, and that trust has to be earned over time. While the United States has done much to promote peace and prosperity in the hemisphere, we have at times been disengaged, and at times we sought to dictate our terms. But I pledge to you that we seek an equal partnership. There is no senior partner and junior partner in our relations; there is simply engagement based on mutual respect and common interests and shared values. So I'm here to launch a new chapter of engagement that will be sustained throughout my administration."

7. April 20, 2009, CIA Headquarters, Langley, VA:

"So don't be discouraged by what's happened in the last few weeks. Don't be discouraged that we have to acknowledge potentially we've made some mistakes. That's how we learn. But the fact that we are willing to acknowledge them and then move forward, that is precisely why I am proud to be President of the United States, and that's why you should be proud to be members of the CIA."

8. Apology for Guantanamo in Washington. President Obama, speech at the National Archives, Washington, D.C., May 21, 2009.

"Unfortunately, faced with an uncertain threat, our government made a series of hasty decisions. ... I also believe that all too often our government made decisions based on fear rather than foresight; that all too often our government trimmed facts and evidence to fit ideological predispositions. Instead of strategically applying our power and our principles, too often we set those principles aside as luxuries that we could no longer afford. And during this season of fear, too many of us — Democrats and Republicans, politicians, journalists, and citizens — fell silent. In other words, we went off course.

There is also no question that Guantanamo set back the moral authority that is America's strongest currency in the world. Instead of building a durable framework for the struggle against al Qaeda that drew upon our deeply held values and traditions, our government was defending positions that undermined the rule of law. In fact, part of the rationale for establishing Guantanamo in the first place was the misplaced notion that a prison there would be beyond the law--a proposition that the Supreme Court soundly rejected. Meanwhile, instead of serving as a tool to counter terrorism, Guantanamo became a symbol that helped al Qaeda recruit terrorists to its cause. Indeed, the existence of Guantanamo likely created more terrorists around the world than it ever detained."

9. May 3, 2013 in Mexico:

"Our attitudes sometimes are trapped in old stereotypes. Some Americans only see the Mexico that is depicted in sensational headlines of violence and border crossings — and let's admit it. Some Mexicans think that America disrespects Mexico, or thinks that America is trying to impose itself on Mexican sovereignty or just wants to wall ourselves off. And in both countries, such distortions create misunderstandings that make it harder for us to move forward together. So I've come to Mexico because I think it's time for us to put the old mind-sets aside. It's time to recognize new realities, including the impressive progress of today's Mexico."

These are only a few representative examples of what Obama really thinks about the United States and our heritage. He lists our mistakes and apologizes for his vision of our shortcomings. He has never spoken of all the good America has done for the world. That list would be endless.

It includes the sacrifice of our soldiers in two world wars. Thousands of patriotic soldiers, airmen and sailors lost their lives storming the beaches to rescue Europe from the evil grasp of the Axis powers. Thousands gave their lives on the beaches on the first day - during only a few hours.

America has given billions of dollars all around the world to help improve people's lives, even much of that money to many countries who hate us and would do us harm with only a little provocation. Does Barack Obama remind those countries he visits of those deeds and sacrifices of America? No! He condemns and criticizes America for what he perceives as ignorance, weakness, and lack of concern for other countries. And this man is our president?

Perhaps Michelle Obama expressed Obama's thoughts of America best when on February 14, 2008, in Milwaukee, Wisconsin, she said,

> "For the first time in my adult life I am proud of my country because it feels like hope is finally making a comeback." Then in Madison, she said, "For the first time in my adult lifetime, I'm really proud of my country, and not just because Barack has done well, but because I think people are hungry for change."

Would Michelle Obama have made this comment in the clear blue without that feeling having been prevalent in their household and their culture? Not likely. Obama continues to express that same lack of pride in America. Michelle Obama's comments were not momentary losses of reality. That was their reality. Even further, during Obama's first few events where it was appropriate to stand and say the Pledge of

Allegiance or to honor the flag, Obama presented only the 'crotch' salute. Someone in his administration must have told him it was proper to show recognition to our flag. For him, it wasn't instinctive or voluntary.

Furthermore, does Obama really recite the Pledge of Allegiance to our flag when it's appropriate? That precious pledge includes the words, 'Under God.' Does he skip that part if and when he cites the pledge? His actions and impulses suggest he has no respect for that God who protects our country, and watches over us in our daily activities. His actions toward God, and country, suggest he is a blasphemer of the worst kind. God will certainly turn His face from a country or a person who turns his face from God. That's clearly written. Examples of his blasphemy are plentiful. Below are described only a few.

On June 28, 2006, during his 'Call to Renewal' speech, he mocked three sections of the Bible, including the Sermon on the Mount, which he called 'so radical.' He asked, mockingly, "Can either of these be used to guide public policy?" Here is that unedited part of the speech:

> "Whatever we once were, we are no longer a Christian nation - not just; we are also a Jewish nation, a Muslim nation, a Buddhist nation, a Hindu nation, and a nation of nonbelievers. And even if we did have only Christians in our midst, if we expelled every non-Christian from the United States of America, whose Christianity would we teach in the schools? Would we go with James Dobson's, or Al Sharpton's? Which passages of Scripture should guide our public policy? Should we go with Leviticus, which suggests slavery is ok and that eating shellfish is abomination? How about Deuteronomy, which suggests stoning your child if he strays from the faith? Or should we

just stick to the Sermon on the Mount, a
passage that is so radical that it's doubtful that
our own Defense Department would survive its
application? So before we get carried away, let's
read our bibles. Folks haven't been reading
their Bibles."

How would one who blasphemes the Bible know what's in
the Bible? Furthermore, why would someone who refuses to
salute our flag, appropriately, use the Bible to try to prove a
political point. Is that, in itself, not blasphemy?

During Obama's remarks at a San Francisco fundraiser
in April, 2008, he attempted to explain the resentment of
many citizens in small towns in Pennsylvania. He stated, "

"You go into these small towns in
Pennsylvania and, like a lot of small towns in the
Midwest, the jobs have been gone now for 25
years and nothing's replaced them. And they fell
through the Clinton administration, and the
Bush administration, and each successive
administration has said that somehow these
communities are gonna regenerate and they have
not. And it's not surprising then they get bitter,
they cling to guns or religion or antipathy toward
people who aren't like them or anti-immigrant
sentiment or anti-trade sentiment as a way to
explain their frustrations." (He associated these
job losses to the Clinton and Bush
administrations. Has he associated himself to the
current major job and economic disaster in
Detroit?)

Again, this is another negative comment about America,
American citizens, and Christianity - which forms the major
principles of our country's foundation. His comment shows
contempt to Americans, and it demonstrates further

blasphemy against God. Although in his admonition to those citizens he does not specifically say "Christians." That is, nevertheless, the religion to which he refers.

In that short statement he criticized Clinton, Bush, and others who shared an interest in trying to improve people's lives. Then he blames their attitudes and opinions on personal characteristics. In his short statement, he equates guns, religion, prejudice (antipathy toward people who aren't like them) Hispanic haters (anti-immigrant sentiment) and anti-trade sentiment (against foreign competition) as an evil embodiment of those citizens. In other words: their attitude is their problem. Does this show love and respect for America and Americans? I think not.

On April 16, 2009, he required the monogram for the name of Jesus be covered before he made his speech at Georgetown University. The monogram above an archway was covered with black painted plywood. Certainly he would not consider this blasphemy against God and the Bible, or an insult to America, whose charter and pledge recognize God as part of our heritage and culture. Does that action by Obama demonstrate his love and care for America?

On November 17, 2011, in Canberry, Australia he made the following remarks in a Campbell High School classroom about American students:

"A lot of poor children don't get the support that they need when they're very young, so by the time they get to grammar school, they're already behind. They don't know their numbers, people haven't read to them, et cetera. So working with programs that are geared to young people -- or very young children, when they're toddlers and infants, to give them a head start. That's pretty important. We're focusing a lot on math and science education, where I think we've fallen behind."

Is this something a responsible American president would say in a foreign classroom about American students? Only if he had no respect for those American students or our country. Those comments were clearly irresponsible, disrespectful, and totally out of place. It made the inference that American students are illiterate, stupid, and uneducated.

Perhaps his comments reflected upon his own understanding and comprehension. Even if his comments were accurate his actions to resolve the problem he announced have been ineffective and insincere. He has gone out of his way to make education effectiveness in America even worse. He chose the worst educator in America to be his secretary of education.

Arne Duncan, the chief administrator of Chicago schools, was Obama's choice to lead education efforts and programs in the United States. Arne Duncan has no history of education success, and certainly has demonstrated that even his basic character is questionable. Why would anyone follow a leader who has demonstrated only incompetence, with a 45-50 percent dropout rate while he was in charge of Chicago schools - and it's still that rate - and speak other falsehoods which is a good indication of his character and intentions.

Arne Duncan recently discredited himself, his country, and our children. One would expect the education leader, the education secretary at the federal level would set an example of honesty to give his department unquestioned credibility. He dishonored that essential standard when he recently lied about results of the 2013 sequestration.

He claimed many teachers had been fired, already given their 'pink slips' because of the sequestration. In fact, no teachers had got their pink slips at that time for that reason. How can students believe in the system to which they must adhere if they know the leader of that system does not tell the truth? If they can't trust him, how can they trust the system that prepares their future? Arne Duncan's selection as secretary of education obviously demonstrates Obama's real ideas about improving education in America.

In a recent entry on my blog site at Authorsden, and in a letter to the editor of a state-wide newspaper, I emphasized that the U.S. Department of Education should be eliminated because it was ineffective, complicated the education process, and does not allow or encourage effective or reasonable education. Now, I've changed my mind. The U.S. Department of Education should be eliminated, destroyed, and totally obliterated; not because it's simply ineffective, but because it's a danger to our national safety and security.

Our education bureaucracy at many levels is ignoring education essentials to develop a successful person. Now, they are focused only on social and cultural aspects. Obama wants a compliant person in accordance with the prevailing plan; whether that be Socialist principles or Islamic dogma.

I repeat; we do not need a national education system. It detracts from educational results rather than supports it. Our education focus must be on our children - not on a system.

At the moment, the only plan by Obama is for our education system to produce more proles so he can increase his authority and influence. Too many educated people are dangerous for his plans - as were educated people in Orwell's book, '1984.' Big Brother could not have risen to power and maintained his influence without first creating enough proles. Education will never be improved under the Obama administration!

And, Obama is reinforcing himself with his disdain of America's past. He has selected Samantha Power for an important position that will allow her to guide his apologies even deeper with other world leaders. He has selected her to be the United States Ambassador to the United Nations. She will have influence and interaction with all countries of the world. Who is Samantha Power?

Samantha Power of the National Security Council might be considered the most extreme of Obama's appointees and advisors. She is extremely anti-Israel and suggests that Israel is the source of most problems in the Middle East. In an interview in 2002 she even said Israel should be invaded to force them to allow Palestine to set up a separate state. She also does not believe Iran is preparing a nuclear weapon and does not pose a real threat to its neighbors.

According to other reports she was also involved with the recent Libya event that resulted in the death of four Americans by Islamic terrorists. It's likely that her selection for the new position at the United Nations is a promotion to reward her for her silence about the Benghazi events. No one has revealed anything about that tragedy. Even Barack Obama, the man most in charge of making decisions during that night of terror, does not reveal his whereabout, or even if he was engaged with those events.

According to Leon Panetta, the Secretary of Defense at that time, he briefed Obama during the Benghazi attack. According to Panetta that was his only conversation with Obama during that night. What happened to Obama? Where did he go? Did he hide in the nearest closet - or was he too busy preparing his tele-prompter speech for his fund-raiser in Las Vegas the next day? He refuses to say. Later, he suggested the slaughter in Benghazi was just a 'bump in the road.' It really wasn't important?

And, where was Hillary Clinton while her subordinates were being massacred? She never said. She never said anything about it except to exclaim when asked before Congress, "What difference does it make!" These are the two people most responsible for those American lives at that time and all they can express is: "It' just a bump in the road," and "What difference does it make."

With these attitudes supporting America and Americans is it any wonder why many feel, as I do, that our country is in grave danger. The president's prime mission - his first priority - is to protect American lives - and all he can do is hide in his closet during the time of most danger then proclaim it only as a bump in the road after the filthy deed is done? What kind of leadership is that? It's either a denial of responsibility - or devising a harmful plan for our country to which the event is only 'a little bump in the road.' Does Obama need Samantha Power in a more important position to continue promoting more little bumps in the road to destroy our freedom?

Philip Klein of the Washington Examiner reports that Samantha Power's mea-culpa doctrine article observes that although the administration mocked Mitt Romney less than a year ago for suggesting that President Barack Obama undertook an "apology tour" to the Middle East in 2009, Samantha Power advocated just that. In a 2003 op-ed attacking the Bush administration in the liberal New Republic, Power proposed a "doctrine of the mea culpa" that would supposedly raise America's stature in the eyes of the world, likening it to the historic example of German Chancellor Willy Brandt kneeling at a Warsaw ghetto memorial. She wrote:

> "We need a historical reckoning with crimes committed, sponsored, or permitted by the United States. This would entail restoring FOIA to its pre-Bush stature, opening the files, and acknowledging the force of a mantra we have spent the last decade promoting in Guatemala, South Africa, and Yugoslavia. A country has to look back before it can move forward. Instituting a doctrine of the mea culpa would enhance our credibility by showing that American decision-makers do not endorse the sins of their predecessors. When Willie Brandt went down on one knee in the Warsaw ghetto, his gesture was gratifying to World War II survivors, but it was also ennobling and cathartic for Germany. Would such an approach be futile for the United States?"

Contrary to Democrat accusations that Romney made up the apology tour scenario out of thin air, Power is on record pushing for U.S. foreign policy to be completely re-worked so as to tell the world we are sorry. Power even implied that the kinds of horrors Nazis committed toward Jews have been carried out by the U.S. against other people around the world. In that context, Obama's visit to Allied-bombed Dresden, on a tour that included the Buchenwald concentration camp, may seem to make sense after all. End of Article.

Clearly, Samantha Power is a real danger to the security of the United States by any exercise of power or influence in or near the White House. Clearly also, her promotion to a higher level and more visible position is her reward for being a 'good soldier' for Obama's plans for America. His plans, certainly most devious, cannot be for the betterment of freedom and democracy. If that's not the case, then why is he keeping so many secrets? Why is everyone in his administration refusing to tell the truth, or anything, about their activities? They are hiding everything. Why?

But, Samantha Power is not the only Obama sidekick who represents hate and danger to America's future. Many more exist - in fact, most of Obama's closest advisors and supporters are guided by backgrounds and influences that are alien to America's heritage and ideals. They hate America and the idealism for which it stands. In summary, here are some of the most notable. More expansive information is about them on the internet.

Cass Sunstein was the Regulatory Czar. His is also married to Samantha Power. He recently resigned because Obama was not moving fast enough toward Sunstein's goals. He doesn't believe the Second Amendment should be an individual right for American citizens. He also promotes the idea that government should regulate all the airwaves under the concept of the 'Fairness Doctrine.'

Todd Stern, as the International Climate Czar, still clings to his climate change agenda. He promotes the idea that an international group should determine and dictate environmental policy, abrogating our national sovereignty under a more socialist dictate.

King Obama

John Holdren, as the Science Czar, promotes a world government that would determine allowable family size; which would be enforced by compulsory abortion, and implanted sterilization capsules and adding sterilizing agents to drinking water and certain food. He is another supporter of the 'world government.'

Mark Lloyd, Obama's Chief Diversity Officer, proposes more diversity and more censorship. He proposed this by fining conservative media to fund media opposing their views. He is also one of many of Obama's appointees who previously worked for George Soros. He also praised Hugo Chavez for his democratic revolution.

David Ogden, as Deputy Attorney General, is a great supporter of American family values. He supports the pornography industry and fought in support of those convicted of child pornography. He also supports the idea that free library computers should have no anti-obscenity filters, and children should be allowed to use them.

Susan Rice, the recent U.S. Ambassador to the United Nations, also has a history of activities opposed to the best interests of America. She firmly believes the United States should follow the dictates and aims of the United Nations, although much of that idealism is extremely anti-United States, including support that favors extremists who plan to harm us. While Ambassador to Sudan, she refused to acknowledge an offer by Sudan to hand over Osama Bin Laden, although he had already initiated attacks against the United States. She didn't think Al-Qaeda was a threat and blamed George Bush for creating problems by not giving full cooperation with the United Nations.

And, we should not forget our number one American patriot, Eric Holder. He doesn't know anything about anything, although his signature turns up in strange places that suggests he should know a few things. There's no doubt he will keep being Obama's attack dog as long as Obama keeps protecting him - a marriage made by a 'strange god'- a Biblical reference.

These are only a few Obama supporters, staff, and advisors who express the same hate toward American idealism as he does. There are many more who can be researched for their backgrounds and thoughts toward America. These include: Elena Kagan, Dawn Johnson, Rosa Brooks, Valerie Jarrett, David Axelrod, Preeta Bansal, Cecilia Munoz, Melody Barnes and Carol Browner.

Another name of great interest connecting Obama and many of his supporters, particularly Valerie Jarrett and David Axelrod, is that of Frank Marshall Davis. He was a card-carrying member of the Communist Party. This research provides some interesting connections and helps explain the many anti-American threats facing America from those within.

And, still another familiar name that we cannot exclude from making claims of atrocities by Americans to discredit America is that of John Kerry. Most people have forgotten his charges against his fellow military personnel. Hating America or making charges against honorable Americans seems to be the primary criteria for choosing someone to support his 'hate America' trend.

We should never forget what John Kerry said about Americans fighting for their lives in the jungles of Vietnam. As its dominant tactic in their battle against the war, the antiwar movement successfully demonized Vietnam veterans by calling a series of "tribunals" or hearings into war crimes. But... they were packed with pretenders and liars -- historian Guenter Lewy, writing in 'America in Vietnam:'

> "John Kerry's lies about the activities of the Swift boats were part of a larger pattern of deception. As a leader of the Vietnam Veterans Against the War (VVAW), Kerry testified before the Senate Committee on Foreign Relations on April 22, 1971, telling the Senators and a national audience that American troops "...had personally raped, cut off ears, cut off heads, taped wires

from portable telephones to human genitals and turned up the power, cut off limbs, blown up bodies, randomly shot at civilians, razed villages in fashion reminiscent of Ghengis Khan, shot cattle and dogs for fun, poisoned food stocks, and generally ravaged the countryside of South Vietnam..." and accused the U.S. military of committing war crimes "on a day-to-day basis with the full awareness of officers at all levels of command."

Kerry's charges were based on a VVAW conference called the "Winter Soldier Investigation" -- a leftist propaganda event funded primarily by Jane Fonda. None of the Winter Soldier "witnesses" Kerry cited were willing to sign affidavits, and their gruesome stories lacked the names, dates, and places that would allow their claims to be tested. Few were willing to cooperate with military investigators. The Naval Investigative Service found that several of the veterans said to have given statements at Winter Soldier were in fact imposters using the names of real veterans.

False testimony and exaggerations were primary characteristics of the war crimes disinformation campaign, and also of the VVAW itself. Executive Secretary Al Hubbard, for example, claimed to have been an Air Force captain wounded in Vietnam piloting a transport plane. In fact, Hubbard had been a staff sergeant who was not a pilot and who was never assigned to Vietnam.

John Kerry and the VVAW worked closely with America's wartime enemies, arranged multiple meetings with the North Vietnamese and Vietcong leadership, and consistently supported their positions. Kerry and his radical comrades also played a key role in defining the false, damaging image of Vietnam veterans as psychologically disabled alcoholics and addicts, haunted by the crimes they had been forced to commit in a "racist" war."

John Kerry reported all this knowledge and activity. Yet,

he   served only four months in Vietnam in 1968-69, as a lieutenant junior grade (Lt. jg.) He still proudly claims to be a real war hero. Is this why Obama chose him to represent our great country? How can Barack Obama select only those who have shown hate toward, or expressed negatively upon America, and then claim to be functioning in the best interests of our great nation? And, if he's not functioning in the best interest of America, what is he really planning and doing?

3

RISE OF BIG BROTHER

Today, many scoff at the idea of 'Big Brother' taking over the United States. But, they scoff at their peril and ours. Too many things are happening, secretly and within our government, that demonstrate we are on a quick and direct path to loss of individualism and personal identity. In the name of safety and security, too many in our society are content to watch freedom and liberty erode. Today, we are watching a replay of the same scenario - only reinforced with higher speed and technology.

To prepare for this book, especially this chapter, I read the complete book by George Orwell, titled: '1984.' It's the book that introduced the concept of 'Big Brother,' written in 1946. While I read the book, I was puzzled by the identification of a class of citizens called 'proles.' I knew it was a word that represented something, and I tried to solve it as a word puzzle. No combination of letters ever resulted in an answer. Finally, just before I began this chapter I went to the internet and was surprised the puzzle had already been solved. It wasn't a word puzzle, after all. It was a short version of the word, 'proletariat.' Why didn't I think of that? I didn't realize Orwell was writing about analytical events of Russia and Germany. The Russians even called their revolution, 'The Rise of the Proletariat."

Perhaps an entry from Wikipedia will help explain Orwell's comments better in their relationship to current events. First, how do proles fit into normal society:

"Orwell refers to the working class of Oceania (one of three divisions of the continent) as the Proletariat. Oceania's society is divided into three distinct classes: "Inner Party," "Outer Party," and proles (with their own upper, middle and lower classes.) The proles constitute 85% of the population; they receive little education, work at manual labor, live in poverty (although in having privacy and anonymity, qualitatively better off than Outer Party members,) and usually die by the age of sixty. As the Party slogan put it: 'Proles and animals are free.'"

My interpretation differed slightly with the interpretation above regarding the upper, middle, and lower classes. That wasn't a differentiation within the proles. It was a differentiation within the total society: the High, Middle, and Low. The Middle was always trying to replace the High. In their efforts to do that, they always used the Low in their dream of having a more fair and just society where everyone would be treated equally and share equally. Once the Middle used the Low for that purpose, they cast the Low back down in the same place they were before. The Low never achieved their position of equal social justice. How were the proles, the Low, controlled to be harmless and subservient? This extract from that book, Part 1, Chapter 7 explains:

"Inner and Outer Party members are under constant

telescreen surveillance in both private and public; by contrast, proles' quarters are generally free of telescreens, since they are not expected to understand their exploitation as cheap labour by the Party, and thereby unable or unwilling to organize resistance. Their functions are simple: work and breed. They care little about anything but home and family, neighbour quarrels, films, football, beer, lottery tickets, and other such bread and circuses. They are not required to express support for the Party beyond mild patriotism; the Party creates meaningless entertainment, songs, novels and even pornography for the proles, all written by machines except for pornography, which is compiled by members of the Outer Party and accessible only by workers in Pornosec. Proles do not wear uniforms, may use cosmetics, and have a relatively free internal market economy. Proles also have liberal sex lives, uninterrupted by the Party, and divorce and prostitution are permitted. Despite these personal freedoms, the "Thought Police" plant agents among the proles to spread false rumours and mark down and/or eliminate any individuals deemed capable of causing trouble. Prole quarters consist of rundown apartment buildings, shops and pubs. Though trade between Outer Party members and proles is nominally prohibited, all Party members participate, as proles are the only source for certain minor necessities (the novel mentions shoelaces and razor blades as examples.)"

Since Orwell used the word 'prole' as a descriptive word for 'proletariat,' obviously he was looking at the events that had recently happened in Russia for the basis for his story. There had been three clear divisions of culture in Russia before the Bolshevik Revolution - the rise of the Proletariat. Czar Nicolas and the Russian aristocrats were the 'High.' The educated who were involved with commerce, trade, and specialties were the Middle, and the working peasants were the Low. The Bolsheviks, finally led by Vladimir Lenin, fueled dissension among the peasants, the Proletariat, to rise to demand more freedom and justice. Everybody knows the result of that action - the Russian aristocracy was overthrown, Czar Nicolas and his family were murdered, the Bolsheviks took over, and the Proletariat, the Low, were returned to their low position.

The Middle rose again to overthrow the High when Boris Yeltzin represented a change the Low had been waiting for to get more freedom and social justice. When Yeltzin challenged the High authority facing the firing end of a tank cannon aimed at his face, the Low rallied to support him, even the troops who had pointed the cannon toward his face. The High was overthrown once again, until a new Middle emerged to once again use the emotions of the Low to gain power. Vladimir Putin still occupies that power. But, when will another Middle come along to challenge that situation? Someone eventually will rise from the Middle to eliminate that High when the Low, the working class proletariat gives enough support to that new challenger.

We should not forget how Adolph Hitler rose to power in Germany. Initially, he was an elected official. When he promised the people more freedom and more prestige in the world, they voted for him. He did not take over Germany by force. The people, the proles, voted him into that high office. Once he was in power, however, he ruled with an iron fist, supported by a large number of people who were determined to see him rule - his Brown Shirt supporters. Once the Brown Shirts eliminated all his potential challengers - the night of the Long Knives - they were then eliminated. Hitler was then in full power. Everyone in his immediate surrounding shared his power lust - and were afraid to challenge him. The Middle had been eliminated, and a new Middle had not had time to take their place.

The great difference in Hitler's high position and that of most is that the Middle didn't recruit the Low to take his place. Before the new Middle formed, Hitler had gone to war with the world. Finally, when Hitler and his immediate subordinates were eliminated, a new hierarchy arose from a few known leaders. A new High and Middle were then formed.

The Low, the proles, remained in their traditional positions and situations of still dreaming for equality and social justice.

So, what do these examples have to do with our current situation here in the United States? Those things could never happen here, because we have a system of checks and balances. We have three branches of government that guarantee one person could never rise to power in such a manner to assume complete control. We have assumed that for many years, and all during that time there has never been a reason to believe otherwise. In most cases, a president never made a serious attempt to circumvent our Constitution and assume some form of dictatorial power. The closest we ever came to even a challenge was during Roosevelt's time in office. He was into his third term when he died. That's when our Constitution was amended to prevent a permanent tenure of power by one person. Perhaps that could change.

Never before has a president said the Constitution stands in the way of things he would like to do. Barack Obama has openly spoken those words. Never before has the president surrounded himself with people who have expressed such disdain and outright hatred for the actions of America and Americans past. Never before have we had a president who, at first, refused to acknowledge the heritage of our flag. Never before have we had a president who said the United States is no longer a Christian nation. Barack Obama spoke those words. Never before have we had a president invite our enemy into our house. Barack Obama has done that with the Muslim Brotherhood, whose ultimate written charter and goal is to destroy us. Never before have we ever had a president who refuses to take responsibility for anything - except killing Osama Bin Laden.

Ordinarily and traditionally, America has been led by leaders who have been guided by love of our country and respect for its institutions. And, generally, within the confines of their philosophies most certainly have tried to do what's right for their country. Nixon was forced to resign, but in retrospect it was not for an actual act against America. He was disgraced when it was discovered he tried to cover for a group of supporters who did perform unlawful acts - the breaking in at Watergate to steal campaign information. His action was not for a personal gain - it was a normal response to friendships and associations. Barack Obama exhibits neither loyalty to friends or love and respect for America. His character is totally dedicated to politics, power, and votes.

Perhaps the perfect example of his loyalty and character was his association with Jeremiah Wright, at that time his pastor and friend. Although, initially Obama said he would never abandon his good friend, his words lasted longer than his actions. Very quickly Wright was suddenly not Obama's close friend, mentor, and pastor. He was cast as a dangerous pariah into the background never to be seen again in Obama's presence.

This was the beginning example of Obama's character and resolve. It put his personal goals before that of long-enduring friendship. He threw Jeremiah Wright 'under the bus' without a single tear of remorse or regret. Wright suffered the fate of a normal prole. He had fulfilled his purpose and was cast aside, as is the normal result for proles. There are many other proles standing in line to be used and cast back into their normal positions by Barack Obama and his dangerous cohorts.

This next article by Patricia Campion on Yahoo Contributor Network is another example of Obama's honesty and character. If character can't be trusted in one event - should it be trusted anywhere?

"We have heard the terms repeatedly from President Barack Obama "millionaires and billionaires" pay "your fair share." He is determined to solve his own fiscal failures by taxing successful Americans -- like "folks in his income bracket" -- who "should pay more taxes. The stunning hypocrisy hidden behind that altruistic facade might surprise you. During Obama's 2008 presidential campaign he said he wanted to raise taxes on those making over $250,000 per year.

In a June press conference Obama called on Congress to raise taxes on those making over $250,000 a year -- to decrease the deficit. In his speech he again described those "folks" as "millionaires and billionaires" and "corporate-jet owners." Obama's FY 2012 budget proposal, which contained the provision for that tax hike, was defeated in the Democrat-controlled Congress 97-0.

Enter, "The Buffett Rule." Named after billionaire Warren Buffett, this measure aimed to force those making more than $1 million a year to pay a minimum tax rate of 30 percent. It too was defeated in the Democrat-controlled Senate on Monday. Which is fine. As reported by the New York Times the estimated $50 billion Obama's tax would generate over the next 10 years wouldn't put a dent in the deficit.

"Do we want to keep giving those tax breaks to folks like me, who don't need them?" Obama asked his student audience on April 10 at Florida Atlantic University in Boca Raton, Fla. Well, obviously not. Hours before the Senate rejected Obama's Buffet Rule a CNN survey showed 72 percent of the respondents favored the bill -- especially Democrats and those making less than $50,000 a year. However, according to Obama's own tax returns he only earned $789,674 in 2011. The Buffet Rule never did apply to "folks like" him. Moreover, as reported by the National Journal, Obama's adjusted gross income in 2010 was $1.7 million. In 2009 it was $5.5 million. Isn't it curious how Obama waited to raise his tax target from those making $250,000 per year to those making $1 million per year until the first year his family income dipped below $1 million since 2006?

Then there's the "secretary" hypocrisy. "Warren Buffett's secretary shouldn't pay a higher tax rate than Warren Buffett," the president said from the White House Rose Garden on Sept. 19. "There is no justification for it." So why does Obama's secretary, Anita Decker Breckenridge, pay higher taxes than he does when she only makes $95,000 a year? And if Obama really wants people to pay their "fair share," how about starting with his fellow Democrats? A November post on Spefriggintacular exposed a list of 10 Democrats caught not paying their "fair share."

* Massachusetts Rep. John Kerry avoided paying $500,000 in taxes on his yacht.

* New York Rep. Charlie Rangel failed to disclose hundreds of thousands of dollars in assets to the IRS.

* Democrat Rep. Claire McCaskill, one of those evil "jet owners" failed to pay over $280,000 in taxes on her personal plane.

* Health and Human Services Secretary Kathleen Sebelius -- the one in charge of making sure every American buys government mandated health insurance or pay a "penalty" -- she and her husband had to pay $7,000 in back taxes.

Of course, Obama's first health and human services nominee -- Tom Daschle -- failed to pay $128,000 in taxes too.

Add to Spefriggintacular's list the name of Democrat Ohio Rep. Sherrod C. Brown. As one of the Senate's strongest advocates for higher taxes, Human Events reported in February that Brown only paid his $892.74 in property taxes on his Seward Square condominium, located roughly a half-mile behind the Capitol -- after he was caught.

Then there's Debbie Wasserman Shultz. She was elected to Congress in 2004. In 2011 she became the Chair of the Democratic National Committee on May 4, 2011. As reported by The Weekly Standard Monday, she makes an annual salary of $174,000 per year. She demanded that GOP front-runner Mitt Romney release his tax returns.

So, in the interest of fair play, her congressional opponent -- Republican Karen Harrington of Florida -- has requested that Wasserman Shultz do the same.

You see, despite her eight years in Congress -- and the requirements that members of Congress disclose assets, holdings and various other financial information reports -- "there are no records of Wasserman Schultz having ever released her personal income tax returns." End article.

These examples of Obama's ideals and financial tax proposals based on his own income, and the income and tax consequences of his friends suggest two important conclusions. First, he has no positive character and is blatantly dishonest. Second, he knows where the proles are and how to use them and deceive them. The real tragedy for our country is that he knows exactly what he's doing; his scheme to deceive the proles is working just like George Orwell said it would.

Beginning into his second administration - not one single person has been helped, or seen their status or economic situation improve since he has been president. As Orwell proposed, the Out Party is Obama's problem. The proles believe, as Obama tells them, that he would do something to help them - but the "greedy rich Republicans will not let him." Their problems are all caused by Republicans who want to keep the good life - fairness, economic equality, and social justice from them.

But what is the real truth? Perhaps we proles should take a deeper and better look at what Obama is really doing to us. Would he be doing this if he loved America and cared about our future - as a country and as individuals? What does it matter to the proles - he keeps promising them more 'free stuff.' But, is that what he's really delivering to them? Perhaps he's taking more from them than giving to them. Even as he talks promises out of one side of his mouth, he steals from them with both hands. As the proles in Orwell's book, they keep waiting for their share and social justice, but all they will ever get is promises. That is, until they realize if they want something they must prepare themselves to be worthy of earning it.

While in principle I agree with Obama that the United States, as well as the world, should move to renewable energy for our long-term energy resources, nevertheless that transition should be in a more controlled and compassionate manner. His exhibited energy policy thus far has been 'full speed ahead with the transition, and American citizens be damned.' While we wait for positive action and support, he gives only false promises to expand his power base. Big Brother can't exist without unquestioning and loyal blind followers - his power base.

His refusal to expand fossil fuel exploration and extraction continues to penalize the weak and the poor, and adds to our national debt every day. Obviously, he's trying to make the transition immediately, which demonstrates either his out-of-touch with reality blind charge into more bankruptcy for our nation - or that's part of his plan to destroy the nation by subterfuge. A reasonable thinking leader would demonstrate more concern and compassion for those depending on that leader for normal existence. A leader who wants more power and control must create a more dependant populace - more proles must be put into a position to expect the government to give them something. A failed economy and a bankrupt nation can offer positive aspirations to no one - only despair and dependency.

Is he not aware that his inactions to make the United States energy independent puts our country in danger both economically and militarily? Or is he aware of the danger, and simply does not care? Any reasonably intelligent person can easily visualize and understand that danger, especially with all the terrorist hazards developing against us throughout the world. Or, is there another possible reason that will be discussed later for his apparent intention to weaken the United States?

King Obama

Reportedly, the United States has more fossil-based resources under our land than Saudi Arabia. Including shale and coal deposits we probably have more energy resources under our dirt and water than all other countries combined. Yet, we continue to import foreign oil and penalize our domestic producers when they venture forth to build America's strength. What is the man's problem with simple logic and simple arithmetic? Let's consider an example of his support for domestic energy production.

One of Obama's senior environmental representatives said they will crucify the first five who try to develop more fossil fuel so America can become fuel independent and prosperous once again. Ah, to digress to world mediocrity and below. Specifically, this is what EPA representative Al Armendariz said in 2010:

"But as I said, oil and gas is an enforcement priority, it's one of seven, so we are going to spend a fair amount of time looking at oil and gas production. And I gave, I was in a meeting once and I gave an analogy to my staff about my philosophy of enforcement, and I think it was probably a little crude and maybe not appropriate for the meeting but I'll go ahead and tell you what I said. It was kind of like how the Romans used to conquer little villages in the Mediterranean. They'd go into a little Turkish town somewhere, they'd find the first five guys they saw and they would crucify them. And then you know that town was really easy to manage for the next few years. And so you make examples out of people who are in this case not compliant with the law. Find people who are not compliant with the law, and you hit them as hard as you can and you make examples out of them, and there is a deterrent effect there. And, companies that are smart see that, they don't want to play that game, and they decide at that point that it's time to clean up. And, that won't happen unless you have somebody out there making examples of people. So you go out, you look at an industry, you find

59

people violating the law, you go aggressively after them. And we do have some pretty effective enforcement tools. Compliance can get very high, very, very quickly. That's what these companies respond to is both their public image but also financial pressure. So you put some financial pressure on a company, you get other people in that industry to clean up very quickly. So, that's our general philosophy."

Perhaps Obama's plans will lead us to even greater environmental progress: candles and bicycles. Who needs electricity, cars, and highways, anyway? Would it be too complicated for Obama to consider that renewable energy must be planned over a longer transition time that allows consistency and dependability without disrupting life as it exists today? That is unless his plan is to create that disruption and to create a lifestyle for all Americans comparable to that of third-world countries. He has never given a strategic plan or any timetable for an energy transition. He keeps proceeding blindly ahead without acknowledging any circumstances from that blind charge.

He also continues to pour millions of taxpayer dollars into those failing renewable energy companies. Is his plan to help create energy or to help expedite bankruptcy of our nation?

He proudly proclaims his zeal to help the middle-class and poor in our society, but is that what he really has in mind? His speeches are all about helping those who have less than the evil rich people get their fair share. Yet, his actions are directly opposed to achieving that humanitarian goal. While he proudly and boastfully talks of putting more money in their front pockets, he steals even more from their wallets and bank accounts - those worshipers fortunate enough to have bank accounts. He robs their few precious assets from them as he convinces them he's their savior that will give them more. How does this happen?

Most people not considered wealthy must put gasoline in

their automobiles to get to work. At least half of what they pay for gasoline is money that Obama's policies strips from their available assets. That's money that could be used for many other things that might help stimulate the economy.

Due to his energy policy of not allowing more oil drilling in and around the United States, gasoline prices have doubled since he became president in 2008. That's doubled! When he took office, gasoline was approximately $1.85 per gallon. At this moment, it's over $3.60 per gallon. That means people are penalized as much as $100.00 to $200.00 a month for gasoline - just to get to their jobs. And those needy people still consider Barack Obama their hero and savior?

Obviously, once a savior is recognized, he is never questioned by his worshipers. "Our economic problems are caused by George Bush and all the evil Republicans." He must keep the proles poor, destitute, uneducated, and without hope, to allow their manipulation and the continued belief that their grief is caused by someone else. It can't be the glorious leader who promises them more, and equality and social justice. One who understands, is involved with everyday events, and who tries to be self-reliant and independent is a threat to a Big Brother manipulator.

His attack on American energy production has increased costs in every sector of the American economy, thereby penalizing the poor and middle-class the most. How? The answer is simple. The cost of energy determines the cost of almost everything in our modern society.

Electricity and power bills have increased for the average consumer because the president has curtailed available energy resources. The poor and middle-class have to pay more for electricity and heat, even if heated by other than electricity. With less production of coal, that cost has also increased, or those who had used coal for heating have had to convert to other heat sources. These increased energy costs are also suffered by businesses and factories who must also increase the cost of their products and services to remain in business.

The falling domino effect runs the course until the final inflated costs reach the consumer - largely the poor and middle class who are hurt the worst. But, by keeping his finger pointed at the wealthy, Obama continues to be the savior of the poor and middle-class; the proles. They close their eyes as they clasp their hands in prayer to him.

And, we should not forget the effects of ethanol. Although this was an active program long before Barack Obama was elected president, he still has done nothing to curtail its devastating effects. Let's consider just a few.

First, many people report engine problems with their automobiles from using ethanol. When ethanol was first introduced it was to support two needs; less reliance on oil, since at that time the oil price was beginning to escalate faster. And, the major purpose for its introduction was to be more environmentally friendly. This was partially in response to the 'climate change' promoters who were determined to make money with their great scare tactics.

Many engines are having to be repaired from the damage created by ethanol use. Many poor people have to use small engines such as lawn mowers, blowers, and chain saws to make a living. Recently, it was announced that ethanol added to gasoline would be increased from 10-percent to 15-percent. How many more poor people will be penalized or damaged? Yet, they continue to worship him.

Again, Barack Obama puts a dagger through the economic hearts of the poor and middle-class, who often can't afford those repairs. Yet, they continue to believe his promises that his sole purpose as president is to give them their 'fair share.' Could he mean a fair share of despair, not their fair share of the country's wealth? A Big Brother, of course, would want the main dish, and would throw his minions the left-over crumbs - if they presented their fair share of personal loyalty to earn those crumbs.

Cost of repairing automobile engines however is not necessarily the greatest disaster created by the use of ethanol against the poor and middle-class. Often, that's a one-time cost that can be absorbed with payments on credit cards or by giving up some other family necessity. The greatest cost to those who can afford it least is the increased cost of food. Even the least wealthy must have food, and nowadays there are not enough personal gardens to fulfill that need. Only a few people now have a garden, a cow, chickens, and pigs from which they can get their food. Most people now must buy their food from the grocery store. So, how does ethanol affect the price of food?

At this time, most ethanol is made from corn. Corn is also used many other ways, especially related to other food, many foods that one would not imagine as an added ingredient for improved taste, firming a product, color, or to create different blends of another food product. Corn is also used as a livestock food. In effect, corn is used in most things related to food and food production.

What happens when much of that corn product is transferred to produce ethanol? Have you noticed the price of food, lately? Are you aware that a gallon of milk has skyrocketed from $1.99 two years ago to over $4.00 today? Have you seen the price of beef, or has that price become so expensive you can no longer buy beef? Have you seen the price of any food product, and can say it has not increased in price at least 25 percent during the past two years? The price of all food has increased, and for four reasons:

First, is the normal rise in inflation. This ordinarily should be no more than 5 percent unless the economy is really booming. Our economy is barely creeping.

Second, is the increased cost to transport that food, because Obama is keeping the price of gasoline too high. It costs more to move that corn to factories and to move those products from factories to the distributors then to the store shelves.

Third, is increased costs of retailers for wages and salaries of workers to meet their increased costs for their gas to get to work, and their cost for higher priced food. Now they will have an added cost to cover the increased health care demands under the new health care law. When that new requirement gets into full bloom, is there any imagination that food prices will not skyrocket even higher?

Fourth, is corn availability, depending upon the financial market and weather. Prices are kept as high as possible by market controllers, and peak prices are compounded even more when a drought, or the threat of a drought occurs. Even at this moment, a drought is forecast for the next corn-growing season. Even during a drought Obama will not be deterred from throwing more money at the basic problem, by corn producer subsidies to keep them in business, so the price of food can remain high.

If the price for a gallon of milk rises to $6.00 a gallon next year, what effect will that have on everyone, especially children who need milk to help develop their bones and teeth? What if the price of all food continues to rise? Will Obama blame those increased costs on normal inflation and price gougers in the marketplace? He certainly will blame it on someone else as he always does, although he is now encouraging the ethanol level to be raised to 15 percent - again devastating the buying power of those who support him most, and even worship him.

Never would he look into a mirror and say, "That's the man who deprives the poor and middle-class from their 'fair share' by raising prices so high that what money they have will buy less of their bare necessities." In effect, Obama's actions regarding his energy policy, or lack thereof, takes money from the pockets of those who need it most.

King Obama

For wealthy people, Obama's energy policy is merely an inconvenience. For the non-wealthy it's a critical burden that restricts their health, their future, and their happiness. Yet, those loyal followers to whom he has made those empty promises believe his every word as if spoken from God. They will continue to keep their eyes closed as he destroys their future, condemns them to poverty, and rips apart the foundation of the United States of America.

Although Obama is their savior, he continues to destroy their well-being by his secrets and deceptions. His followers are blindly oblivious to the fact that his war on wealthy people is a war on all people. His blind followers will continue to suffer most. He must maintain this rift between economic classes to continue his total takeover of America.

Barack Obama knows exactly what he's doing to create his role as Big Brother of our once-wonderful and free country. He's following the example formed by Vladimir Lenin, Adolph Hitler, and described by George Orwell in his book, '1984.' He's the majestic Pied Piper leading his band of 'Proles' over the 'Freedom Lost' cliff. How far will he go, and what perils will his actions present. It will not be a positive venture for any true American.

King Obama

4

DECEIT IS HONESTY

How many different ways can our government watch us and gather information about us? How can they and how will they use that information? We already knew the government had great capability to gather information about every person, but we had no idea how much information they could gather and maintain - or how deeply the system peered into our daily activities. Thanks to whistle-blowers, we are beginning to have a good idea.

Government leaders tell us the only people really targeted for surveillance and scrutiny are those who fit certain criteria and signs of abnormal activity - geared to certain events or certain key words. Should we believe those who tell us that? Only to our peril should we believe them, now. Our government, since Obama has been in office, has done nothing to support the idea or the words that they even understand the concept of honesty and patriotism. Our country has changed right before our eyes.

We have watched that deterioration, and we have done nothing about it. Most citizens now accept the erosion of our Constitution and its protections as nothing extraordinary. Why is our Constitution being attacked? Who is leading that attack? How are they succeeding in destroying our great country, while at the same time trying to convince us they are examples of 'good Americans?' Perhaps deceit is honesty - if it's aimed at that negative and unseen target, instead of the one used as a distraction.

Perhaps the real target of the Obama administration is either Socialism or Islam. Having two possible targets makes the real one more difficult to detect. Perhaps the one that prevails in the end is Obama's real   target. According to George Orwell's concepts, this really could be considered 'Deceit is Honesty' in his book. Let's begin with a few examples.

The first is the 'Beer Summit.' This was Obama's first reaction to suggest his racist and preferential views, and his inability to react in a presidential manner in a situation that should have been analyzed by one occupying that position.

In an article by John Sexton at Brietbart.com, he describes one of the first comments by Barack Obama that indicates his propensity toward racism, and a lack of respect for our Constitution. It also gives an opinion by one of the first important members selected by Obama for his first administration - Van Jones. Sexton's article began:

"In an April 3rd, 2012 appearance on the Democracy Now TV show, Van Jones has offered his own behind-the-scenes take on an incident that made race a political issue three years before the Trayvon Martin case. As Jones describes it, the infamous "beer summit" on the White House lawn was a case where President Obama was "forced" into a meeting with a "racist" police officer.

In July 2009, while Jones was working at the White House, Sgt. James Crowley responded to a call of a possible break-in at a Cambridge, MA home. In reality, the person a neighbor thought might be a burglar was the homeowner, Harvard professor Henry Louis Gates, with another man helping him enter the house. When Sgt. Crowley arrived at the home, he asked Professor Gates for ID. Gates reportedly responded, "Why? Because I'm a black man in America." Gates initially refused to produce an ID. Once he did, the police report indicates Crowley left the home. However, Professor Gates followed him outside and continued to "yell" at Sgt. Crowley. Crowley claims to have warned Gates in front of several neighborhood witnesses before arresting Gates for disorderly conduct.

After word of the arrest broke, the president weighed in during a press conference saying that while he didn't have all the facts, "the Cambridge police acted stupidly." The White House quickly tried to walk back the remark and eventually proposed a meeting on the White House grounds which came to be known as the "beer summit." No reporters were present, but photos of the president, Vice President Biden, Prof. Gates, and Sgt. Crowley sharing a beer were widely circulated.

While neither side agreed to apologize to the other at the time of the beer summit, several months later Professor Gates appeared on the Oprah television show and told the host that he and Sgt. Crowley had developed a "really good relationship." Crowley gave Gates the handcuffs used in the arrest and Gates said he planned to donate them to the Smithsonian. A report issued one year after the arrest placed blame on both Gates and Crowley for failing to de-escalate the situation.

But according to Van Jones, the beer summit was not a chance for both sides of the disagreement to take stock, but a media event which forced the president to "sit humbly" across from a "racist" police officer: "The right wing and the law enforcement establishment brought the wrath of God down on the White House, I was there, and suddenly he's forced to do a beer summit to sit eye to eye with a racist police officer... as a black man, even the most powerful man in the world, can not speak about race and if he does he's then forced to sit humbly across the table from a racist police officer."

Jones goes on to describe the beer summit as a "terrifying, shocking" revelation about the state of race relations in America. At this point, the Democracy Now host attempts to draw Jones out further about what advice he gave the President. Jones declines, saying he doesn't want to talk "out of school."

This is quite a different perspective on the story than the one the White House presented to the media at the time. In 2009, the President called the beer summit a "teachable moment" and clearly wanted to be seen as someone who could bring the two sides together after the firestorm caused by his initial remarks. But apparently, that view was not shared by everyone in the White House.

Did the president himself agree with his employee Jones' private assessment of Sgt. Crowley? Was the beer summit something the president felt forced into by "the right wing and the law enforcement establishment"? These questions might be worth asking now that the White House is once again taking sides in a case with obvious racial overtones. End of article.

What was Obama's instinctive reaction to that event before he even questioned what had happened? His first and basic instinct was to blame the white police officer: "The Cambridge police acted stupidly." As president of the United States, or as any non-judgmental person, should he not have asked for the facts before he made a condemnation of anyone? That's the responsibility of a leader - any leader. Not only did he fail as a leader in that situation, he set the example of his following decisions and activities.

This sets the example of things and decisions to follow. That being: Does he have the ability and the instincts to make fair, just, and equitable decisions for America - or is that his purpose and goal? Even up to the present day, that answer is a resounding, no! And, we cannot forget Obama's typical selections for people as his close advisors. Van Jones is a typical example. Who is Van Jones?

A Washington Post article on September 6, 2009, by Scott Wilson and Garance Franke-Ruta gives information about Van Jones, who resigned after a simmering controversy over his past statements and activism erupted into calls for his ouster from Republican leaders. Their report stated:

"White House spokesman Robert Gibbs on Sunday explained the resignation on ABC's 'This Week with George Stephanopoulos," saying, "Van Jones decided was that the agenda of this president was bigger than any one individual." The president does not endorse Jones's past statements and actions, "but he thanks him for his service," Gibbs said.

A White House official, who spoke on condition of anonymity to discuss a personnel matter, said Jones's past was not studied as intensively as other advisers because of his relatively low rank. Jones's position did not require Senate confirmation, so he avoided the kind of vetting Cabinet officials were subjected to. In addition, as an adviser to the Council on Environmental Quality, rather than to Obama directly, his past was not reviewed to the same degree as the more senior "assistants to the president" and other top advisers inside the West Wing.

The result was the revelation of a controversial past that, administration officials acknowledge, caught the White House off guard. "He was not as thoroughly vetted as other administration officials," the official said. "It's fair to say there were unknowns."

The announcement that Jones was stepping down came minutes after midnight Sunday morning. "On the eve of historic fights for health care and clean energy, opponents of reform have mounted a vicious smear campaign against me," Jones said. "They are using lies and distortions to distract and divide." He continued: "I have been inundated with calls -- from across the political spectrum -- urging me to 'stay and fight.' But I came here to fight for others, not for myself. I cannot in good conscience ask my colleagues to expend precious time and energy defending or explaining my past. We need all hands on deck, fighting for the future."

Jones, who joined the administration in March as special adviser for green jobs at the CEQ, had issued two public apologies in recent days, one for signing a petition in 2004 from the group 911Truth.org that questioned whether Bush administration officials "may indeed have deliberately allowed 9/11 to happen, perhaps as a pretext for war" and the other for using a crude term to describe Republicans in a speech he gave before joining the administration.

His one-time involvement with the Bay Area radical group Standing Together to Organize a Revolutionary Movement (STORM), which had Marxist roots, had also become an issue. And on Saturday his advocacy on behalf of death-row inmate Mumia Abu-Jamal, who was convicted of shooting a Philadelphia police officer in 1981, threatened to develop into a fresh point of controversy.

Fox News Channel host Glenn Beck launched the drive against Jones and all but declared war on him after a group Jones founded in 2005, ColorofChange.org, led an advertising boycott against Beck's show to protest his claim that Obama is a racist.

Rep. Mike Pence (R-Ind.) called on Jones to resign Friday, saying in a statement, "His extremist views and coarse rhetoric have no place in this administration or the public debate." Senator Christopher S. Bond (R-Mo.) urged Congress to investigate Jones's "fitness" for the position, writing in an open letter, "Can the American people trust a senior White House official that is so cavalier in his association with such radical and repugnant sentiments?" On Saturday, Sen. John Cornyn (R-Texas), chairman of the National Republican Senatorial Committee, wrote on his Twitter account, "Van Jones has to go."

Jones's resignation was foreshadowed Friday when Gibbs gave only tepid support for him when pressed, saying that

Jones "continues to work for the administration." He declined
to state that the adviser enjoyed the full support of President
Obama, instead referring questions to the environmental
council where he worked.

Jones, a towering figure in the environmental movement,
had worked for the White House Council on Environmental
Quality since March. He was a civil-rights activist in
California before turning his focus to environmental and
energy issues, and he won wide praise before joining the
Obama administration for articulating a broad vision of a
green economy Democrats could embrace.

White House adviser David Axelrod, on NBC's "Meet the
Press," said Sunday he had not spoken with the president
about Jones. "The political environment is rough, and so
these things get magnified. But the bottom line is that he
showed his commitment to the cause of creating green jobs
in this country by removing himself as an issue, and I think
that took a great deal of commitment on his part," he said.
End of article.

Another advisor to Obama, Anita Dunn, was also hand-
picked by Valerie Jarrett, as was Van Jones. She also exposed
her Communist leanings when she expressed her admiration
for Mao Je Tung as her 'favorite philosopher.' While making
this statement to a group of high school graduates, she didn't
mention the fact that Mao was responsible for the deaths of
70 million of his fellow Chinese. Mao eliminated these fellow
citizens because they didn't support his Communist regime -
or were suspected of not supporting his Communist regime.

Anita Dunn's connections go even deeper. She is married
to Robert Bauer. According to reports in 2009, It was Bauer
who lobbied the Justice Department unsuccessfully during
the 2008 presidential campaign to pursue a criminal probe of
American Issues Project (AIP), an independent group that
sought to run an ad spotlighting Obama's ties to Weather
Underground terrorist Bill Ayers. It was Bauer who attempted
to sic the DOJ on GOP donor Harold Simmons, and sought

his prosecution for funding the ad. It was Bauer who tried to compel television stations across the country to pull the spot. All this on Barack Obama's behalf.

Bauer's specialty is stifling dissent. He's married to the woman Obama picked to stop information being promoted against him - especially by Fox News. He was appointed as Barack Obama's personal counsel in 2009. Was Bauer's attempt to stifle information about Obama's connection with Bill Ayers honest? Let's examine.

Obama claims he hardly knew his good friend and party pal, Bill Ayers, the man who expressed his patriotism with bombs against America. He is also the man, along with his father, who is thought to have helped launch Obama's political career. What was the ultimate purpose? Was it to support Bill Ayers' continued hate and aggression against America?

He claimed to know Ayers only as someone he casually saw in the neighborhood. He failed to reveal that he was on two boards with Bill Ayers, the Annenberg Project and the Woods Foundation, and that on at least one occasion he attended a party at Bill Ayers' home. Why did he not tell the whole and revealing truth about his association with Bill Ayers? Why did he keep that information a secret even if it were a casual acquaintance or an incidental event? What was he afraid of? If he were that non-associated with Bill Ayers why did he not say so and reveal the whole truth? What were the hidden secrets? Does not a minor deception require more questions? Obama's relationship with Ayers goes even deeper, and represents even more hidden danger to our national security.

This is another article, published by Aaron Klein, January 23, 2013, that shows the insidious attack on our education system - and America, by the Islamists. Aaron Klein is WND's (WorldNetDaily) senior staff reporter and Jerusalem bureau chief. He also hosts 'Aaron Klein Investigative Radio' on New York's WABC Radio.

The article begins: "A Muslim Brotherhood-linked

organization has partnered with the U.S. Department of Education and the State Department to facilitate an online program aiming to connect all U.S. schools with classrooms abroad by 2016." Vartan Gregorian, a board member of the organization, the Qatar Foundation International, was appointed in 2009 to President Obama's White House Fellowships Commission. WND previously exposed that Gregorian served as a point man in granting $49.2 million in startup capital to an education-reform project founded by former Weather Underground terrorist William Ayers and chaired by Obama.

Documentation shows Gregorian was central in Ayers' recruitment of Obama to serve as the first chairman of the project, the Chicago Annenberg Challenge – a job in which Obama worked closely on a regular basis with Ayers. Obama also later said his job at the project qualified him to run for public office, as WND previously reported."

Yet, Obama claims he hardly knew Bill Ayers. This falsehood, in itself, is not necessarily important. The important point is that the president of the United States, Barack Obama, is not honor bound to be guided by truth. He has demonstrated too many times that his words cannot be trusted. How can a leader lead if he or she is not guided, at least to some degree, by honesty? America cannot be at its best and highest if its leader is not at least partially honest, and demonstrates the best interest of the United States as his guiding principle.

Barack Obama does not do that. He hides other dark secrets known only to a few. And, these secrets suggest even more dangerous connections - beginning with Valerie Jarrett.

Valerie Jarrett has an all-inclusive title with which to advise Obama. It's Senior Advisor and Assistant to the President for Public Engagement and Intergovernmental Affairs. With that title, part of her function is to review and approve all others appointed to advise and counsel the president. Although she knew about Van Jones' connection to the Communist Party, she was nevertheless exuberant to have him join the Obama team. Finally he was discovered and had to resign. He suffered the same loyalty fate as did Obama's other great friend and mentor, Jeremiah Wright. For Obama, personal ambition seems to have greater influence than does friendship and honesty.

Who is Valerie Jarrett? Her father-in-law, Vernon Jarrett, was a friend and comrade of Communist Party leader Frank Marshall Davis. She married Vernon's son and some time later became Mayor Richard Daley's Deputy Chief of Staff. She was active in that position at the time of its greatest big city corruption phase. Incidentally, Frank Marshall Davis, the Communist leader, was one of Barack Obama's early and closest mentors. He was also a good friend of Obama's grandfather. So, is there any question how Barack Obama and Valerie Jarrett are so closely associated? Although they met when Michelle Obama applied for a job at the City of Chicago, with Jarrett, it seems they might have similar and close Communist ties from long before. And, there's even another tie that makes this connection a trio - David Axelrod.

Reviewing Axelrod's past gets very cloudy and complicated. To try to make this review short and as simple as possible, it can be said that he was trained in many left-wing and Communist situations. The most interesting note, however, is that there is a related Communist association among Obama, Jarrett, and Axelrod.

The Communist card-carrying member Frank Marshall Davis who was Obama's mentor and friend also worked with the Canter family. The Canter family mentored David Axelrod in Communist theory and doctrine. According to another source, Axelrod's mother wrote for a New York City tabloid called, PM Magazine, which often promoted the Communist Party line. A wealthy donor, Marshall Field, who helped fund the magazine, also funded the Saul Alinsky training school.

Does a dangerous pattern begin to show itself? This dangerous plot grows thicker. It seems a man named George

Soros appears in many of these environments to provide funds whenever necessary to continue the progression. Just curios, I wonder where Obama got the funds to buy his large house before he became president. Where did he get the funds to take foreign trips while he was in college? (And, what country of origin was printed on his passport when he took all those foreign trips? No one knows. He will not let that information be released to the public.)

But, why is all this deception so difficult to interpret. On the basis of the relationships exposed above, one would imagine we are being led straight to socialism or communism, or somewhere in between - if that difference can even be discerned. There are many self-proclaimed Communists and Socialists in Obama's administration. Not one - not a single one - has ever professed, "I am proud to be an American, and I support the American way of life." Not even John Kerry, who charged his comrades-in-arms, fighting for their lives in Vietnam, as cold, ruthless killers.

He was later rewarded for his anti-American dogma by having everything given to him on a 'silver platter.' Now, he's America's representative to the world. Is he the 'new' John Kerry, or the 'old' John Kerry? What does the rest of the world think about us, knowing that our 'out-front' representative proclaims his fellow Americans as ruthless killers?

There are also many Islamists in Obama's administration. This conundrum of confusion allows Obama to shift back and forth so he can't be tied to either - either which is a direct threat to the perpetuation of our democracy. But, these are good Muslims - not radical Muslims. They worship from the same written source document, so that means when they destroy all non-Muslims, they will do it in a kinder, gentler way. Perhaps they will use a sharper sword than the radical Muslims, who will use a dull sword. They are deceiving the world, and Barack Obama is their greatest promoter. Or, is he using them merely as a distraction while he ventures onward toward his self-perceived destiny? Only six of his most prominent appointments are shown next, but they are typical of his many Muslim appointments to critical positions.

Arif Alikhan – Assistant Secretary for Policy Development for the U.S. Department of Homeland Security.

Arif Alikhan played a key role in the removal of the LAPD "Mapping" Plan which involved mapping Muslim communities in an effort to identify potential hotbeds of extremism. LAPD officials said that it was crucial for them to gain a better understanding of isolated parts of the Muslim community because those groups can potentially breed violent extremism.

Alikhan reportedly helped raise funds for Muslim Public Affairs Council (MPAC) that has labeled a deadly anti-U.S. terrorist attack a legitimate operation, referred to terrorists as "freedom fighters" and equated Muslim jihad with the sentiments of American statesman Patrick Henry. He joined MPAC on April 11 for a special fundraiser called "Be the Change" to support what the group calls its innovative leadership development programs.

Mohammed Elibiary – Homeland Security Adviser. According to information reported in an article by the Investigative Project on Terrorism, Mohamed Elibiary has defended Muslim Brotherhood luminary Sayyid Qutb, Ayatollah Khomeini, and radical New York Imam Siraj Wahhaj. He has asserted conspiracy theories, supported terror-related individuals and organizations and accused the government of mounting a war against Islam.

Despite all this, he was appointed by Department of Homeland Security (DHS) Secretary Janet Napolitano to the Homeland Security Advisory Council (HSAC).

Elibiary is the co-founder, president and CEO of the Freedom and Justice Foundation (F&J), founded in November

King Obama

2002 "to promote a Centrist Public Policy environment in Texas by coordinating the state level government and interfaith community relations for the organized Texas Muslim community." F&J's nonprofit status was revoked by the IRS in May 2010 for failure to file the requisite 990 forms that would reveal the entity's source of income. Similarly, according to the Texas Comptroller of Public Accounts, F&J has not filed a Texas Franchise Tax Public Information Report.

The North Texas Islamic Council (NTIC), also called the "Texas Islamic Council," is an affiliate organization of F&J. Elibiary is the registered agent for the NTIC, and one of the directors is H. Mustafaa Carroll, who is also the executive director of the Houston chapter of the Council on American-Islamic Relations (CAIR). CAIR is a Muslim Brotherhood-linked group in the U.S. that was formed as part of a Hamas-support network in the U.S.

Elibiary was a Fellow in 2008-2009 with the American Muslim Civic Leadership Institute (AMCLI), "housed at the University of Southern California's Center for Religion and Civic Culture (CRCC), which works in partnership with the Prince Alwaleed Bin Talal Center for Muslim Christian Understanding (ACMCU) at Georgetown University." This is the center where Obama had the Christian icon covered with black plywood before he made his speech there in April, 2009.

Elibiary was featured in a CNN piece in December 2009 as a "deradicalizer." He likened the allure of radicalism among American Muslim teens to "at-risk gangbangers, who want to stand up for their community, to address grievances of the global Muslim community more effectively than they've seen the elder generation."

Elibiary has defended Sayyid Qutb, the Islamist ideologue credited with inspiring the Muslim Brotherhood and terrorist groups including al-Qaida. He recommends Qutb's writing as offering "the potential for a strong spiritual rebirth that's truly ecumenical allowing all faiths practiced in America to enrich us and motivate us to serve God better by serving our fellow

79

man more."

Rashad Hussain – Special Envoy to the (OIC) Organization of the Islamic Conference. A Global Muslim Brotherhood Daily Report took a look at Hussain's official biography and found several concerning affiliations. The first is that in October 2000, Hussain spoke at a conference sponsored by the Association of Muslim Social Scientists, which was listed in an internal Muslim Brotherhood document as one of "our organizations and the organizations of our friends," and the Prince Alwaleed Center for Muslim-Christian Understanding of Georgetown University, which receives Saudi funding and is directed by prominent Muslim Brotherhood advocate, John Esposito.

In September 2004, Hussain played a role in the Muslim Students Association's annual conference, which was founded by Muslim Brotherhood in 1963 and is also listed as one the group's fronts in its own documents. Since then, many of its nearly 600 college chapters have engaged in extremism and the group closely collaborates with the other Brotherhood fronts. For example, MSA was part of an umbrella organization called the American Muslim Taskforce that led a campaign against the FBI's use of informants in mosques and accused the agency of anti-Muslim activity. Several Brotherhood affiliates are in this including the Muslim-American Society, the Islamic Circle of North America, the Islamic Society of North America, the Muslim Public Affairs Council and the Council on American-Islamic Relations.

At this conference, Hussain spoke alongside the daughter of Professor Sami Al-Arian, who was convicted of being a key leader of the Palestinian Islamic Jihad terrorist group and later admitted to being a member of the Muslim Brotherhood. Hussain also defended Al-Arian and described his prosecution as being a "politically-motivated persecution."

The network of Brotherhood-affiliated groups has consistently been on his side throughout the entire ordeal and celebrated his release. Interestingly, the story in The Washington Report on Middle East Affairs that quoted Hussain's defense of Al-Arian has been altered since its original publication. A cnsnews article reports that the quote was removed "sometime after October 2007" and that the reporter who wrote the article expressed surprise but said she no longer worked at WRMEA and could not explain the edit.

Last May, Hussain spoke at a conference sponsored by several Brotherhood affiliates, including the Muslim Public Affairs Council, an organization whose extremism has been catalogued in a A series by The Investigative Project on Terrorism and the Council on American-Islamic Relations. The latter was listed by the federal government in 2007 as an 'unindicted co-conspirator' in the terrorism financing trial of The Holy Land Foundation, another Muslim Brotherhood front that was found to be financing Hamas. Its founders are former officials at the Islamic Association of Palestine, a Brotherhood front shut down for supporting Hamas and are said by the FBI to be members of the Brotherhood's Palestine Committee in the United States.

Hussain's view on the cause of terrorism is important to note as it will play a significant role in the Obama Administration's outreach to the Muslim world. He quoted a study that concluded that 'The primary cause of broad-based anger and anti-Americanism is not a clash of civilizations but the perceived effect of U.S. foreign policy in the Muslim world.' In this statement, it appears that he believes that terrorism is the product of opposition to foreign policy, rather than the product of a politico-religious totalitarian ideology, which explains his opposition to terms like "Islamic terrorism."

On the other hand, Hussein does support the use of the term "Hamas terrorists," so he cannot be said to be a supporter of Hamas, which grew out of the Muslim Brotherhood. He has an entire section in his paper titled, 'Discrediting the Terrorist Ideology.' He opposes making democracy promotion a central part of that goal, saying that it can be interpreted as imperialism and an attempt to bring about freedom that enables immorality, but admits that it may be part of the solution. He instead suggests that the government use Muslim voices to argue that Islam forbids acts of terrorism and extremism.

One other important part of his paper is when he proposes that the U.S. build a Muslim coalition "not limited to those who advocate Western-style democracy, and avoid creating a dichotomy between freedom and Islamic society." This would set the stage for a partnership with the Muslim Brotherhood. Rather than focusing on supporting elements that will genuinely argue that democracy is compatible with Islam, his standard for allies is that they just oppose terrorism and extremism. Apparently, those who pursue Sharia Law through other methods do not fit his version of 'extremist.'

Salam al-Marayati – Obama Adviser, founder of Muslim Public Affairs Council and its current executive director. This is an article by the Militant Islam Monitor, on May 11, 2013, regarding al-Marayati:

"Salam Al Marayati, the director of the Muslim Public Affairs Council (MPAC), is scheduled to be on a panel at the upcoming National Homeland Security Conference in June in LA. The panel discussion is about "Public and Private" Partnerships. The program tracks "Interoperability, Information Sharing and Intelligence".

Arif Alikhan ,who was responsible for derailing the LAPD's plans to monitor activities within the Muslim community is also a speaker at the conference, He was appointed as assistant secretary for the Office of Policy Development in Barack Obama's Department of Homeland Security in 2009. According to 'Discover the Networks': MPAC has defended the use of terrorism and Al Marayati said on the radio on 9/11 that Israel could have been behind the attacks." In a November 1997 speech at the University of Pennsylvania,

MPAC Co-Founder and Executive Director Salam Al-Marayati steadfastly refused to call Hezbollah a terrorist organization; he justified the existence of Hamas as a political entity and a provider of social programs and "educational operations" and he equated jihad with the sentiments of the American statesman Patrick Henry, whose "Give me liberty or give me death" declaration was, in Al-Marayati's view, "a way of looking at the term 'jihad' from an American perspective."

Al-Marayati will be participating in the NHS conference under the aegis of the Muslim American Homeland Security Congress an Islamist organization which attempts to prevent law enforcement scrutiny of Muslims, deny any Islamic connection to terrorism and hinder government efforts to educate people about the jihadist threat. Among the MAHSC listed board members is the Council on American Islamic Relations (CAIR) a Saudi funded front group for Hamas and an unindicted co-conspirator in the Holyland Foundation Hamas funding trial.

It should come as no surprise that Haroon Azar,the DHS Security Regional Director for Strategic Engagement, has worked with MPAC in the past. Haroon Azar took part in an MPAC teleconference aimed at portraying Muslims as victims of a non existent backlash after the Boston terrorist attacks. Azar is also speaking on the same panel as Al Marayati at the upcoming NHS conference.

To have a documented Islamist leader of a major Muslim organization with known terrorist sympathies and Muslim Brotherhood ties on a panel at a NHS conference is further proof that our security apparatus is being manipulated by and adopting a jihadist perspective while doing everything it can to deny and obscure the threat which radical Islam poses to the security of the United States.

Imam Mohamed Magid – Obama's Sharia Czar, Islamic Society of North America. A PJ Media report on July 5, 2012 gave the following information about Mohamed Magid and his support for other radical Islamists:

"Mohamed Magid is the Obama administration's go-to guy for Muslim outreach and advise on international affairs and counterterrorism. He is a regular visitor to the White House (even when the administration wants to conceal it,) attends important administration speeches on the US Middle East policy at the State Department, he counsels the Department of Justice to criminalize defamation of Islam, he entertains the deputy national security adviser at his DC-area mosque, and he serves on the Department of Homeland Security's Countering Violent Extremism Working Group. He also advises the FBI and many other federal agencies. He has also been profiled by Time Magazine and the Huffington Post has even dubbed him "America's Imam." His ubiquitous presence across the Obama administration undoubtedly makes him the most influential and sought after Muslim authority in the country.

Imam Magid also serves as the president of the Islamic Society of North America (ISNA). In that capacity last weekend he presided over ISNA's "Diversity Forum" held in Dearborn (where Muslim residents were recently video recorded stoning Christian protestors). One of the speakers at the ISNA Diversity Forum was CAIR-Michigan executive director Dawud Walid. Imam Magid even gave a "diversity award" to Walid.

Walid, too, is popular with the Obama administration, taking two taxpayer financed trips overseas on behalf of the State Department. But just a little over a month ago Dawud Walid gave a sermon at the Islamic Organization of America (IONA) mosque in Warren, Michigan. As noted by an Investigative Project report issued just days after Walid's appearance, during the sermon he asked, "Who are those who incurred the wrath of Allah?" Answering his own question in Arabic, he replied, "They are the Jews, they are the Jews." Walid also took aim his imagined enemies, saying:

"One of the greatest social ills facing American

King Obama

today is Islamophobia, and anti-Muslim bigotry. And if you trace the organizations and the main advocates and activists in Islamophobia in America, you will see that all those organizations are pro-Israeli occupation organizations and activists."

So not only are the Jews the cursed of Allah, but the Jews are also behind "Islamophobia" — reviving longtime Islamic blood libels. As the Investigative Project report goes on to note Walid has also taken to Twitter to correctly source and affirm Islamic authorities who called for killing Jews.

Imam Magid's endorsement of Walid's outspoken Jew-hatred raises some serious questions about who Obama is getting his advice from, but it does answer some questions about the inspiration for the Obama administration's ongoing "Islamophobia" witchhunt. But handing a "diversity award" to an unashamed Jew-hater doesn't make Dawud Walid a diversity hero. It does, however, say something about Obama's Shariah czar Mohamed Magid."

Eboo Patel – Advisory Council on Faith-Based Neighborhood Partnerships. Named by US News & World Report as one of America's Best Leaders of 2009, Eboo Patel is the founder and Executive Director of Interfaith Youth Core (IFYC), a Chicago-based institution building the global interfaith youth movement. Author of the award-winning book 'Acts of Faith: The Story of an American Muslim, the Struggle for the Soul of a Generation,' Eboo is also a regular contributor to the Washington Post, National Public Radio and CNN. He is a member of President Obama's Advisory Council of the White House Office of Faith Based and Neighborhood Partnerships, and holds a doctorate in the sociology of religion from Oxford University, where he studied on a Rhodes scholarship.

Although nothing specific has been reported to suggest he has the same Islamic inclinations as the others reported above, his inclusion in Obama's close administration must still be suspect. The idea of a 'global interfaith youth movement' itself could be suspect considering all the other aspects of Islam. Their ultimate goal is to turn everyone into Islamists. And, combine this approach with the global internet connection with all schools - they have the perfect vehicle to begin that insidious project.

Barack Obama and his administration have supported and promoted many of these Islamists under the guise of peace building and inclusion. But is that what's really happening? Let's analyze the organizations these Islamists openly support - especially the ISNA.

The 'Investigative Project on Terrorism' discovered a plan for the silent Islamic Jihad in America. The plan was written in May, 1991, and is titled: 'An Explanatory Memorandum On the General Strategic Goal for the Group In North America.'

This May 1991 memo was written by Mohamed Akram, a.k.a. Mohamed Adlouni, for the Shura Council of the Muslim Brotherhood. In the introductory letter, Akram referenced a "long-term plan approved and adopted" by the Shura Council in 1987 and proposed this memo as a supplement to that plan and requested that the memo be added to the agenda for an upcoming Council meeting. Appended to the document is a list of all Muslim Brotherhood organizations in North America as of 1991. These are some notable quotes from the document:

"Enablement of Islam in North America, meaning: establishing an effective and stable Islamic Movement led by the Muslim Brotherhood which adopts Muslims' causes domestically and globally, and which works to expand the observant Muslim base, aims at unifying and directing Muslims' efforts, presents Islam as a civilization alternative, and supports the global Islamic state, wherever it is.

In order for Islam and its Movement to become "a part of the homeland" in which it lives, "stable" in its land, "rooted" in the spirits and minds of its people, "enabled" in the live

[sic] of its society and has firmly-established organizations on which the Islamic structure is built and with which the testimony of civilization is achieved, the Movement must plan and struggle to obtain "the keys" and the tools of this process in carry [sic] out this grand mission as a "Civilization Jihadist" responsibility which lies on the shoulders of Muslims and "on top of them" the Muslim Brotherhood in this country.

The process of settlement is a "Civilization-Jihadist Process" with all the word means. The Ikhwan must understand that their work in America is a kind of grand Jihad in eliminating and destroying the Western civilization from within and "sabotaging" its miserable house by their hands and the hands of the believers so that it is eliminated and God's religion is made victorious over all other religions. Without this level of understanding, we are not up to this challenge and have not prepared ourselves for Jihad yet. It is a Muslim's destiny to perform Jihad and work wherever he is and wherever he lands until the final hour comes, and there is no escape from that destiny except for those who chose to slack. But, would the slackers and the Mujahedeen be equal."

The document also recommends that all the Muslim related organizations must be organized together under one banner for the common cause, and should work in the same spirit. That common cause is to "destroy America from within." The Islamic Society of North America (ISNA) is probably the most dangerous to our existence as Americans.

Established in 1981 by the Saudi-funded Muslim Students' Association of the U.S. and Canada (MSA), the Islamic Society of North America (ISNA) calls itself the largest Muslim organization on the continent. ISNA was created by MSA with the help of one of Palestanian Islamic Jihad's founding students, Sami Al-Irian. Another noteworthy founding member of ISNA was Mahboob Khan.

Today ISNA's annual conventions draw more attendees, usually over 30,000, more than any other Muslim gathering in the western hemisphere. ISNA's mission is to function as "an association of Muslim organizations and individuals that provides a common platform for presenting Islam, supporting Muslim communities, developing educational, social and outreach programs and fostering good relations with other religious communities, and civic and service organizations."

ISNA focuses heavily on providing Wahhabi theological indoctrination materials to a large percentage of the mosques in North America. Many of these mosques were recently built with Saudi money and are required, by their Saudi benefactors, to strictly follow the dictates of Wahhabi imams; an edict that affects the tone and content of the sermons given in the mosques, the selection of books and periodicals that may be read in mosque libraries or sold in mosque bookshops, and the policies governing the exclusion or suppression of dissenters from the congregations.

Through its affiliate, the North American Islamic Trust, a Saudi government-backed organization created to fund Islamist enterprises in North America, the Saudi-subsidized ISNA reportedly holds the mortgages on 50 to 80 percent of all mosques in the U.S. and Canada. Thus the organization can freely exercise ultimate authority over these houses of worship and their teachings.

Writes Kaukab Siddique, the editor of 'New Trend,' an Islamic periodical of extremist views that is nonetheless opposed to Wahhabi domination of American Islam: "ISNA controls most mosques in America and thus also controls who will speak at every Friday prayer, and which literature will be distributed there."

Islam scholar Stephen Schwartz describes ISNA as "one of the chief conduits through which the radical Saudi form of Islam passes into the United States."Adds Schwartz, "Our view is that the number of mosques under Wahhabi control actually totals at least 600 out of the official total of 1,200, while, as noted, Shia community leaders endorse the figure of 80 percent Wahhabi control. But we also offer a number of 6,000 mosques overall, including small and diverse congregations of many kinds."

According to Sufi leader Sheikh Muhammad Hisham Kabbani's testimony before a State Department Open Forum on January 7, 1999, extremists have taken over "more than 80 percent of the mosques in the United States. This means that the ideology of extremism has been spread to 80 percent of the Muslim population, mostly the youth and the new generation." Kabbani based his statement on his personal investigation of 114 American mosques. "Ninety of them," he said, "were mostly exposed, and I say exposed, to extreme or radical ideology, based on their speeches, books and board members." This is largely due to the efforts of ISNA.

According to terrorism expert Steven Emerson, ISNA "is a radical group hiding under a false veneer of moderation;" "convenes annual conferences where Islamist militants have been given a platform to incite violence and promote hatred" (for instance, al Qaeda supporter and PLO official Yusuf Al-Qaradhawi was invited to speak at an ISNA conference); has held fundraisers for terrorists (after Hamas leader Mousa Marzook was arrested and eventually deported in 1997, ISNA raised money for his defense); has condemned the U.S. government's post-9/11 seizure of Hamas' and Palestinian Islamic Jihad's financial assets; and publishes a bi-monthly magazine, 'Islamic Horizons,' that "often champions militant Islamist doctrine."

Many more Islamic organizations, almost all in fact, that are aimed at the one goal of a silent Jihad of changing America to Sharia from within. They have all assigned themselves to that charter - and Barack Obama is helping them achieve that goal. The hard truth is: they could not accomplish that Jihadist goal without Obama's help. Is he helping them destroy the United States from sheer stupidity, or is he really part of that Jihad, himself? Perhaps he really does understand what he's doing. Or, is he perhaps guided in his relationship with Muslim terrorists by a statement he made in 2007.

On November 21, 2007, then-candidate Obama said on

New Hampshire Public Radio that his Muslim experience would make us safer:

"I truly believe that the day I'm inaugurated, not only the country looks at itself differently, but the world looks at America differently. If I'm reaching out to the Muslim world they understand that I've lived in a Muslim country and I may be a Christian, but I also understand their point of view.

My sister is half-Indonesian. I traveled there all the way through my college years. And so I'm intimately concerned with what happens in these countries and the cultures and perspective these folks have. And those are powerful tools for us to be able to reach out to the world.Then I think the world will have confidence that I am listening to them and that our future and our security is tied up with our ability to work with other countries in the world that will ultimately make us safer."

Is Obama delusional, or is he lost in la-la land? The radical Muslim terrorist goal is to destroy us and anyone else who is not or does not convert to Islam. Why does he think his relationship with them, or who he is, will change that dogma?

King Obama

5

COOPERATING WITH TERRORISTS

Like ISNA, many other Islamic organizations are connected in a significant way to the Muslim Brotherhood. The May 1991 Muslim Brotherhood document discovered by the Investigative Project on Terrorism, revealed the Brotherhood's 29 like-minded "organizations of our friends" that shared the common goal of destroying America and turning it into a Muslim nation. Some other organizations included in this list, who hold similar charters and purposes, are:

Foundation or International Development (FID)
Islamic Housing Cooperative (IHC)
ISNA FIQH Committee
ISNA Political Awareness Committee (IPAC)
Islamic Education Department (IED)
Muslim Arab Youth Association (MAYA)
Malasian Islamic Study Group (MISG)

Islamic Association For Palestine (IAP)
United Association For Studies and Research (UASR)
Occupied Land Fund (OLF)
Mercy International Association (MIA)
Islamic Circle of North America (ISNA)
Baitul MAL Inc. (BMI)
International Institute For Islamic Thought (IIIT)
Islamic Information Center (IIC)

The Investigative Project on Terrorism discovered this Islamic conspiratorial plan for the silent Islamic Jihad in America. Clearly and explicitly the proposal, and acceptance by most if not all, of these organizations is to destroy the United States and its religious foundation from within. What is Barack Obama's reaction to their plan and his attitude toward their approach? He embraces them - in his own words. This is from an interview with Steve Kroft, on 60 Minutes, where Obama made the 'bump in the road' comment after four Americans were murdered in Benghazi, and he refused to blame Islamic radicals. He said:

> "Well, I've said even at the time that this is going to be a rocky path. The question presumes that somehow we could have stopped this wave of change. I think it was absolutely the right thing for us to do to align ourselves with democracy, universal rights, a notion that people have to be able to participate in their own governance.
>
> But I was pretty certain and continue to be pretty certain that there are going to be bumps in the road because you know, in a lot of these places the one organizing principle has been Islam, the one part of society that hasn't been controlled completely by the government. There are strains of extremism, and anti-Americanism, and anti-Western sentiment. And you know can be tapped into by demagogues.

There will probably be some times where we bump up against some of these countries and have strong disagreements, but I do think that over the long term, we are more likely to get a Middle East and North Africa that is more peaceful, more prosperous and more aligned with our interests."

Let's repeat for clarity, ("the one organizing principle has been Islam, the one part of society that hasn't been controlled completely by the government.")

Obama's comments fall right in line with that report of the Muslim Brotherhood. It's the 'smoking gun' that links Obama directly to the Muslim Brotherhood intentions. He is sending them millions of our honest American dollars - while he wants more American dollars from more 'rich people.'

Not once in his administration has he criticized either of these organization, their leaders, or the radical Islamists who expressly proclaim from every hilltop in America that they plan to destroy America. He even refuses to acknowledge that Islamic terrorists exist who promise to kill us. From his support of the Islamists, and from his lack of interest in curtailing their plan, one can make only one important conclusion:

Obama clearly supports actions by the Muslim Brotherhood. The Muslim Brotherhood's expressed goal is to "destroy America from within."

We must again ask that question: why did he bow to the Saudi king, the leader of Wahabbism, the most radical of Islamism? This is an article copied from Brietbart that further discloses this plan by the Muslim Brotherhood - supported by Barack Obama - weakening the United States as we know it:

"In the Spring of this year, US Army Lieutenant Colonel

Matthew Dooley was condemned by the Joints Chiefs of Staff (JCS) and relieved of teaching duties at Joint Forces Staff College for teaching a course judged to be offensive to Islam.

The course he taught, 'Perspectives on Islam and Islamic Radicalism', was an elective course that Lt. Col. Dooley's superiors judged as presenting Islam in a negative way. His superiors were persuaded to come to this conclusion after receiving an October, 2011 letter in which 57 Muslim organizations claimed to be offended by the course.

The fact that Lt. Col. Dooley is a highly decorated combat veteran with nearly 20 years of service under his belt apparently held little or no sway with the JCS. As a matter of fact, JCS Chairman General Martin Dempsey personally attacked Lt. Col. Dooley on C-Span on May 10, 2012, during a Pentagon News Conference.

Yet the craziest part of all this is that "the course content, the guest speakers, and the method of instruction" for the course was all approved by the Joint Forces Staff College "years ago."

Former CIA agent Claire M. Lopez commented on the state of things: "All US military Combatant Commands, Services, the National Guard Bureau, and Joint Chiefs are under Dempsey's Muslim Brotherhood-dictated order to ensure that henceforth, no US military course will ever again teach truth about Islam that the jihadist enemy finds offensive (or just too informative)."

Of course this action against Lt. Col. Dooley is outrageous just on the face of it. But one must delve much deeper to understand the grave danger America now faces. The conspiracy is deep and multi-faceted, and is supported even by those who have taken an oath to "protect and defend the United States against all enemies - foreign and domestic."

Of course, Obama's policies created this travesty against Lt. Col. Dooley, but in my mind Obama's character is no better than that. That action can be expected by one of such little character. To me, the real travesty is from the actions by

General Dempsey.

I spent 21 years in the U.S. Air Force, serving a year of that in Saigon, Vietnam. At that time, and ever before and ever since, I have always had a high regard for military officers. They were expected, even of themselves, to be honest and honorable at all times - even under the most dire and self-incriminating situations.

To me, General Dempsey violated that military standard - that code. I realize he was following orders from either the secretary of defense or the president. I absolutely cannot believe he took that action against Lt. Col. Dooley of his own initiative and beliefs. Any honorable military officer would have resigned before committing that unwarranted assault against another military person - especially one of junior rank.

That makes General Dempsey just as culpable in supporting the silent American Jihad as the president. Who is General Dempsey, anyway? He is an unknown who came out of nowhere - selected, of course, by Barack Obama. General Martin Dempsey has violated his oath as one pledged to defend the Constitution of the United States when he did not protect Lt. Col. Dooley from charges by those who plan to destroy us.

Obama's association and cooperation with Islamic terrorists' interests are growing even closer and closer as he gets well into his second term. Perhaps he gets bolder as his time for more open actions becomes more critical. An example is a recent formal meeting with a high-level terrorist by senior administration officials. A report by Investors.com, a part of Investors Business Daily, on June 26, 2013, disclosed the following information:

"In a new low for an administration that courts U.S. enemies, the White House has met secretly with the deputy of a Muslim cleric who has called for the killing of U.S. troops. On June 13, of all things the National Security Council hosted Sheik Abdullah bin Bayyah for a West Wing chat, where the radical Islamist asked for more support for Hamas and Syrian "rebels," i.e. al-Qaida terrorists.

President Obama's envoy to the Muslim world, Rashad Hussain, and senior NSC aide Gayle Smith reportedly asked for the meeting as a learning session. Well, here's what the administration apparently didn't learn or did find out and still didn't care when it vetted the sheik: Bin Bayyah works for Yusuf al-Qaradawi, who supports suicide bombings and issued a fatwa calling for attacks on U.S. soldiers in Iraq. Al-Qaradawi, who happens to be the spiritual leader of the radical Muslim Brotherhood, also once vowed to "conquer" America.

His boss is considered so dangerous the State Department has banned him from entering the U.S. every year since 1999. Yet it apparently had no reservations granting a visa to his right-hand man. Why?

In 2004, bin Bayyah joined a radical pro-jihad group, the International Union of Muslim Scholars which has supported Palestinian terrorists and called for the destruction of the state of Israel. Last year, the sheik participated in a conference in Mauritania sponsored by the Islamic Society of North America, which the Justice Department has blacklisted as a Hamas front group and named an unindicted terrorist co-conspirator. (Do you remember this member of Obama's inner circle described in the last chapter - also a member of ISNA? Imam Mohamed Magid – Obama's Sharia Czar, Islamic Society of North America.)

During his trip to Washington, bin Bayyah also visited the ADAMS Center, a northern Virginia mosque whose leaders' homes and businesses were raided by federal agents after 9/11 for terrorist connections. It strains credulity that the White House was in the dark about this creep. His statements and videos and associations are readily available on the Internet.

Yet it rolled out the red carpet, legitimizing him and his group "basically the equivalent of inviting al-Qaida to the White House," said Steve Emerson of the Investigative Project on Terrorism, which exposed the secret White House meeting. We join Emerson in calling for Congress to investigate not only why the Secret Service OK'd a known jihadist's White House visit, but also why Homeland Security signed off on his visa." End of article.

Why does Barack Obama and his administration continue to court and placate the Muslim Brotherhood and known terrorists who proclaim loudly across the world, verbally and in writing , that they plan to 'destroy us, our religion, and our way of life?' If they succeed, and if they fully carry out their promises, will God-fearing Americans who refuse to worship the beast really be beheaded? It's proclaimed and it's written - why should we not believe it?

There are too many examples of Obama's support for Muslims who have expressed their plans and desires to kill Americans (Westerners and non-believers) to list in this book. All the examples on the internet would fill many volumes and many books. These examples are only short representatives. How can anyone not believe he is an ardent Muslim terrorist supporter? He will not offend them - because he must need them for his plans for the future: The Great Imam - President for Life - King - or one identified in the Bible's Book of Revelation?

Perhaps that conclusion about Obama and his plans and actions for America must be made and accepted within each individual American heart. That thought is too dire, it's too unbelievable, to be expressed in written words in this insignificant and probably never-to-be-discovered book. But, let's look even further into Obama's acceptance of and cooperation with those who have clearly stated they intend to do harm to America.

Soon after he became President of the United States, he immediately began his silent war on Christians. Although he claims to be a Christian, that's clearly a guise to hide his real Muslim following. If he were to proclaim he is a Muslim, that would reveal the ulterior purpose for his rise to such a high worldly leadership position. Certainly, he didn't get to that position only by his own guile and actions. It took a greater force to put him there. It took a larger plan - beginning with his keynote speech during the previous Democratic National Convention. Who put him there in that position to make that speech? No one had ever heard of him. He was a great speaker, saying the right things to a large following.

He quickly revealed his large appeal plans to his proles when he began his campaign for president for the 2008 election. It was "fair share" and "spread the wealth around." Of course, those voters didn't consider themselves 'proles' as identified by George Orwell. His followers were clearly thinking only of themselves and what was in it for them, personally and individually. They were blinded to the needs and the support for America's needs to support the Constitution. His supporters were diverse groups who made the election more personal - for their perceived needs and social justice.

That election was far removed from American concepts and ideologies of self-determination and self-reliance. It was guided by the concept of 'me.' Most who voted for him were blinded by his promises to do something for them - not for America. They functioned perfectly in their place in Orwell's outline of a three-tiered society.

Of course, nearly every black person voted for Obama. It was something new and revolutionary. One who represented them and their heritage had finally made it to the top - his blackness had been recognized as good and positive. It negated the long-standing stereotype that had plagued them for generations. They had no choice. Had the roles been reversed, had the whites been in the minority without what they considered due recognition and status, they would have had the same feeling and the same obligation. Whites would have voted for a white candidate, regardless of the outlook for the future. It was a representative vote, not a personal candidate vote. For black voters it was for history - not for the best outlook for the future.

Although I know of no surveys to prove or disprove it, but from casual readings of blogs and other postings, certainly all homosexuals voted for Obama simply on the idea that he would support their personal cause. They were so attuned to that one point that other ideas and statements he expressed had no relevance. That was their focus - the prosperity and well-being of the United States was totally irrelevant in their desperation to find someone who would give them "equality and fairness."

The third group to support Obama without consideration of a future based on ideological American principles were the Hispanics. Too many were citizens and wanted a more open and free flow across the border so their relatives and friends could join them in the new 'promised land.' Obama made them feel he would support their instant citizenship plans with his great speeches of fairness, equality, and social justice. He had their unquestioned votes locked in even before the campaign began.

Those three voting blocks were solidly locked in for Obama even before the campaigning began. But, that still wasn't enough by itself to get him elected. He still needed many of the independent voters to make his campaign successful. Two things were in his favor. First, the economy had plummeted and many desperate people were looking for anything to change their economic future. Many needed a job. This is where his promise of a 'fair share' and 'spread the wealth around' mantra offered an alternative to those desperate people. He said the right words at the right time.

Although he was unproven, untested, and inexperienced, he said what they wanted to hear. It was the basic socialistic call to the proletariat - the proles. It was his basic 'rise of the proletariat' call to defeat the evil and unfair upper class and 'rich people' who were cheating them - not allowing them to be successful. In Orwellian language, he was targeting the 'High.' Along with this group were many of those who voted for a black man, any black man, to prove to themselves they were not prejudiced. It was a social conscious relief.

No one in these groups asked what was the best decision for the advancement and prosperity of America. They simply voted for Barack Obama because he was 'that man.' On the other hand, he didn't really have an opponent for his first election once he got past Hillary Clinton in the primary.

John McCain had such a weak campaign that it seemed he didn't even really want to win the election. Who wants to vote for someone who gives the impression that he doesn't really want to win? I voted for McCain only because there was no other choice. Perhaps many others voted for Obama for that same reason. I knew Barack Obama planned to weaken our American heritage, and the strength of the United States while he was campaigning.

He did not then, and still does not today, encourage people to accomplish something to support themselves, to improve their personal lives. He avoids promoting traditional American values and ideals. Instead, he keeps dividing America by blaming the hardship of the poor on those greedy rich people - the High. Even if greedy rich people were the cause of some poverty, an individual still must rely on himself or herself to at least try to improve his or her conditions. The alternative is a Socialist or Communist society. Every day his actions and comments support the idea that his plans are not in the best interests of our country.

It's these large and dedicated voting blocks that gave Barack Hussein Obama his great power in the United States. It's these same voting blocks that give him the confidence to ignore American fundamentals and charge ahead with his agenda that's most dangerous to our national survival. His goal is to change America to another purpose other than freedom. It's an accepted idea that the United States could never be conquered by an outside force.

Even our forefathers, the founders of our great country, warned us that the inside threat was the most dangerous. Barack Obama is in a position to prove them correct. He is the most likely nightmare they warned us about. And, he is accomplishing that goal most deceitfully. As he distracts with the fear of a one-world order and socialism, he is helping the radical Islamists slip in the back door. The signs are all around.

In my previous book, 'Obama's Ring: The Seat of Satan,' I referenced many of those signs to specific verses and chapters in the Bible. Although I have intentionally avoided those references in this book, there are two that are too important - and relevant - to ignore. For those who are Bible-haters, and vehemently anti-Christian, please skip this part. It will only cause you much anger and frustration - because there is no denying what it says - or that it is not a clear prophesy that can be related to current times. These two references must be considered together to understand this current information:

Revelation, Chapter 20,Verse 4 says the souls of those who are beheaded by the beast because they had not worshiped him or his image, or had not received his mark upon their foreheads or in their hands would live and reign with Christ a thousand years. This is after the beast and the false prophet are both "cast alive into a lake of fire burning with brimstone." The souls of those who are killed for refusing to worship the beast are resurrected first. So, what is the pertinent information here? In today's world the only people who behead other people are Muslims. That means a Muslim will be the beast who promotes those beheadings.

Daniel, Chapter 11, Verses 38 and 39 state, "But in his estate shall he honour the God of forces; and a god whom his fathers knew not shall he honour with gold, and silver, and with precious stones, and pleasant things. This shall he do in the most strong holds with a strange god, whom he shall acknowledge and increase with glory; and he shall cause them to rule over many, and shall divide the land for gain."

Barack Obama seems to want more dedicated followers with their minds focused on him and their efforts on giving him more influence and power. He has destroyed the essence, the foundation that makes America strong by these promises and actions that divide Americans. He has divided this land for his gain, his gain in more power. But, for what purpose does he turn American against American? Is it to lead them to another god or eventually to look toward him as their god? Was this one of the warnings given to Daniel?

If this is the case, if Barack Obama is using promises and actions of those pleasant things to increase another strange god or himself with glory, who is that strange god to whom he offers those things? It can only be one other, and that's the one he calls Allah, the god of Islam. He can run and hide from this concept all he wants, but many American citizens have already looked behind his facade of claiming to be a Christian. They know. He is 'dividing the land for gain' to gather enough followers to make that transition, either to that other 'strange god,' or to himself.

Why did the prophet Daniel identify this future god as a 'strange god?' Because the god is Islam did not appear until six-hundred years later. At the time Daniel wrote this message the other gods in his area were Roman gods. At that time they were not 'strange.' Only that god to arrive six-hundred years later would not have an identification at the time of Daniel.

When the numbers are large enough he will transition the United States from what was a 'Christian' nation into a Muslim nation or that godless nation of the strange god. At the moment, he has proclaimed that we are neither, but only a mixture of many. He has pushed the influence of Christianity out the back door. Or perhaps he considers growing more worthy of occupying that high place himself without another god above him. Until that happens, however, he will need the cooperation of his Muslim brothers to help him reach that decision point.

There are two things he must have to maintain his power base. He must have an active terror threat; and he must have the support of Muslims who present the facade of being cooperative and peace-loving. Now he has both.

First, he must have an ever-present danger to distract citizens that will not allow them to look toward a bright and safe future. A bright and safe future would allow American citizens to focus on more positive things such as self-improvement, country advancement, comfort and prosperity. These are the things that define who we are - Americans.

According to Maslow's 'Heirarchy of Needs' theory those higher order things cannot be approached until the safety need is fulfilled. Obama must keep the fear factor as the dominant focus so he will know exactly where the control points are - only on that one important thing to every American citizen. Perhaps that explains why he refuses to label those groups who do harm to Americans as terrorists. He does not want to alienate them as a formal group. Perhaps he doesn't want to be seen as their adversary. To call them 'terrorists' would place a label on them that they could later use against him. But, how soon will he need them?

Of course, no one could even guess or predict that exact time. However, one might guess the conditions that would create that symbiotic relationship. It would be at the rise of the Antichrist, or as described in Revelation - the beast. That will happen when the seven continents become ruled by a central authority, as in a one-world government. That's when Satan will give that one-world leader his 'great authority.' That's when he will become 'the' Antichrist.

Historically, we have already had 'many' Antichrists, but not one with world authority. Their followers have been as few as a dozen or so, and as many as several thousand. But, they have never had a total world stage with many millions of followers and devotees. Most Antichrists in the past have led many of their followers to their deaths - such as Jim Jones and David Koresh.

There is another important clue that reveals Obama's support of and association with those Islamic terrorists whom he placates and supports. He refuses to call them what they have time and time again proven to be. Never forget that he

King Obama

refuses to call them Islamic terrorists. Why?

6

DEADLY SECRETS

At the beginning of his first administration, in 2008, Barack Obama promised to have the most transparent government ever. In a conversation in February, 2013 he commented on that promise as Thehill.com reported:

"President Obama on Thursday hailed his administration for its transparency. "This is the most transparent administration in history," Obama said during a Google Plus "Fireside Hangout."

"I can document that this is the case," he continued. "Every visitor that comes into the White House is now part of the public record. Every law we pass and every rule we implement we put online for everyone to see." The president said this holds true even on the issue of the attack on a U.S. Consulate in Benghazi, Libya, a controversy which he said was "driven by campaign politics" and one that Congressional

Republicans were clinging to even though they've "run out of questions." He recently referred to it as a "phony scandal." This tactic is in accordance with Alinsky's Rule 5: "Ridicule is man's most potent weapon." There is no defense. It's irrational. It's infuriating. It also works as a key pressure point to force the enemy into concessions. The purpose for Rule 5 is to create anger or fear. Obama plays it very well.

Which transparency is more important: letting citizens know who visits the White House - or enforcing policies that prevent deaths of brave Americans? Did he tell the truth?

Unfortunately, for us, all indications and suggestions are the answer is a clear and resounding - NO! Everything Obama's administration does and says exposes an ever-present dangerous leaning. They are incapable and indisposed to tell the truth about anything. To them, everything must remain a secret - even if they must use deception to prevent the truth from being revealed. Let's use two clear and blatant examples to show how their lack of transparency result in loss of life - of American citizens and others. Operation 'Fast and Furious' and the Benghazi event are two examples that directly resulted in deaths.

Operation Fast and Furious

What was 'Operation Fast and Furious?' According to Wikipedia, it was part of a 'Gunwalking' program used by the Arizona Field Office of the U.S. Bureau of Alcohol, Tobacco, Firearms and Explosives (ATF.) They ran a series of "gunwalking" sting operations between 2006 and 2011 in the Tucson and Phoenix area where the ATF "purposely allowed licensed firearms dealers to sell weapons to illegal straw buyers, hoping to track the guns to Mexican drug cartel leaders." These operations were done under the umbrella of Project Gunrunner, a project intended to stem the flow of firearms into Mexico by interdicting straw purchasers and gun traffickers within the United States.

The stated goal of allowing these purchases was to

continue to track the firearms as they were transferred to higher-level traffickers and key figures in Mexican cartels, with the expectation that this would lead to their arrests and the dismantling of the cartels. The tactic was questioned during the operations by a number of people, including ATF field agents and cooperating licensed gun dealers. During Operation Fast and Furious, by far the largest gunwalking probe, the ATF monitored the sale of about 2,000 firearms, of which only 710 were recovered as of February 2012. A number of straw purchasers have been arrested and indicted; however, as of October 2011, none of the targeted high-level cartel figures had been arrested.

Guns tracked by the ATF have been found at crime scenes on both sides of the Mexico-United States border, and the scene where Border Patrol agent Brian Terry was killed. The gunwalking operations became public in the aftermath of Terry's murder. Dissenting ATF agents came forward to Congress in response. According to Humberto Benitez Trevino, former Mexican Attorney General and chair of the justice committee in the Chamber of Deputies, related firearms have been found at numerous crime scenes in Mexico where at least 150 Mexican civilians were maimed and killed. Revelations of gunwalking led to controversy in both countries, and diplomatic relations were damaged.

As a result of a dispute over the release of Justice Department documents related to the scandal, Attorney General Eric Holder became the first sitting member of the Cabinet of the United States to be held in contempt of Congress on June 28, 2012. Earlier that month, President Obama had invoked executive privilege for the first time in his presidency over the same documents.

How anxious and desperate is Obama and his administration to keep secrets from American citizens. Not only did Eric Holder refuse to give information to Congress, who represents us as 'having a right to know,' and not only did Obama refuse to allow Holder to disclose that information, his administration also targets people who try to let Americans know what happened. They target whistleblowers and try to silence them with intimidation. A perfect example is a report by Alex Newman in 'New American' on May 28, 2013:

"As if there were not already enough scandals plaguing the Obama administration, the federal Fast and Furious operation that armed Mexican drug cartels is back in the news after the Justice Department Inspector General released a report blasting a government leak intended to smear a key ATF whistleblower. The leaked memorandum was apparently aimed at discrediting Special Agent John Dodson and contradicting his explosive testimony before Congress, which blew the lid off of a federal program that put thousands of high-powered weapons into the hands of deadly criminals in Mexico.

The latest twist in the scandal surrounds disgraced former U.S. Attorney Dennis Burke, one of the officials at the center of the administration's lawless gun-trafficking scheme. The ex-prosecutor, who resigned in August of 2011 along with acting ATF boss Kenneth Melson, was furious after learning that brave whistleblowers had gone to Congress and the media, documents show. He was particularly upset because Dodson, one of the crucial figures in exposing Fast and Furious, had written a memo outlining a plot to let guns "walk" across the border into Mexico — and into the hands of known criminals.

Special Agent Dodson, however, said he had been alarmed about the idea from the start, only putting the plot down on paper in an effort to show superiors how preposterous it really was. When the ATF agent went to Senator Charles Grassley (R-Iowa) and CBS News to blow the whistle, Burke wanted desperately to protect his reputation. The then-U.S. attorney, who worked in Arizona, learned that Fox News reporter Mike Levine was working on a story about the issue. Burke then leaked the Dodson memo to Levine.

"We also concluded that Burke's disclosure of the Dodson memorandum to Levine was likely motivated by a desire to undermine Dodson's public criticisms of Operation Fast and Furious," the Justice Department's Office of the Inspector General (OIG) said in its report. "Although Burke denied to congressional investigators that he had any retaliatory motive for his actions, we found substantial evidence to the contrary."

Official sources, for example, told the OIG that "Burke disclosed the document to help the U.S. Attorney's Office defend against what were considered hypocritical criticisms being made by Dodson," the report explains. "That disclosure occurred less than two weeks after Dodson's public testimony before Congress." Others interviewed during the investigation also confirmed that Burke was "frustrated" with the whistleblower's "highly critical" congressional testimony about Fast and Furious.

Burke refused to be interviewed for the investigation. However, he admitted in his own account of the conversation with Levine that he believed the Fox reporter was working on a story that would expose what Burke considered to be Dodson's "hypocrisy," the OIG noted. As such, the former U.S. Attorney claimed that he simply released the memo in question — a violation of Justice Department policy at the very least — in an innocent but misguided effort to provide "context" for the story.

Neither Dodson nor the inspector general bought those excuses. "We believe that this explanation, taken together with the other evidence cited above, demonstrate that Burke's conduct in disclosing the memorandum to Levine was likely motivated by his desire to undermine Dodson' public criticisms," the OIG report said, adding that the ATF whistleblower had raised very serious concerns about Fast and Furious.

Among the most interesting findings in the Inspector General investigation was Burke's sense that he was being sacrificed by the administration. Quoted in the OIG report, Burke explained that "several U.S. Attorneys commented to me that the Department was throwing my office under the bus." The Inspector General report noted: "Burke's statements to the Department reflected a belief that he could not rely on the Department to respond to criticism of his office's handling of the Fast and Furious investigation, and we found that he responded to this belief by deciding to defend the office himself through, in part, the unauthorized disclosure of information to the media."

The report savages the former U.S. attorney in its conclusions, stating that Burke violated Justice Department policy by leaking the memo and that his excuses "were not credible." The OIG also "rejected" Burke's explanations, adding that the former U.S. attorney took "calculated measures" to reduce the chances of being caught: sending the document from a private e-mail account to a friend who passed it on to the Fox reporter.

"First, regardless of whether Burke in fact believed Levine or Congress already had the memorandum, that belief would not excuse his failure to comply with Department policy," the report said, citing DOJ policies on media relations that were violated. "Second, we found that Burke disclosed the Dodson memorandum despite knowing he was under investigation at the very same time by OPR for virtually the same alleged misconduct."

The misconduct described in the report is "particularly egregious," the OIG continued, "because of Burke's apparent effort to undermine the credibility of Dodson's significant public disclosures about the failures in Operation Fast and Furious." In the end, the actions were found to be "inappropriate for a Department employee and wholly unbefitting a U.S. Attorney." As such, the problem will be reported to state Bar associations where Burke is licensed to practice law.

In an August 2011 memo to his staff at the U.S.

Attorney's office about his resignation, Burke, who previously worked for current Homeland Security boss Janet Napolitano, claimed that it was time to move on. "My long tenure in public service has been intensely gratifying," he said. "It has also been intensely demanding. For me, it is the right time to move on to pursue other aspects of my career and my life and allow the office to move ahead."

The latest OIG report is not the first time Burke has come under fire for his controversial handling of the press after the Fast and Furious scandal emerged. In December of 2011, for example, the administration was forced to release more than 1,300 pages of documents related to the gun-trafficking program. The subpoenaed records revealed frantic e-mail communications between senior officials about how vigorously to defend the operation, as well as concerns about the veracity of some of the proposed defenses.

The documents showed that DOJ officials were worried that if the administration were to cooperate with the congressional investigation, Congress would press for even more information. Others highlight the general fear among those involved that exposure would damage the image of the Bureau of Alcohol, Tobacco, Firearms, and Explosives (ATF).

One of the most explosive e-mails was actually from Burke, who recommended sending a "stern missive" to the Arizona Republic newspaper for exposing the scheme. "Just baffling that they refuse to engage even just to protect the integrity of the agency," he wrote in a February 1 e-mail to Justice Department Criminal Division boss Lanny Breuer, as if the media's job were to protect government rather than expose its shady dealings. In another e-mail, Burke complained that congressional investigators were acting as "willing stooges" for defenders of the right to keep and bear arms.

Burke, of course, was also not the only top official who has been caught trying to retaliate against the whistleblowers. After the scandal was publicly exposed, the ATF retaliated against the brave agents who told Congress and the media. The agency got caught, but its new acting chief subsequently released a video threatening other agents not to blow the whistle again. Lawmakers were outraged, yet the lawlessness continues.

Meanwhile, the establishment press has continued to ignore the most important elements of the scandal, pretending that Fast and Furious was simply a "botched" operation in which low-ranking administration bureaucrats inadvertently "lost" the weapons. In reality, multiple White House officials had been briefed about the scheme, the supposed "targets" of the alleged "investigation" were drug lords already on the FBI's payroll, and top administration officials have been caught lying repeatedly — resulting in disgraced Attorney General Eric Holder being held in criminal contempt of Congress for the ongoing cover up.

Incredibly, the violence from Fast and Furious — U.S. law enforcement officers killed, hundreds of Mexicans massacred, and more — was used to push more gun control in the United States, official documents showed. The e-mails exposing the administration's scheme to use the bloodshed to assault the Second Amendment backed up assertions made by the numerous analysts and experts including the National Rifle Association.

Finally, evidence continues to emerge that Fast and Furious was in fact much bigger than the press and the administration have admitted. Mexican drug lords, for example, have said that the U.S. government was shipping weapons to their cartels and allowing them to bring drugs across the border in exchange for information. The CIA's involvement also continued to be largely concealed. However, with Fast and Furious seemingly taking a back seat to other major scandals - Benghazigate, spying on journalists, IRS abuse, and more - justice for the Fast and Furious victims may never be truly served.

On 12 September, 2012, Gerardo Reyes and Santiago

Wills, from ABC News, reported five other facts about Fast and Furious:

"The U.S. government's botched Fast and Furious gun-trafficking operation left a trail of bullets and bodies in Mexico. In a special investigation by Univision News, which aired Sunday night, several new revelations came to light. Here are five worth knowing.

1. Fast and Furious Guns Used in Infamous Massacre. Mexican military reports show that at least three guns from North America were used in the Salvarcar massacre in 2010. A total of 15 people died in that incident, most of them teens. They were gunned down by the Juarez cartel, which mistook the group for rival Sinaloa cartel members. According to one document, the weapons entered Mexico illegally through a border point near Columbus, New Mexico.

2. 57 Previously Unidentified Weapons Surface. Univision cross-referenced the serial numbers off guns used in Fast and Furious against guns seized in Mexico. Nearly 100 of those weapons were used in crimes, and 57 of them were not mentioned in an investigation carried out by the U.S. Congress.

3. Mexico Knew About Fast and Furious. Univision News obtained the list of Fast and Furious weapons and a list containing almost 60,000 recovered firearms compiled by Mexico's SecretarÃa de la Defensa Nacional (SEDENA)."

4. U.S. Gun-Walking Operations Extended to Other Countries. Fast and Furious was not the only ATF operation of its kind that went awry. A dailycaller.com report, July 13, 2011 asked: "did-operation-fast-and-furious-have-a-tampa-twin-operation-castaway?" Under Operation Castaway, Hugh Crumpler, a former ATF informant, told Univision News the ATF deliberately allowed guns to pass into Honduras, Puerto Rico and Colombia. Several of those weapons have already been found at crime scenes and in the hands of local cartels.

In an email message, the ATF claims that they "found out about the weapons when they had already been shipped."

5. U.S. Agents Were Attacked with U.S. Weapons. Victor Avila and Jaime Zapata, two U.S. Federal Agents assigned to the U.S. Embassy in Mexico, were in the process of transporting surveillance equipment when their vehicle was surrounded by cartel members and shot more than 90 times. Zapata died and Avila was seriously wounded.

Prior to traveling into the region, Avila reached out to a supervisor expressing concerns over security that were backed by a U.S. State Department document which forbade U.S. Embassy employees from traveling in that area. The reason: It was heavily controlled by the Zetas cartel. According to an exclusive interview with Avila, the supervisor did not share his concerns. Three of the guns used in this shootout were also from a gun-walking operation, but not Fast and Furious.

The end result of Fast and Furious is that many people, including American agents, were killed by an ill-conceived and preposterous idea and plan. Worse yet, Barack Obama and his administration show little concern about those deaths or in giving any valid information to explain what happened, who was responsible, and why an event such as that should never be attempted again.

They have thumbed their noses at Congress and the American people. How much power do they think they have? How much power do they think they should be allowed? This contempt for Congress and the American people has set a dangerous precedence. It's only the first of many. They continue to show their irresponsibility and contempt regarding the Benghazi incident.

The Benghazi Incident

What was the 'Benghazi Incident?' An article in Wikipedia gives this brief synopsis:

"The American diplomatic mission at Benghazi, in Libya, was attacked on September 11, 2012 by a heavily armed group. The attack began during the night at a compound that is meant to protect the main diplomatic building. A second assault in the early morning the next day targeted a nearby CIA annex in a different compound. Four people were killed, including U.S. Ambassador J. Christopher Stevens. Ten others were injured. The attack was strongly condemned by the governments of Libya, the United States, and many other countries throughout the world.

Many Libyans praised the late ambassador and staged public demonstrations against the militias that had formed during the civil war to oppose leader Colonel Mummar Gaddafi. The Libyan government also began attempts to disband many of the groups. The United States increased security worldwide at various diplomatic and military facilities and began investigating the attack.

At various times between September 11th and 17th, eight other diplomatic missions in the Middle East, Asia, and Europe were subject to protests and violent attacks in response to an inflammatory video, 'Innocence of Muslims.' Initially, it was suggested that the attack arose in similar circumstances, but an investigation by the U.S. State Department determined that there was no such protest and that the attack was premeditated and was launched without warning by Islamist militants. The video and the resulting anger may have provided an opportunity for the attackers; according to some eyewitnesses, they used the video as justification for the attack.

Some Republican politicians, conservative media figures, and other critics immediately accused the Obama administration of mishandling the attack and its aftermath and of over-emphasizing the role of the video. As the incident became a focus of political discussion on the right, some Republican members of Congress launched their own independent investigations and hearings on the subject in the following months. These investigations are currently ongoing, and are a matter of great controversy in the American political sphere. Weapons used in the attack were: rocket-propelled grenades, hand grenades, assault rifles, 14.5 mm anti-aircraft machine guns, truck mounted artillery, diesel canisters and mortars. "

This question about Benghazi goes deeper and further with many considerations. This is perhaps the most significant political event of our time and should never be forgotten or overlooked, until all the facts are known - by all American citizens. Presently, it seems there's a desperate attempt by a secretive group - the Obama administration - to cover up something insidious that would not be supported by American history, heritage, or expectations of a free democracy. They even perpetrated an outrageous falsehood to cover it up. What have they done to America? How have they violated and compromised American principles of honor and justice?

A May 16, 2013 report by J.B. Williams at NewsWithViews.com, titled: 'Benghazi: Where are Gen. Ham and Adm. Gaouette?' gives another view and more information:

"Who knows the whole truth about why Navy SEALs Tyrone Woods and Glen Doherty, along with State Department officials Chris Stevens and Sean Smith died in Benghazi, 11 September 2012? It's now public knowledge that the ever evolving official administration stories on Benghazi are all bold faced lies.

It's clear that the four Americans who were brutally murdered in Benghazi did not have to die. What's not clear yet, is who is responsible for these murders? Nothing the

Obama administration has told the people about Benghazi is true. but who is responsible? General Carter Ham and Admiral Charles M. Gaouette know the answer to this question. Where are Ham and Gaouette today? Why hasn't Issa's investigative committee called these decorated military officers to testify before the committee investigating Benghazi?

We have known since 30 October, 2012 that these two officers who were ordered to STAND DOWN in Benghazi ignored those orders and were relieved of duty for refusing orders to STAND DOWN. We know from the unclassified cables between Benghazi and DC and the subsequent Executive Brief, that cables were firing in all directions in the hours before and during the Benghazi attack that ended in the brutal death of four Americans. General Ham was head of AFRICOM and commander of the 2011 US-NATO operation to depose Gadhafi in Libya. Rear Admiral Charles M. Gaouette was in command of the Carrier Strike Group Three (CSG-3), then deployed in Middle Eastern waters during the attack on Benghazi.

Both Ham and Gaouette reported receiving the same desperate cables for additional security and backup that Obama administration officials received and ignored from Benghazi. They did not ignore those desperate calls for help ringing out from the Benghazi installation on 11 September, 2012. No, both Ham and Gaouette attempted to launch ready response teams in the region capable of provided the much needed assistance during the seven hour long assault on Benghazi. Both were then relieved of command for their actions, described by the US military as allegations of inappropriate leadership judgment.

General Ham immediately had a rapid response unit ready, and communicated to the Pentagon that he had a unit ready to deploy to Benghazi. Then, General Ham received the order to stand down. His response was "screw it" - he was going to help anyway. Within minutes after issuing an order to deploy his ready response team, Ham's second in command apprehended the General and told him that he was now relieved of his command. Ham knows who issued the order to STAND DOWN as well as the order to relieve him of his command at AFRICOM.

Admiral Gaouette had also received the startling requests for support as the attack unfolded in Benghazi. Like Ham, he readied a response from Carrier Strike Group Three (CSG-3). Gaouette was also ordered to STAND DOWN and like Ham, he decided to refuse those orders. Gaouette readied vital intelligence and communications operations for an extraction effort to be launched by Ham.

'Stars and Stripes' reported October 18, 2012 that General Ham is being replaced by Gen. David Rodriguez. They also reported on October 27, 2012 that Adm. Gaouette is being replaced by Rear Adm. Troy M. Shoemaker. The Navy stated that it was "replacing the admiral in command of an aircraft carrier strike group in the Middle East, pending the outcome of an internal investigation into undisclosed allegations of inappropriate judgment."

What were the "inappropriate judgments" of these two decorated military leaders? Rear Adm. John Kirby, the Navy's chief spokesman, declined to discuss the investigation. What we know is that these two highly unusual acts to remove two highly decorated commanders is related to the 11 September, 2012 strike on Benghazi. We also know that the congressional investigation has not yet called these valiant men (at the date this article was written) in to give testimony. We know that months' worth of warnings and requests for additional security at Benghazi were ignored and denied by the Clinton run State Department and that someone gave the DoD order to STAND DOWN when American troops were in the region and ready to assist.

We know that the Obama administration manufactured a lie about some obscure anti-Islam youtube clip that had nothing whatsoever to do with the events of 11 September, 2012 Benghazi. We know that the Obama administration is holding that filmmaker in prison today. We know that Benghazi survivors have been threatened and silenced. But most of all, we know that Gen. Ham and Adm. Gaouette can provide very real answers to a laundry list of very important questions regarding the Benghazi attacks and Issa's alleged investigation. Five House Committees investigating Benghazi issued a joint Interim Progress Report. In it, all five committees fail to ask the right questions and all five demonstrate a clear intent to keep the truth about Benghazi under wraps, though the report does confirm almost everything stated herein.

State Department official, and Benghazi 'whistle-blower' Gregory Hicks said the special forces personnel were "furious" that they were not allowed to go. The testimony raises a key question--who gave the "stand down" order? In the chain of command, the three possibilities are President Obama, Sec. of Defense Leon Panetta, and commander of AFRICOM Gen. Carter Ham. These are the three who could have given a "go" or "stand down" order, although Gen. Ham's authority to do so would have been limited to the window of time between which he gained knowledge of the events in Benghazi and the time President Obama learned of the same. Unless, of course, Obama gave a standing order at the outset forbidding the Sec. of Defense and AFRICOM from sending military force.

Another option is that an agreement banning the use of U.S. special forces, or U.S. military force in general, for certain parts of Libya was negotiated between the Obama administration and the Libyan government after Muammar Gaddafi was overthrown. No one has denied or confirmed this, but if it were the case, Sec. of State Hillary Clinton would have had to re-negotiate the agreement to open the door for the use of force, after which Obama, Panetta, or Ham could have given the "go" or "stand down" order. The testimony is a gray area that needs to be cleared up." End of article.

Another article by Debra Saunders at Real Clear Politics,

on May 14, 2013 gives another view of the attempted cover-up by the Obama administration:

"Last Sept. 11, a terrorist attack left four Americans dead at the Benghazi, Libya, diplomatic mission. The next day, a State Department official wrote in an email, "The group that conducted the attacks, Ansar al-Sharia, is affiliated with Islamic terrorists." Days later, however, U.S. Ambassador to the United Nations Susan Rice went on Sunday talk shows and blamed an anti-Islam video for the violence, even though others in her own department knew better.

The administration later claimed that Rice simply was following CIA talking points. But last week, The Weekly Standard and ABC released revised versions of the documents -- and they don't mention the video. Early versions of the talking points do mention Ansar Al-Shariah, however, even if Rice did not.

At a news conference Monday, President Barack Obama talked of a pledge he made the day after the deaths of Ambassador J. Christopher Stevens, Sean Smith, Tyrone Woods and Glen Doherty. Obama said that he promised to the American people "that we would find out what happened, we would make sure that it did not happen again, and we would make sure that we held accountable those who had perpetrated this terrible crime."

Really? Eight months later, there have been no arrests, even though some of the perpetrators can be seen on camera. (The FBI waited until May 1 to release photographs of three people of interest.) The only guy Washington has put behind bars is Nakoula Basseley Nakoula, the man who shot the video that did not spark the Benghazi violence, for violating conditions of his parole.

Last week, former U.S. deputy chief of mission in Libya Gregory Hicks told the House Oversight and Government Reform Committee that the FBI had not interviewed him. That's not good. From Benghazi, Stevens had phoned Hicks in Tripoli to alert him of the attack. Hicks also testified under oath that he believes that the State Department demoted him because he complained about Rice's scapegoating the video.

Hicks was enraged because he believes that Rice's comments, which directly contradicted those of the Libyan president, hindered the FBI probe. Perhaps as an act of payback, the Libyan government kept FBI investigators in Tripoli for more than two weeks.

Obama did mention Accountability Review Board recommendations, which his administration is implementing so this sort of thing won't happen again. That's good, but the board predetermined not to fix responsibility on anyone higher than the assistant secretary level. So I'm not impressed.

To recap: No bad guys brought to justice, a snail's-pace FBI probe and not-too-high-up bureaucratic review. The public still hasn't heard a good reason for why Washington didn't even try to rush a military presence to Benghazi in time perhaps to save Doherty and Wood.

Some apologists have argued that the military could not have arrived in time, but Hicks' attorney, Victoria Toensing, observed, "When you're in the middle of an attack like that, you don't know when it's going to end."

Former Rep. Dennis Kucinich, D-Ohio, said on Fox News Channel: "We went into Benghazi under the assumption that somehow there was going to be a massacre in Benghazi. So we went there to protect the Libyan people. We couldn't go into Benghazi to protect our own Americans who were serving there?" End of article.

That's the question this administration does not want to answer. In fact, although those radicals continue to slaughter and maim people - including many innocent bystanders and children - Obama still refuses to call them what they are, "terrorists." As a result of the pressure on the Benghazi event, he finally mentioned terrorism in an indirect manner - but he still did not directly call them "terrorists." To Obama, instead of those terrorists killing four good Americans, they merely created a "bump in the road."

And, what did Hillary Clinton say about the event - the one that was under her direct supervision, monitoring, and control? She denied knowledge of the events as they were happening - and later responded, "At this time - what difference does it make?"

All the senior administrators responsible for what happened in Benghazi had disavowed that responsibility because they claimed they were not directly involved and didn't know what was happening. Does anyone in their right mind believe they are telling the truth? One might also ask is it possible they are even capable of telling the truth.

Perhaps the destination Obama is leading us has no place for truth, honor and justice. Perhaps he and his ardent 'worshipers' are taking America to a place it's never been - a place we have always feared as free Americans. Perhaps exhibition of truth, integrity, and honor from those leaders would relieve that fear.

On the other hand, perhaps there are too many prole citizens, according to George Orwell, who don't really care and who don't take the time to ask questions. They just follow the man in their own little imagined world. Our forefathers warned us.

If Barack Obama and his administration have been so open and transparent, then why are there so many unanswered questions about very serious and deadly matters? But to some, it doesn't matter - his proles just keep following along worshiping everything he has to say. The one who promises them everything can do no wrong.

7

DANGEROUS DECEPTIONS

What should we sacrifice for safety? Should our concern for safety rise above all our other human concerns? Should we blindly follow as Obama and his administration continue to subjugate our freedoms to promise us more safety? This is what a wise man had to say about those questions:

"Those who surrender freedom for security will not have, nor do they deserve, either one."

Benjamin Franklin

This is an article by Donna Anderson, at Infowars.com, on June 12, 2013:

"In response to media concerns over reports that the NSA has been spying on communications between millions of law-abiding American citizens, President Obama said, "You can't have 100-percent security and also have 100-percent privacy and zero inconvenience. We're going to have to make some choices as a society." But is the promise of security really worth sacrificing our freedoms?

During an appearance on the Alex Jones show, Rep. Steve Stockman (R-Texas) said the NSA (National Security Agency) spying scandal was par for the course. "It follows with Obama's intent to focus on the citizens as the criminal and the terrorists are not to be investigated. The Tea Party and average citizens have become the target. It's alarming that we do live in an Orwellian world where good is bad and bad is good, and it's now targeting American citizens over the terrorists."

Stockman also said he didn't understand why more Americans weren't outraged. "What I don't understand is, people outside of your listeners, you interview them or talk to them, it's puzzling to me at what degree they're willing to give up their individual freedoms for the perception of security, and we both know that when you give up your individual liberties you soon have neither."

In a series of Tweets sent after the announcement of the NSA spy scandal, Stockman reminded followers, "The Democrats defending IRS abuses and illegal spying programs are the same ones who insist they would never abuse a gun registry data base."

Obama isn't the first president to spy on American citizens. The Bush administration ordered the NSA to engage in warrantless surveillance of U.S. citizen's phone calls and emails in response to the 9/11 terrorist attacks. In 2008, legislation was passed that permitted the NSA to seek a generalized warrant from the court to allow surveillance on anyone the agency "reasonably" believed to be involved in terrorism, whether they were a U.S. citizen or not.

In 2009, the NSA admitted they'd reached well beyond the boundaries set forth in 2008 and engaged in "overcollection" of communications belonging to U.S. citizens without any connection to terrorism at all. So Obama isn't the first, he's merely the president who plans to put the icing on the cake.

In 2010, under Obama, the FBI proposed expanding the 1994 Communications Assistance for Law Enforcement Act, a law that requires phone and network carriers to build interception capabilities into their systems. Under the existing law, the FBI must have a search warrant and currently, judges simply ask the service providers to comply with law enforcement. The provider can always use the excuse that he doesn't have the capability to comply.

Just last month, buried under the news of the AP and IRS scandals, Obama moved closer to endorsing legislation that will make it even easier to put a tap on anyone he wants. Under the new law, judges will no longer request, they'll order providers to comply, and if they don't they'll face fines starting at $25,000 per day.

The new plan will also require Internet giants like Facebook and Google to build back doors into their systems that will enable government surveillance at-will. By criminalizing those Americans who disagree with him and classifying anyone who speaks against his plans for takeover as an "extremist," Obama and his administration have convinced Americans that he's only looking out for their best interests and the safety of our country.

But Stockman reminds us that we need to look beyond the smoke and mirrors. "The NSA can keep tabs on anyone including federal judges, senators and average citizens. This is massive abuse. These are the same guys who want you to register your guns. They can't keep this data private so how can they keep gun registrations private?" End of article.

This article inherently asks the greatest and most important question of our time; and for that matter at any time for any country. That question is: Are our leaders acting in the best interests of us - the citizens? Fundamentally, can we trust our government to protect us? Is our government concerned more about citizen Americans - or are they more concerned about themselves, their comforts and their future? All my research suggests Obama and his administration , his cohorts, couldn't care less about American citizens - except to suppress their American idealism, and use them for their own personal goals and aspirations - to have them as 'proles.'

The fundamental considerations regarding these questions are: to whom do Obama's administration and his close supporters owe their allegiance - and what is their vision of America's future? Is it their own vision, or does it support the Constitution? Perhaps the Constitution is a hindrance to their plans. Recent scandals and actions by the Obama administration certainly suggest a lack of citizen concern. Consider two attacks against American citizens - beginning with the IRS scandal.

The IRS Scandal

Not only do we have dishonesty and deception from our government with serious and deadly matters such as the gunrunning operation 'Fast and Furious' and the Benghazi event; other events of dishonesty, deceit and fraud make themselves known almost every day. Consider the revelations about the IRS tactics against Conservative groups, IRS waste and abuse of money, NSA overreach, and use of drones. Each has a different consequence; nevertheless, all are important to demonstrate lack of transparency that Obama promised. Perhaps we should begin with the IRS situation first. It represents a dangerous abuse of power and waste of taxpayer money. For an overview to explain the abuse of power by the current IRS scandal, let's use the summary from Wikipedia:

"Beginning in March 2010, the IRS more closely scrutinized certain organizations applying for tax-exempt status under Section 501(c)(4) of the Internal Revenue Code by focusing on groups with certain words in their names. In May 2010, some employees of the "Determinations Unit" of the Cincinnati office of the IRS, which is tasked with reviewing applications pertaining to tax-exempt status, began developing a spreadsheet that became known as the "Be On the Look Out" list.

The list, first distributed in August 2010, suggested intensive scrutiny of applicants with names related to the Tea Party movement and other Conservative causes. Eventually, IRS employees in at least Cincinnati, Ohio; El Monte, California; Laguna Niguel, California; and Washington, D.C. applied closer scrutiny to applications from organizations that:

1. Referenced words such as "Tea Party," "Patriots," "Israel," "progressive," "occupy," or "9/12 Project" in the case file.

2. Outlined issues in the application that included government spending, government debt, or taxes.

3. Involved advocating or lobbying to "make America a better place to live."

4. Had statements in the case file that criticized how the country is being run.

5. Advocated education about the Constitution and the Bill of Rights.

6. Were focused on challenging the Patient Protection and Affordable Care Act — known by many as Obamacare.

7. Questioned the integrity of federal elections.

Over the two years between April 2010 and April 2012, the IRS essentially placed on hold the processing of applications for 501(c)(4) tax-exemption status received from organizations with "Tea Party," "patriots," or "9/12" in their names. While apparently none of these organizations' applications were denied during this period, only 4 were approved. During the same general period, the agency approved applications from several dozen presumably liberal-leaning organizations whose names included terms such as "progressive," "progress," "liberal," or "equality." However, the IRS also targeted several progressive- or Democratic-leaning organizations for increased scrutiny, leading to at least one such organization, called Emerge America, being denied tax-exempt status. Instructions to screeners obtained by The National Review obtained instructions to IRS screeners, and NR's reading of the instructions was that conservative and liberal groups were treated differently. The instructions stated that applications of tea-party groups should be sent "to group 7822" for additional scrutiny, but the National Review's interpretation was that screeners could approve liberal groups on the spot.

Senate and House Democrats in early 2012 continued to press the IRS to investigate abuses of 501(c)(4) tax-exempt status by organizations engaged in political activity. In a February 2012 letter to then-IRS Commissioner Douglas Shulman, several Democratic senators led by Senator Chuck Schumer wrote:

"We urge you to protect legitimate section 501(c)(4) entities by preventing non-conforming organizations that are focused on federal election activities from abusing the tax code."

The senators also urged the IRS to issue new rules to prevent this type of abuse. In a follow-up letter sent in March 2012, the senators asked the IRS to clearly define the amount of political activity that is permissible for "social welfare" groups under 501(c)(4) rules, to require the groups to document in their IRS filings the exact percentage of their activity that is dedicated to "social welfare," and to require the groups to notify their donors of what percentage of donations could be claimed for tax deductions. The senators promised to introduce legislation to accomplish these aims if the IRS did not do so itself by promptly issuing new administrative rules. None of these letters called for the targeting of groups on the basis of political ideology."

So, how was the IRS targeting of Conservative groups discovered, and what started the investigation? Some questions and answers by New York Times reporters, on May

20, 2013, help explain that time line. Their report begins, "Congressional Republicans investigating targeting of political groups by the Internal Revenue Service are focused on what government officials knew about the department's actions, and when they found out about it." They listed the following questions with appropriate responses:

When did the possibility that the IRS was improperly targeting conservative groups first become public? The first reports emerged in February 2012 on conservative Web sites like The Blaze. The New York Times first reported on the issue on March 6, 2012. "In recent weeks, the IRS has sent dozens of detailed questionnaires to Tea Party organizations applying for nonprofit tax status, demanding to know their political leanings and activities."

Why did the issue then remain quiet for more than a year? It was not yet clear in early 2012 that the IRS was specifically targeting conservative groups. Groups allied with the Tea Party made that accusation. But the issue remained clouded by a larger debate over politically oriented groups that seek nonprofit tax status. To receive such status, according to the IRS, a group must be "primarily engaged in the promotion of social welfare." Such organizations can engage in some political activity "so long as, in the aggregate, these nonexempt activities are not its primary activities." The standard for what constitutes a "primary" activity remains unclear, and many outside experts believe that political groups, on both the right and left, take advantage of the uncertainty.

When did an official investigation of the IRS behavior begin? The staffs of Representative Darrell Issa of California, the chairman of the House Oversight and Government Reform Committee, and Representative Jim Jordan, Republican of Ohio, contacted the Treasury Inspector General for Tax Administration in March 2012 to explore an investigation of allegations of abuse by IRS officials reviewing applications for tax exemption by conservative groups. That spring, the inspector general's staff developed an audit plan. With that plan complete, the lawmakers formally requested an audit on June 28, 2012. It asked that the audit cover the IRS oversight of organizations applying for tax-exempt status. The inspector general, J. Russell George, formally notified the lawmakers on July 11, 2012, that he had begun his "Document: Inspector General's Report" Mr. George also let the Treasury general counsel know of his audit in June 2012 and Deputy Treasury Secretary Neal S. Wolin shortly after.

White House officials have emphasized Mr. Issa's early involvement. Why have they done so? One of the Republican targets of inquiry is to ask how much the White House knew about the IRS activities and whether administration officials should have taken action to stop it once they knew. By pointing out that Mr. Issa was aware of the IRS audit in the summer of 2012, White House officials are hoping to show that the Republican outrage is manufactured.

White House officials argue that both they and Republicans knew about the audit in 2012, but no one yet knew what it would conclude. It ultimately found that officials in the Cincinnati office acted wrongly and that higher-level IRS officials attempted to stop the inappropriate practices once they knew of them.

What is the Republicans' response to that argument? Republicans say that of course Mr. Issa and Mr. Jordan knew; they requested the audit. They kept quiet as the audit unfolded to avoid even the appearance of trying to shape its outcome, Republicans say. And they say that members of Congress being aware of an audit into behavior by the executive branch is very different from members of the executive branch failing to stop that behavior.

Where does the matter go from here? The biggest open questions involve whether any White House officials or other senior Obama administration officials had reason to suspect inappropriate behavior at the IRS in 2012 or, even worse, had any role in influencing that behavior. Obama administration officials say they did not, and no evidence has yet emerged to the contrary.

Again, this is where all the secrets, deceptions, and lack of transparency apply for Obama's administration. Nothing can specifically be tracked because so many people were involved. Therefore - where is the promised transparency? And, there are many players involved in the IRS targeting, although only three names thus far have been subjected to scrutiny: Lois Lerner, Doug Shulman and Steven Miller.

First, who is Lois Lerner? She is, or was, the Internal Revenue Service's director of Exempt Organizations, who is at the center of the controversy after the agency targeted conservative organizations for gratuitous scrutiny. She invoked her Fifth Amendment right against self-incrimination at a congressional hearing examining the IRS scandal, on May 22, 2013.

She swore to tell the truth, read a brief statement saying she had done nothing wrong, broken no laws, or had violated any rules or regulations, or had not provided false information to this or any other congressional committee. Then she said, "I'm asserting my constitutional right not to testify or answer questions related to the subject matter of the hearing." Her right not to testify was challenged since she had made statements during the opening comments declaring that she was innocent of any wrongdoing. At the time of this writing, further action regarding her right not to testify are still pending.

The major question is as the supervisor of that unit, did she make the decision to target conservative applications - or was she acting on behalf of, or at the suggestion of a person more senior? This is the purpose of the congressional committee.

Douglas Schulman is another part of the puzzle who refused to give transparent information regarding this scandal when he appeared before a Congressional committee in May, 2013. How is Schulman involved?

An article by Susam Ferrechio of the Washington

Examiner, June 21, 2013, gives more information about the scope of these events. It explains Schulman's role and his refusal to give complete information before Congress:

"While congressional lawmakers are questioning why former Internal Revenue Service Commissioner Douglas Shulman paid dozens of visits to the White House during his tenure, Shulman's top political aide seems to have spent even more time working side-by-side with members of the Obama administration. White House visitor logs show Shulman's chief of staff, Jonathan M. Davis, appears to have visited the White House and adjacent Eisenhower office building as many as 310 times between the fall of 2009 and February 2013. Davis described his position at the IRS on the business social networking site LinkedIn as "strategy lead and adviser to IRS Commissioner" between 2008 until 2012, with a focus on modernizing the agency's technology and implementing "significant new economic programs."

The White House logs list Davis' "time of arrival" for 85 visits, but that does not necessarily mean Davis was present for all or some of the other 225 meetings. Only a handful of meetings are listed as cancelled. Neither the White House nor the IRS responded to requests about the frequency or nature of the visits.

Shulman and other IRS staff say many of their visits centered around implementation of the health care law and since Davis is skilled in data and technology development, he may have been working with the administration to modernize the IRS, which will play a primary role enforcing the health care law. Many of the meetings Davis attended took place in the Eisenhower Executive Office Building, which is part of the White House campus. Other meetings took place within the White House.

Shulman's tenure at the IRS ended in 2012. He was succeeded by Steven Miller, who was recently forced to resign following the revelation that IRS agents were targeting conservative groups seeking tax-exempt status. (Miller was pointed as the scapegoat to the scandal - and was already planning to leave that position in about two weeks.)

During hearings before Congress on the IRS scandal, in May, 2013, one of the Congressman questioning former IRS Commissioner Douglas Shulman alleged that White House Visitor Logs showed that he had visited the White House 157 times between January 2009 and November 2012 when he left office at the end of his term. Shulman testified that the only truly memorable visit he could recall at the time was attending the White House Easter Egg Roll. He refused to give any reason for any other visit or who he visited."

What are Lerner and Schulman hiding? Why won't they give Congress, and the American people, the information to explain why certain people with leanings against the Obama administration were targeted for more scrutiny and harassment, and those who showed inclinations toward supporting the administration were not? If Obama wants to live up to his promise of 'transparency' why doesn't he ask those people who are hiding that information to tell the truth. Obama remains silent. Is Obama an honest man - or is he a deceiver? What are his ulterior motivations? Are his motives counter to everything America stands for?

NSA (National Security Agency) Scandal

Although the secret, and possibly illegal, activities by the NSA aren't as clear and specific as the IRS event, it could nevertheless be more dangerous and far-reaching. Perhaps secrecy knows no bounds or limits. The following is a blog I posted on my site at Authorsden regarding NSA and a new center they are building in Utah. The question being - did Edward Snowden release any classified information about NSA information gathering that was not already commonly known or suspected:

"Barack Obama and his minions are now trying to track down and capture the "traitor" Edward Snowden for leaking America's secrets to our enemies, particularly China and Russia. This important chase causes me to ask two questions. First, what information did Snowden reveal that has not been already known publicly. Second, who is (are) the real American traitors?

Those actions by NSA were announced way before Snowden's revelations. My blog on May 25th, titled: The Looming Big Brother, reported a story by Wired Magazine that gave essentially the same information. It said the whole world was 'being hacked.' This is the important paragraph from that blog:

> 'A new story in Wired Magazine reveals details about how the National Security Agency is quietly building the largest spy center in the country in Bluffdale, Utah, as part of a secret surveillance program codenamed "Stellar Wind." According to investigative reporter James Bamford, the NSA has established listening posts throughout the nation to collect and sift through billions of email messages and phone calls, whether they originate within the country or overseas.'

Who are America's real traitors - if that's the word the Obama administration chooses to use? Could we consider Joe Biden and Barack Obama? They have done more damage to American citizens than Edward Snowden could ever do.

On May 1, 2011, Barack Obama personally and proudly gave the announcement on the killing of Osama Bin Laden. That briefing contained 'classified' information. Then on May 3, only three days later at a Washington event, Joe Biden announced the raid was carried out by SEAL Team 6. That was even more dangerous 'classified' information. Within hours, a member of SEAL Team 6 called his mother and told her to "wipe every piece of information regarding the family on social media, Facebook and Twitter." According to the mother, he said, "Mom, we're picking up chatter. We're not safe. You're not safe. Delete everything."

On Aug. 6, 2011, a Chinook helicopter carrying 30 U.S. service members — including 15 SEAL Team 6 members — was shot down in Afghanistan. Everyone on board was killed. The Chinook was shot down by a Taliban rocket-propelled grenade in Wardak province. Taliban fighters were waiting on three sides for the aircraft as it approached. The Chinook was a sitting duck as it hovered in the sky. The evidence is overwhelming and disturbing: SEAL Team 6 members were ambushed. It was America's single greatest loss of life in Afghanistan and the largest number of SEALs ever killed in one incident in history. The strange part is that some of the Afghan soldiers on the helicopter were replaced just before the helicopter took off.

And, to show his true 'patriotism' Barack Obama has appointed five Islamists as czars and senior advisors to his administration. They are all connected with the Islamic Society of North America (ISNA) whose WRITTEN GOAL is to make America a Sharia nation. They are: Imam Mohamed Magid, Salam al-Marayati, Rashid Hussain, Mohammed Elibiary, and Arif Alikhan. Several are appointed to Homeland Security.

So, of these three people, who has done the most damage to American citizens? Who has the greatest potential to destroy the America we know and love? " End of blog.

The program, Stellar Wind, supposedly secret was already publicized as a huge information gathering center - whose capability was almost unlimited. Just this announcement alone would have alerted any simpleton, not to mention security and spy agents around the world, that their phone and computer information could be hacked.

Perhaps Snowden's information release just confirmed what they already had been told, and gave other countries an opportunity to criticize what they already knew the United States government was doing. Perhaps the only real damage is if undercover agents and other identification systems are identified, that could be killed or otherwise neutralized or bypassed. On the other hand, did Obama and Biden release information that caused the deaths of fifteen SEAL Team Six members?

How are the NSA scandal and Stellar Wind related? This is a brief summary from Wikipedia:

"Stellar Wind was the open secret code name for four surveillance programs by the United States National Security Agency (NSA) during the presidency of George W. Bush and revealed by Thomas Tamm to The New York Times reporters James Risen and Eric Lichtblau. The operation was approved by President George W. Bush shortly after the September 11 attacks in 2001. Stellar Wind was succeeded during the presidency of Barack Obama by four major lines of intelligence collection in the territorial United States, together capable of spanning all modern telecommunications.

The program's activities involved data mining of a large database of the communications of American citizens, including e-mail communications, phone conversations, financial transactions, and internet activity. William Binney, a retired Technical Leader with the NSA, discussed some of the architectural and operational elements of the program at the 2012 Chaos Communication Congress.

There were internal disputes within the Justice Department about the legality of the program, because data are collected for large numbers of people, not just the subjects of Foreign Intelligence Surveillance Act (FISA) warrants.

During the Bush Administration, the Stellar Wind cases were referred to by FBI agents as "pizza cases" because many seemingly suspicious cases turned out to be food takeout orders. According to Mueller, approximately 99 percent of the cases led nowhere, but "it's that other 1% that we've got to be concerned about." One of the known uses of these data was the creation of suspicious activity reports, or "SARS", about people suspected of terrorist activities. It was one of these reports that revealed former New York governor Eliot Spitzer's use of prostitutes, even though he was not suspected of terrorist activities.

In March, 2012 Wired magazine published "The NSA Is Building the Country's Biggest Spy Center (Watch What You Say)" talking about a vast new NSA facility in Utah and says "For the first time, a former NSA official has gone on the record to describe the program, codenamed Stellar Wind, in detail," naming the official William Binney, a former NSA code breaker. Binney went on to say that the NSA had highly secured rooms that tap into major switches, and satellite communications at both AT&T and Verizon. The article suggested that the otherwise dispatched Stellar Wind is actually an active program. This conclusion is supported by the exposure of Room 641A in AT&T's operations center in San Francisco, and by information released by NSA leaker Edward Snowden.

The potential danger of this program is described even deeper in a report from Adan Salazar at Infowars.com, on August 28, 2012. This was well before Edward Snowden's name became known:

"A new mini documentary by Academy Award-nominated documentary filmmaker and journalist Laura Poitras blows the lid off the US government's secretive domestic spy program – a system currently storing all electronic communications and analyzing it in real time, thereby building dossiers on virtually every American. Poitras, who says she is on the government's "watch-list" after a documentary she made criticized the US occupation of Iraq, has personally been detained and questioned about 40 times at different airports.

"The Program" documentary reveals the Stellar Wind program's highly classified nature, undoubtedly due to its blatant violation of individual privacy rights. In Poitras' film, William Binney details his work in developing a program meant to intercept and monitor Soviet communications. Binney has direct insider knowledge, having worked for the NSA for a staggering 32 years as former technical director.

Binney says the domestic spy program – code-named Stellar Wind, or simply "The Program" as known to insiders – gathers data from individuals, storing it in massive databases and allowing customized profiles for each person to be queried à la search engine-style. He says Stellar Wind's sole purpose is to monitor what everyone is doing.

Unwittingly, Binney says he built the back-end for a program that has since been redirected towards the American people, tracking and logging every citizen's phone calls, texts, emails, Google searches, and even social network history. In a short video interview, Binney briefly summarized the NSA's spy program:

> "Domestically, they're pulling together all the data about virtually every U.S. citizen in the country and assembling that information, building communities that you have relationships with, and knowledge about you; what your activities are; what you're doing. So the government is accumulating that kind of information about every individual person and it's a very dangerous process."

The central hub for all recorded activities is said to be a data storage facility in Bluffdale, Utah with, reportedly, the capacity to store 100 years worth of data. In addition, Binney says his position as chair of the Technical Advisory Panel, the NSA's foreign relations council, allowed him to oversee the transfer of eavesdropping technology into the hands of Israeli intelligence, who he suspects then passed the technology on to Israeli companies – manifesting itself in the form of the Israeli company Narus – thus, inadvertently granting the Israeli government unlimited access to critical military, economic, and diplomatic information.

In June, the NSA refused to provide details on its highly secret domestic spy apparatus, arguing that to do so would compromise the privacy of Americans. Judging by what we've recently witnessed with the unlawful detainment of veteran Brandon Raub and numerous others, it is safe to assume that information gathered is being stored for use as opportunistic leverage to crush dissenting voices and go after citizens choosing to exercise constitutional rights.

And there's another part of the spy program. There's more. Talkleft.com on June 7, 2013, cited a CBS report that gave even more pertinent information. It was concerned with a part of the NSA program called 'PRISM.' CBS reported that PRISM is an arm of the Stellar Wind program.

This top-secret arm of the Stellar Wind program was set up in the wake of 9/11 is allowing the National Security Agency and the FBI to tap directly into the central servers of nine major Internet companies to extract audio, video, photos, emails and documents that let analysts track an individual's communication.

PRISM was established in 2007, according to The Washington Post, which broke the story Thursday evening. CBS News senior correspondent John Miller said it doesn't deal with names but was designed as a way for the government to track suspected terrorists. It culls metadata from Microsoft, Yahoo, Google, Facebook, PalTalk, AOL, Skype, YouTube and Apple and will soon include Dropbox.

The Stellar Wind program was revealed a few years ago by NSA Whistleblower William Binney and James Banford. He says it is a domestic spying program:

"Domestically, they're pulling together all the data about virtually every U.S. citizen in the country and assembling that information, building communities that you have relationships with, and knowledge about you; what your activities are; what you're doing. So the government is accumulating that kind of information about every individual person and it's a very dangerous process."

In May, 2012, in response to an inquiry by Senators Mark Udall and Ron Wyden, Charles McCullough, Inspector General of the Intelligence Community wrote:

"Thank you for your 4 May 2012 letter requesting that my office and the National Security Agency (NSA) Inspector General (IG) determine the feasibility of estimating "how many people inside the United States have had their communications collected or reviewed under the authorities granted by section 702 of the FISA Amendment Act (FAA). On 21 May 2012, I informed you that the NSA Inspector General, George Ellard, would be taking the lead on the requested feasibility assessment, as his office could provide an expedited response to this important inquiry. The NSA IG provided a classified response on 6 June 2012. I defer to his conclusion that obtaining such an estimate was beyond the capacity of his office and dedicating sufficient additional resources would likely impede the NSA's mission. He further stated that his office and NSA leadership agreed that an IG review of the sort suggested would itself violate the privacy of U.S. persons." In summary, the answer to the two senators was a non-answer.

PRISM was launched from the ashes of President George W. Bush's secret program of warrantless domestic surveillance in 2007, after news media disclosures, lawsuits and the Foreign Intelligence Surveillance Court forced the president to look for new authority.
Binney is one of a few NSA whistleblowers who has helped the Electronic Frontier Foundation (EFF) with their lawsuits. He's been raided, but never arrested.

The Electronic Frontier Foundation is the non-profit that's been beating the drum about the importance of digital rights, privacy, and metadata for decades. And in recent years, one of the EFF's causes has been to shed more light on the United States's National Security Agency (NSA) and specifically its use of the Foreign Intelligence Surveillance Act (FISA) to essentially spy on the telecommunications and web activity of millions of innocent Americans under the guise of keeping them safe.

How does National Intelligence Director James Clapper play into this? An article by Kimberly Dozier of the Huffington Post, July 2, 2013 gives more information about his role:

"WASHINGTON -- Director of National Intelligence James Clapper has apologized for telling Congress earlier this year that the National Security Agency does not collect data on millions of Americans, a response he now says was "clearly erroneous." Clapper apologized in a letter to Senate Intelligence Committee Chairwoman Dianne Feinstein. His agency posted the letter Tuesday on its website.

Leaks by former NSA systems analyst Edward Snowden have revealed the NSA's sweeping data collection of U.S. phone records and some Internet traffic every day, though U.S. intelligence officials have said the programs are aimed at targeting foreigners and terrorist suspects mostly overseas. Clapper was asked during a hearing in March by Sen. Ron Wyden, an Oregon Democrat on the Intelligence Committee, if the NSA gathered "any type of data at all on millions or hundreds of millions of Americans." At first, Clapper answered definitively: "No."

Pressed by Wyden, Clapper changed his answer. "Not wittingly," he said. "There are cases where they could inadvertently perhaps collect, but not wittingly."

Last month, in an interview with NBC News after revelations about the program, Clapper said: "I responded in what I thought was the most truthful, or least untruthful, manner, because the program was classified. In his letter to

Feinstein, Clapper wrote that he was thinking about whether the NSA gathered the content of emails, rather than the metadata of the phone records, the record of calls to and from U.S. citizens and the length of those phone calls.

"I realized later Sen. Wyden was asking about ... metadata collection, rather than content collection," Clapper wrote. "Thus, my response was clearly erroneous, for which I apologize."

Feinstein said in a statement Tuesday: "I have received Director Clapper's letter and believe it speaks for itself. I have no further comment at this time."

Wyden spokesman Tom Caiazza said Tuesday that when Wyden staffers contacted Clapper's office shortly after the hearing, his staffers "acknowledged that the statement was inaccurate but refused to correct the public record when given the opportunity."

"Sen. Wyden is deeply troubled by a number of misleading statements senior officials have made about domestic surveillance in the past several years. He will continue pushing for an open and honest debate," Caiazza said.

In the letter, Clapper said he could now publicly correct the record, because the existence of the metadata collection program has been declassified since the deluge of leaks from Snowden. A copy of the letter posted on the DNI website was stamped June 21 but made public on Tuesday."

Since the revelations, the Obama administration has said the leaks have caused damage to national security, including tipping off al-Qaida and other terrorist groups to specific types of U.S. electronic surveillance. But under pressure from lawmakers and privacy activists, the administration took the extraordinary step of declassifying many of the details surrounding the surveillance programs and how they work, to explain to Americans that NSA is not spying directly on them, which would violate its charter.

In an affidavit by Binney, in an EFF lawsuit, he states:

"The NSA has the capability to do individualized searches, similar to Google, for particular electronic communications in real time through such criteria as target addresses, locations, countries and phone numbers, as well as watch-listed names, keywords, and phrases in email. The NSA also has the capability to seize and store most electronic 5 communications passing through its U.S. intercept centers. The wholesale collection of data allows the NSA to identify and analyze Entities or Communities of interest later in a static database. Based on my proximity to the PSP and my years of experience at the NSA, I can draw informed conclusions from the available facts. Those facts indicate that the NSA is doing both."

In conclusion, how much can we trust our government to perform their duties under the auspices of our U.S. Constitution which is designed to protect our privacy and our rights? Learning what we have from whistleblowers and Congressional questioning - should we trust our government?

Shouldn't a president set the tone and the example for those in his administration under his leadership to follow? All indications are that Barack Obama has set the example for his staff, and they are following it very well - in the direction not suggested by our Constitution. The next chapter will give an example of where his leadership might be taking us - as citizens of the United States.

King Obama

8

A POLICE STATE

What's happening to our great country? It's not the free country we used to know and respect. It's not the country that welcomed you to come outside and smell the roses, and find ways to enjoy life - just for the sanctity of living and sharing with other people around you. Now, we've been influenced to believe that freedom is no longer free - the roses don't smell the same. We must clean the rose with an antibacterial before we should smell it.

We are now under the influence to believe that every thing around us is a threat that must be analyzed and purified. In effect, we are fast becoming a police state. This fear was recognized in an article by Representative Ron Paul, on August 10, 2004, titled: 'The Police State USA,' he stated:

"Last week's announcement that the terrorist threat

warning level has been raised in parts of New York, New Jersey, and Washington, D.C., has led to dramatic and unprecedented restrictions on the movements of citizens. Americans wishing to visit the U.S. Capitol must, for example, pass through several checkpoints and submit to police inspection of their cars and persons.

Many Americans support the new security measures because they claim to feel safer when the government issues terror alerts and fills the streets with militarized police forces. As one tourist interviewed this week said, "It makes me feel comfortable to know that everything is being checked." It is ironic that tourists coming to Washington to celebrate the freedoms embodied in the Declaration of Independence are so eager to give up those freedoms with no questions asked.

Freedom is not defined by safety. Freedom is defined by the ability of citizens to live without government interference. Government cannot create a world without risks, nor would we really wish to live in such a fictional place. Only a totalitarian society would even claim absolute safety as a worthy ideal, because it would require total state control over its citizens' lives. This doesn't stop governments, including our own, from seeking more control over and intrusion into our lives. As one Member of Congress stated to the press last week, "people who don't want to be searched don't need to come on Capitol grounds." What an insult! The Capitol belongs to the American people who pay for it, not to Congress or the police.

It is worth noting that the government rushes first to protect itself, devoting enormous resources to make places like the Capitol grounds safe, while just beyond lies one of the most dangerous neighborhoods in the nation. What makes Congress more worthy of protection from terrorists than ordinary citizens?

To understand the nature of our domestic response to the Sept. 11, 2001 attacks, we must understand the nature of government. Government naturally expands, and any crises – whether real or manufactured – serve to justify more and more government power over our lives. Bureaucrats have used the tragedy of 9/11 as an excuse to seize police powers sought for decades, such as warrantless searches, Internet monitoring, and access to bank records. It should be no surprise that the recently released report of the 9/11 Commission has but one central recommendation: bigger government and more spending at home and abroad.

Every new security measure represents another failure of the once-courageous American spirit. The more we change our lives, the more we obsess about terrorism, the more the terrorists have won. As commentator Lew Rockwell of the Ludwig von Mises Institute explains, terrorists in effect have been elevated by our response to 9/11: "They are running the country. They determine our civic life. They shape our private life. They decide how public resources are spent. They may dictate who gets to be the next president. It should be obvious that the government doesn't object. Not at all. The government benefits, by getting ever more reason for ever more money and power."

Every generation must resist the temptation to believe that it lives in the most dangerous time in American history. The threat of Islamic terrorism is real, but it is not the greatest danger ever faced by our nation. This is not to dismiss the threat of terrorism, but rather to put it in perspective. Those who seek to whip the nation into a frenzy of fear do a disservice to a country that expelled the British, fought two world wars, and stared down the Soviet empire.

Liberty is lost through complacency and a subservient mindset. When we accept or even welcome automobile checkpoints, random searches, mandatory identification cards, and paramilitary police in our streets, we have lost a vital part of our American heritage. America was born of protest, revolution, and mistrust of government. Subservient societies neither maintain nor deserve freedom for long."

In Ron Paul's statement, one important idea must be considered by every American citizen that respects freedom and individualism. This is that statement. It Incorporates every aspect of our lives - no matter what age:

> "Only a totalitarian society would even claim absolute safety as a worthy ideal, because it would require total state control over its citizens' lives. This doesn't stop governments, including our own, from seeking more control over and intrusion into our lives."

This idea doesn't refer only to safety checks at airports, or other places where large numbers of people gather to keep them safe from terrorists. As government gains more control in those areas, their concern turns into arrogant zeal. Once they feel the necessary power they claim, there becomes no limit to other areas in which they feel they must control. After all, in their position of care do they not lose the real basis for that care. For example, consider the power and control they are gaining in just the simple matter of school lunches.

Nanci Hellmich published this article in USA Today, on January 26, 2012. It reveals the government's role in more and more controlling our everyday lives:

> "Today the government is releasing new nutrition standards for school meals that spell out dramatic changes, including slashing sodium, limiting calories and offering students a wider variety and larger portions of fruits and vegetables. These changes will raise the nutrition standards for meals for the first time in more than 15 years.
>
> "When we send our kids to school, we expect that they won't be eating the kind of fatty, salty, sugary foods that we try to keep them from eating at home," first lady Michelle Obama said in a statement. She is announcing the new standards today along with Agriculture Secretary Tom Vilsack:
>
> Require schools to offer a minimum number of leafy green

vegetables, red-orange vegetables, starchy vegetables and legumes each week.

Require that after the two years of implementation, all grains offered to students must be rich in whole grains such as brown rice. Breads, buns, cereals and pastas must list whole grain as the first ingredient.

Require milk to be either low-fat (1%) or fat-free. (That is already in effect.) Flavored milk, such as chocolate, must now be fat-free.

Require that foods that are served contain no trans fats.

The new standards for lunch take effect the next school year. Changes for breakfast will be phased in."

Of course, this activity by the federal government sounds great. It demonstrates they care for the safety and health of American citizens. But, is it really necessary? What are the probable consequences? Although this simple action might be well-intentioned, these well-intentioned activities always have off-setting consequences.

First, who will monitor and control all these new requirements? Of course, it will be the government. That means more people will be hired into the government workforce. Then, the automatic chain-reaction occurs: taxes must be raised to hire those additional people, when those additional people are hired they must justify their jobs more thoroughly, to justify their jobs they must create more 'safety' regulations, then those regulations become so burdensome the government must hire more people. The vicious circle continues - until most people are working for the government. That results in more control by the government - moving us even closer to the total police state. Yes, it's happening even today.

Second, costs are always increased in these regulated

activities. Since available quantities of required products are less than more general products, the prices always are increased. More tax revenues are needed to provide those specialized items. More tax revenues place a heavier burden on ordinary taxpayers - people working for a decent living. Part of their livelihood is taken from them.

Third, and as in many special programs promoted by the government, special products or items always end in fraud and public abuse. Special subsidies and price support are almost always given to special friends of politicians to continue their financial support for their votes - from both parties. Neither Democrats or Republicans have a special entitlement to this fraudulent process. For example, special financial support might be given to the farmer who produces the most 'program supported green leafy vegetables.'

Where there are special requirements for a government program there is always preferential abuse. But, in the name of supporting a program that 'makes our children healthier' who can criticize that program? Our government will continue to abuse society as long as we have no serious objections to their 'safety and care for society programs.'

The more American citizens accept, the deeper our government will gain more control. Although the new and growing 'Police State' of America sliding into every corner of society, it seems to be making its greatest moves in our schools. Our children are most vulnerable and the easiest for tyranny to infect. Consider an article by Calltodecision.com published on February 28, 2013. It's titled, '11 Reasons to Get Your Kids Out of Government Schools.' It reads:

"It should be painfully obvious to everyone by now that it is time to get all of our kids out of the government schools. The public school system in the United States has been dramatically declining for a long time, and in most areas of the country the public schools are open sewers at this point.

Yes, there are some U.S. public schools that are still very good and that do a decent job of preparing our young people for their adult lives. But those good schools are the exception to the rule. Hopefully the school shooting that just happened in Ohio will be a wake up call to millions of parents out there. Drugs, sex and violence are rampant in American public schools today. The "teachers" are endlessly pushing specific political and social agendas down the throats of our kids, and the skills that our children really need such as reading, writing and mathematics are often badly neglected. Hopefully we can get more parents educated about what is really going on in these schools. After all, why would any parents want to send their children into an environment that is going to be highly destructive for them for six to eight hours a day?

Sadly, "destructive" is not too hard a word to use for the environment in these public schools. I went to public schools all my life, and they were absolutely horrible. Unfortunately, they have gotten even worse since the time that I left them.

The following are 11 reasons to get your kids out of the government schools:

#1 You Could Be Arrested For Something That Your Child Does. Yes, you read that correctly. If your child writes a story or draws a picture which a teacher or an administrator takes the wrong way, you could end up in jail. The following example is from thestar.com:

A Kitchener father is angry at police after he was arrested at his child's school and later strip-searched at the police station, all because his 4-year-old daughter drew a picture of a gun in class.

"I'm picking up my kids and then, next thing you know, I'm locked up," Jessie Sansone, 26, said of his ordeal on Wednesday. "I was in shock. This is completely insane."

The school principal, police and child welfare officials, however, all stand by their actions. They say they had to investigate to determine whether there was a gun in Sansone's house that children had access to.

#2 Your Child Could Be Arrested While At School For Just About Anything These Days. As I have written about previously, children all over the United States are being arrested by police in government school classrooms for some absolutely crazy things. Just check out the following examples:

A 12-year-old girl named Sarah Bustamantes was recently arrested for spraying herself with perfume at a public school in Texas.

A 13-year-old kid attending a public school in Albuquerque, New Mexico was recently arrested by police for burping in class.

A 12-year-old girl at a school in Forest Hills, New York was marched out of her public school in handcuffs by police just because she doodled on her desk. "I love my friends Abby and Faith" was what she reportedly scribbled on her desk.

When a little girl recently kissed a little boy at one Florida elementary school, it was considered to be a "possible sex crime" and the police were called out.

#3 Your Child Might Be Bodily Harmed By Security Thugs. All over the nation, public schools students are being bodily injured (sometimes permanently) by school security thugs. The following are a couple of examples:

A security thug at one school in California actually fractured the arm of one 16-year-old girl because she left some crumbs on the floor after cleaning up some cake that she had spilled.

In Allentown, Pennsylvania a 14-year-old girl was tasered in the groin area by a school security thug even though she had put up her hands in the air to surrender to him.

#4 Virtually Everything That Your Child Does At School

Is Being Put Into A Database Somewhere. As I described in a previous article, public schools (in conjunction with the federal government) have become obsessed with watching, monitoring and recording the activities of our kids.

According to the New York Post, the Obama administration is planning a vast new database which will collect all sorts of information about our children. Is this the kind of information that you want the federal government to keep track of?

The administration wants this data to include much more than name, address and test scores. According to the National Data Collection Model, the government should collect information on health-care history, family income and family voting status. In its view, public schools offer a golden opportunity to mine reams of data from a captive audience.

#5 Our Kids Are Not Learning Anything In These Public Schools. As I have documented before, American public school students are being dumbed-down and millions of them end up dumb as a rock and yet still are able to graduate from high school somehow. The following are some of the absolutely amazing results of a study conducted a few years ago by Common Core:

Only 43 percent of all U.S. high school students knew that the Civil War was fought some time between 1850 and 1900.

More than a quarter of all U.S. high school students thought that Christopher Columbus made his famous voyage across the Atlantic Ocean after the year 1750.

Approximately a third of all U.S. high school students did not know that the Bill of Rights guarantees freedom of speech and freedom of religion.

Only 60 percent of all U.S. students knew that World War I was fought some time between 1900 and 1950.

Sadly, we are rapidly falling behind the rest of the globe.

At this point, 15-year-olds that attend U.S. public schools do not even rank in the top half of all advanced nations when it comes to math or science literacy.

#6 Our Public School Kids Are Being Forced To Take Large Numbers Of Vaccines. All over the nation, children that have not received all of the "required vaccines" are being banned from school. Many parents do not want dozens of toxic vaccines injected directly into the bloodstreams of their kids, but in many states today you will not be able to send your kids to the public schools if they don't submit to the shots. This is just another reason why all American families should pull their kids out of these government schools immediately.

#7 Exposed To Rampant Sexual Promiscuity. When you send your kid to a government school, you are sending them into an environment where they will be exposed to rampant sexual promiscuity on an endless basis. When the kids around you are constantly talking about sex and joking about sex, it makes it nearly impossible to escape it. What makes things even worse is that the "sex education" courses are becoming more detailed and more graphic than ever. One example of this phenomenon was detailed in the New York Times -

"IMAGINE you have a 10- or 11-year-old child, just entering a public middle school. How would you feel if, as part of a class ostensibly about the risk of sexually transmitted diseases, he and his classmates were given "risk cards" that graphically named a variety of solitary and mutual sex acts? Or if, in another lesson, he was encouraged to disregard what you told him about sex, and to rely instead on teachers and health clinic staff members?"

In some U.S. public schools, kids are even having sex in the school bathrooms. Do you want that to happen to your kid?

#8 Teachers Are Having Sex With The Students. It seems like almost every single day there is another news story about teachers having sex with public school students. The following are just a few of the headlines that I found from this week:

-"More California Teachers Accused Of Sex Crimes"
-"Teacher Accused Of Sex With Student Appears In Court"
-"Queen's Teacher's Aide Charged With Child Sex Abuse"
-"Teacher Caught In Bed With Teen Student"

#9 U.S. Public Schools Are Dominated By Radical Control Freaks That Are Teaching Our Kids How To Live Like Slaves. The level of control that is exerted over the lives of children in many of our public schools is absolutely frightening. I know that I have mentioned the following example several times, but it is worth repeating because it shows just how far things have gone. One 4-year-old girl recently had her lunch confiscated by a control freak at one U.S. preschool because it did not meet USDA guidelines. These are the details:

'A preschooler at West Hoke Elementary School ate three chicken nuggets for lunch Jan. 30 because the school told her the lunch her mother packed was not nutritious. The girl's turkey and cheese sandwich, banana, potato chips, and apple juice did not meet U.S. Department of Agriculture guidelines, according to the interpretation of the person who was inspecting all lunch boxes in the More at Four classroom that day.

The Division of Child Development and Early Education at the Department of Health and Human Services requires all lunches served in pre-kindergarten programs – including in-home day care centers – to meet USDA guidelines. That means lunches must consist of one serving of meat, one serving of milk, one serving of grain, and two servings of fruit or vegetables, even if the lunches are brought from home.'

Do you want sick control freaks inspecting the lunches that your kids bring from home every single day? If not, perhaps it is time to pull them out of the government schools.

#10 Specific Social And Political Agendas Are Being Shoved Down The Throats Of Our Kids In U.S. Public Schools. If you think that the government schools are "neutral places" where all social, political and religious beliefs are tolerated, then you are either ignorant or you are delusional. The truth is that very specific social and political agendas are built into the curriculums of most public schools. Often, these social and political agendas are the same ones that are being force-fed to public school children in other western nations.

If your children are attending a government school, a system of "right and wrong" is being pounded into their heads that may be very different from what you would teach them. In one recent New York Times article, a district superintendent admitted that particular agendas are integrated into classroom instruction anywhere that they will fit.

"We're trying to integrate it into anything where it naturally fits," said Jackie Taylor, the district's superintendent. "It might be in a math lesson. How much water are you really using? How can you tell? Teachers look for avenues in almost everything they teach."

If you want to see where all of this is going, just check out what is going on in Europe. In the UK, teachers that don't promote the "correct agenda" face harsh disciplinary action. Those that control the public schools don't just want to "educate" your children. They want to indoctrinate them.

#11 If Your Children Attend Public Schools They Could

End Up Dead. Sadly, the school shooting that just happened in Ohio reminds us all once again that this is a matter of life and death. Our schools are not safe and they are becoming less safe all the time. While the odds are not great that your children will actually be murdered in our public schools, the truth is that there is a very good chance that they could be scarred for life by the destructive environment in these schools. Most Americans that have gone through the public school system emerge from it with deep emotional scars. If you have some of these emotional scars you know exactly what I am talking about.

The vast majority of our public schools are horrible places. Just ask kids that are going to public high schools right now. Most of them hate it. Sometimes people argue that we should keep our children in the public schools so that they can be a "light" and so that they can be a good influence.

(Author observation: This concept is what started school integration in the 1960s. The 'good students' were expected to share their 'social capital' as described by Professor James Coleman's Equal Education Opportunity Survey (EEOS) of 1965.)

Unfortunately, that is just not the reality of the situation. Our kids go there to be taught, and it is the teachers that have the authority. Our children are far more likely to be changed by their teachers and their friends than they are to significantly change the system around them.

When you are young and insecure, it can be incredibly difficult to take a stand for what is right when all of your teachers and all of your friends are going the other way. We need to protect our children and we need to put them into environments where they will be safe, protected and will receive a quality education. Growing up is hard enough without having to spend 30 to 40 hours a week in a nightmarish hell hole where you will be physically, mentally and emotionally tortured. End of article.

But, these actions of contempt and more control by

government officials don't involve only children and students. These restrictive activities and pressures against Americans are now being forced upon those who have sacrificed most to earn those freedoms our government is restricting - our veterans. An article by Investors.com on February 28, 2013 explains how they are compromising veterans' rights to possess weapons. The article begins:

"Guns: Veterans who bore arms to defend their country are receiving letters that they may be declared mentally incompetent and have their Second Amendment right to keep and bear arms stripped from them. Welcome home.

The contempt by the Obama administration for our Constitution and our rights has reached a new low with news the Veterans Administration has begun sending letters to veterans telling them they will be declared mentally incompetent and stripped of the Second Amendment rights unless they can prove to unnamed bureaucrats to the contrary.

On Thursday, Michael Connelly, executive director of the United States Justice Foundation, said veterans have begun getting warning letters from the Veterans Administration (VA). The letters inform the recipients that he or she must provide evidence to the contrary within 60 days. If the veteran desires a hearing, they must inform the VA within 30 days. The letter reads:

"A determination of incompetency will prohibit you from purchasing, possessing, receiving, or transporting a firearm or ammunition. If you knowingly violate any of these prohibitions, you may be fined, imprisoned, or both pursuant to the Brady Handgun Violence Prevention Act, Pub.L.No. 103-159, as implemented at 18, United States Code 924(a)(2)."

The VA states on its Fiduciary Program website that, according to the Brady Handgun Violence Prevention Act, signed into law in 1993, being determined as unable to manage your benefits prevents you from owning and possessing a firearm or ammunition. While mental health is a factor in the current gun control debate and recent mass shootings in Newtown, Conn., and Aurora, Colo., and elsewhere have in common the questionable mental state of the shooters, to single out returning vets from Iraq and Afghanistan this way is unconscionable and unconstitutional.

No one wants the mentally unstable to possess firearms, but neither do we want to see the presumption of innocence or the right to due process guaranteed under the U.S. Constitution taken away. The Fifth Amendment states that no person shall "... be deprived of life, liberty, or property without due process of law." The VA seems to be violating these rights to take away those guaranteed under the Second Amendment.

Returning vets were seen as vulnerable to "right-wing extremists" in an April 2009 report by Janet Napolitano's Homeland Security Dept., titled "Rightwing Extremism: Current Economic and Political Climate Fueling Resurgence in Radicalization and Recruitment".

"Returning veterans possess combat skills and experience that are attractive to right-wing extremists," it says. "Department of Homeland Security's Office of Intelligence and Analysis is concerned that right-wing extremists will attempt to recruit and radicalize veterans in order to boost their violent capacities." End of article.

This is a clear example of 'government gone wild,' and it has many implications. First, it implies that veterans returning from combat - or involved in combat - or under the auspices of combat control - are incapable of sound reasoning as are other United States citizens. The truth of the matter is that, possibly except in very unusual circumstances, those targeted veterans are the most stable and loyal Americans to ever exist. They risked their lives to defend our country and our Constitution. They faced the enemy - the one they could see and understand - and they tried to defeat it. Perhaps their real enemy was at their backs - such as a government administration that sneers at our Constitution.

Another implication concerns the fidelity, honor, and honesty of those who are to make judgements about a veterans patriotism and stability? If Janet Nepolitano, (or now her replacement) through the Homeland Security Department, orders the VA to declare all veterans an imminent threat to national security - what would the VA do? What does any governmental agency do? They comply without question. Superficially, and after much consideration, this appears to be a first major step to gun control by Obama's administration. It's an easy first step. If these actions continue - who is most to fear?

In his 'Call to service' speech on July 2, 2008 in Colorado Springs, then presidential candidate Barack Obama said,

> "We cannot continue to rely on our military in order to achieve the national security objectives we've set. We've got to have a civilian national security force that's just as powerful, just as strong, just as well-funded."

What did he mean by that? What would be the purpose of that civilian national security force? He has never explained, but recent events suggest he is beginning to act on that plan he revealed during that speech.

Recently, the Department of Homeland Security, operating under strict Obama policies bought 1.6 billion (that's billion - with a B) rounds of high-powered ammunition, 7000 full-auto assault rifles, and 2700 armored vehicles. There's still some uncertainty about the vehicles, but the Department of Homeland Security has not revealed the purpose for the other weaponry.

Is it to be used against drug smugglers crossing our southern borders? Is it to be used against radical jihadists

King Obama

led by the ghost of Osama Bin Laden wading ashore at the Boardwalk in Atlantic City? Or is to be used against those rowdy grandmothers who don't win enough when they play 'Bingo' at the community center? Who are these weapons to be used against? Department of Homeland Security, just tell us an answer that makes sense. Our Founding Fathers spoke against a force such as this and said it would be dangerous to its citizens. Is it? New revelations reveal that possibility. Here's more about DHS ammunition purchases:

An article by Paul Joseph Watson, of PrisonPlanet.com on March 25, 2013 revealed that while the Department of Homeland Security continues to ignore members of Congress demanding to know why the federal agency is engaged in an apparent arms build-up, the DHS has just announced it plans to purchase another 360,000 rounds of hollow point ammunition to add to the roughly 2 billion bullets already bought over the past year.

As reported elsewhere, some of this purchase order is for hollow-point rounds, forbidden by international law for use in war, along with a frightening amount specialized for snipers. Also reported elsewhere, at the height of the Iraq War the Army was expending less than 6 million rounds a month. Therefore 1.6 billion rounds would be enough to sustain a hot war for over twenty years.

A solicitation on the Federal Business Opportunities website details the DHS' plan to purchase 360,000 rounds of "Commercial leaded training ammo (CLTA) Pistol .40 caliber 165 grain, jacketed hollow point." The bullets are to be delivered to the Federal Law Enforcement Training Center in Artesia, New Mexico, the same destination for 240,000 hollow point rounds which were purchased only last month.

Although the DHS has attempted to explain its mammoth purchase of ammunition by claiming the bullets are being acquired in bulk to save money and that they are for training purposes only, this has been disputed by reputable voices such as former Marine Richard Mason, who told reporters

161

with WHPTV News in Pennsylvania earlier this month, "We never trained with hollow points, we didn't even see hollow points my entire four and a half years in the Marine Corps."

Hollow point bullets are almost twice as expensive as full metal jackets, therefore the DHS' explanation that it is buying huge quantities in bulk to "save money" doesn't make sense.

(Author's note: For those who are not aware of the difference in hollow point bullets and regular bullets, the difference is great. Although the DHS claims these bullets are for "training purposes only" that reason is pure and blatant deception. Hollow point bullets are never used for training - and for two reasons. First, is the cost; they are much more expensive, and since the purpose for target practice is to improve one's aim, hollow points do not improve that purpose. In a normal paper target the hollow point could never be discerned. It would simply pass through a piece of paper like a finger, pencil, pen, or regular bullet.

The second reason is safety. As stated above, in a paper target it couldn't be discerned if it were a hollow point or a regular bullet. To tell the difference, a hard target must be used. And, practicing with hollow point bullets at a hard target would be too dangerous. Upon hitting a hard target the hollow point bullet expands or explodes - to create more impact and damage. Ricochets and flying fragments from the shattered bullets would spread in all directions creating a hazard zone for anyone in the immediate area.

Simply, hollow point bullets would never be used for training purposes. If the DHS is giving this reason for purchasing hollow point bullets then they are claiming that American citizens are stupid.)

According to Watson's article ,Retired United States Army Captain Terry M. Hestilow sent a letter to Sen. John Cornyn (R-TX) warning that the ammo purchases represent "a bold threat of war by that agency (DHS), and the Obama administration, against the citizens of the United States of

America." Questions from members of Congress about why the federal agency is buying up ammo, exacerbating shortages across the country, have been met with silence.

* Kansas Congressman Timothy Huelscamp said last week that threats should be made to withdraw funding from the DHS if it didn't explain why it was purchasing so many bullets, remarking, "They have no answer for that question. They refuse to answer that."

* Earlier this month, New Jersey Congressman Leonard Lance said, "Congress has a responsibility to ask Secretary Napolitano as to exactly why these purchases have occurred," signaling his intention to get answers.

* Californian Congressman Doug LaMalfa and 14 of his House colleagues have written a letter to the Department of Homeland Security asking if the purchases are, "being conducted in a manner that strategically denies the American people access to ammunition."

Although members of Congress are treating the matter with the seriousness it deserves, the mainstream and leftist media have attempted to ridicule the entire issue as a conspiracy theory, with Atlantic Wire even suggesting that the story had its origins in a debunked email, a report that completely failed to even mention the admitted fact that the DHS had purchased around 2 billion bullets.

While the DHS continues to purchase bullets in large quantities, police departments have been forced to barter amongst each other in a desperate scramble to meet their ammo needs.

In August, 2012 the Department of Homeland Security censored information relating to the amount of bullets purchased by the DHS on behalf of Immigration & Customs Enforcement, citing an "unusual and compelling urgency" to acquire the bullets, noting that there is a shortage of bullets which is threatening a situation that could cause "substantial safety issues for the government" should law enforcement officials not be adequately armed.

But who are they arming against? Who is their enemy? It seems they are arming against those dangerous 'right wing terrorists - those returning veterans.' Perhaps many of us who respect our Constitution might also be those targets.

According to Ben Shapiro, Editor-At-Large of Breitbart News, "The attempt by the left - to minimize the threat of Islamic terror inside the United States and to maximize the threat of 'right-wing extremism' is all too obvious. By using the label 'right-wing extremism' to apply to everything from neo-Nazis to anarchists, the left seeks to smear the right, the same way it smeared the right with the shooting of Gabrielle Giffords.

The truth remains that the Islamist threat in the United States is very real – and that only the dedication of law enforcement has stopped substantially more Islamist attacks. After the Boston Marathon bombings that killed three and wounded well over 170, only a truly philosophically perverse publication would claim that right-wingers are actually more of a threat to public safety than Islamists."

This is another comment, by the Huffington Post on April 14, 2009 regarding the supposed right-wing extremism, "If you think the conservative 'Tea Party' movement is daunting, take a look at a new report issued by the Department of Homeland Security that says right-wing extremism is on the rise throughout the country.

In the report, officials warn that right-wing extremists could use the bad state of the U.S. economy and the election of the country's first black president to recruit new members to their cause.

In the intelligence assessment issued to law enforcement last week, Homeland Security officials said there was no specific information about an attack from right-wing extremists in the works.

The agency warns that an extended economic downturn with real estate foreclosures, unemployment, and an inability to obtain credit could foster an environment for extremists to recruit new members who may not have been supportive of these causes in the past."

So, who is this massive group of 'dangerous right-wing terrorists' the DHS warns us about? How is this group so dangerous DHS must order two billion rounds of ammunition, including hollow point, to stop? In almost every example they use, it's not a group who perpetuates a criminal act - of which they can classify any way they desire. Ordinarily, it's a criminal act such as bank robbery, domestic violence, racially-motivated, or settlement of a grudge. Also considered are the 'skin-heads' and neo-Nazis.' Nevertheless, the DHS has no clear and indisputable examples of 'right-wing' terrorism.

The major question remains - why is the DHS buying so many bullets - especially hollow point bullets? Could there, even in one's wildest imagination, be that many right-wing terrorists who threaten our security? Who are to be the targets of those bullets?

King Obama

9

A NEW AMERICA

Perhaps the most profound and prophetic statement of all time regarding the events and progress in America was the statement by Nancy Pelosi on March 9, 2010. In reference to the pending healthcare bill she said, "We have to pass the bill so that you can find out what is in it." Perhaps she knew at that time that our government would surprise us with many more secrets.

What was Pelosi implying when she made that statement? Was she suggesting that perhaps common citizens were not intelligent enough to comprehend what was going into the bill until the 'intelligentsia' of the Obama administration could later explain it to us? Or, was she suggesting it really would be a surprise? Or according to George Orwell, was she simply making 'thought-speak' which had no meaning?

Obviously, she didn't understand the bill, herself, along with her other Democrat cohorts who bought their way to its passage. Did they pass that bill with good positive intentions - or was it part of a grand design to give more proles more safety and security - when combined with other 'most helpful' programs?

This more safety - this more control - is on a hazardous course for United States citizens. Whether it's a grand design by Barack Obama, by evil forces around him, or by a movement that's taken a life of it's own that no one can influence or stop, it's nevertheless a huge wave that's growing out of control.

Movements are well on the way to make every American subjected to a machine - a computer - that will monitor and control every activity of their lives. Since Barack Obama could easily stop this process, but doesn't, suggests he must be at the helm to chart it's fullest course - a most dangerous course for every citizen, prole or otherwise.

What are the four components of this movement? The components are the four parts of central government control: the healthcare law, the IRS, the new NSA center (Stellar Wind) and drones. With the combination of these four components the government can control every part of every person's life. The major component of this dangerous movement, however, is the lack of recognition or respect for our United States Constitution. Obama has demonstrated he has neither. Consider his following comments and actions that demonstrate he does not regard the Constitution as currently relevant.

In a 2012 interview with Matt Lauer, Barack Obama said, "Our Founding Fathers designed a system that makes it more difficult to bring about change than I would like." What oath of office does a president take at the inauguration? Obama said, "I, do solemnly swear (or affirm) that I will faithfully execute the office of President of the United States, and I will to the best of my ability, preserve, protect, and defend the Constitution of the United States."

So, is his comment that the Constitution is against the things he wishes to accomplish the same as 'defending' that

Constitution? What are his other ideas and comments about the Constitution? Let's consider just how dedicated he is to respecting and following the plan designed by that Constitution. This is an article published by Wordpress.com:

"For some insight into his current thinking, Obama, while in the Illinois senate, in a 2001 interview, said that the Chief Justice Earl Warren court failed to 'break free from the essential constraints' in the US Constitution and launch a major redistribution of wealth. 'It didn't break free from the essential constraints that were placed by the Founding Fathers in the Constitution... that generally the Constitution is a charter of negative liberties. Says what the states can't do to you. Says what the federal government can't do to you, but doesn't say what the federal government or state government must do on your behalf.'

That thinking is exemplified by his 'We can't wait' campaign to circumvent the US Constitution, to bypass Congress, and do whatever he pleases to extend 'positive' rights when he thinks they're required. If Congress and the US Constitution get in his way or don't give him his way, he ignores them. He says 'We can't wait' and does what he wants.

Article II, section 1, of the US Constitution clearly states about the president: Before he enters on the Execution of his Office, he shall take the following Oath or Affirmation: 'I do solemnly swear (or affirm) that I will faithfully execute the Office of President of the United States, and will to the best of my ability, preserve, protect and defend the Constitution of the United States.' That is the oath that Obama voluntarily took.

Further, Article I, section 1, states 'All legislative Powers herein granted shall be vested in a Congress of the United States, which shall consist of a Senate and House of Representatives.' So when he says 'We can't wait,' is he hiding behind the phrase 'to the best of my ability?' Does his ability include in what he believes? And how does he get around the phrase 'faithfully execute the Office?' Does he think he is faithfully executing his duties when he invokes his "We can't wait" stratagem?"

Wordpress.com continues with some examples of Obama's 'We can't wait' strategy and executive fiat:

"In October, 2011, Obama, seeking to circumvent congressional opposition and to jump-start the economy, pushed a series of "executive branch steps," beginning with 'new rules' to make it easier for homeowners with little or no equity to refinance their federally funded mortgages, through Fannie May and Freddie Mac, which posted larger losses than expected, sought $6 billion in additional aid.

In July, 2011, Obama told the National Council of La Raza that the idea of 'doing things' on his own was 'very tempting' when it came to bypassing Congress on immigration.

In September, 2011, Obama told the Congressional Hispanic Caucus he'd like to work his way 'around Congress.'

In July, 2011, during the debt limit debate, Obama asked lawyers if there was a way to interpret the 14th Amendment so as to get around Congress and establish a 'long-term extension of the federal borrowing limit' on his own.

Before Obama was president he said he wanted to bankrupt the coal industry by imposing a cap and trade system that would be so harsh that 'electricity costs would necessarily skyrocket.' Unable to get that bill through Congress, Obama bypassed them and used Environmental Protection Agency (EPA) regulations to accomplish his goals. According to an analysis released in October, 2011, by the Institute for Energy Research, the EPA is 'leading the Obama administration's assault on coal with a number of new regulations.'

Blatant subversion: Lybia war – In Article I, section 8 (Powers of Congress) of the US Constitution, there is the phrase "To declare War…" But Obama said the US actions in Lybia didn't amount to war, so he didn't need the approval of

Congress. And he ignored the War Powers Act."

And there's more on Obama's disdain of our Constitution. On June 12, 2013, Infowars.com published another article reinforcing the idea that Obama has no respect for it. Their article reiterated, "Long before he was president, Barack Obama was already plotting to overturn the Constitution of the United States. In a chilling 2001 public radio interview, Obama said the Constitution was a 'charter of negative liberties,' full of constraints imposed upon us by our Founding Fathers." He used a recent event to support his thoughts that our Constitution's support of privacy was not important. The Infowars article added:

"In response to outrage over Edward Snowden's revelation that the NSA was conducting warrantless wiretaps across a variety of networks, President Obama said, 'You can't have 100-percent security and also have 100-percent privacy and zero inconvenience. We're going to have to make some choices as a society.'

According to a Washington Post-Pew Research Poll published on June 10, 2013, a full 56 percent of Americans polled agree with Obama and considered the NSA's spying efforts an 'acceptable way for the federal government to investigate terrorism.'

Those 56 percent of Americans who agree that it's OK for President Obama to ignore our Constitutional right to privacy pride themselves on being forward-thinkers and relish standing alongside Obama while he criminalizes Edward Snowden and his supporters. They're also the same people who agreed with Obama back in 2001 (when he made that comment detailed above about the U.S. Constitution - the one that began, 'The Supreme Court never ventured into the issues of redistribution of wealth, and of more basic issues such as political and economic justice in society...')

At the time, Obama was referring to the changes brought about by the civil rights movement. Obviously, though, over the years his opinion remains unchanged and he still has no respect for the Constitution – or the citizens – of the United States.

But when it comes to security vs. privacy, the Constitution guarantees that Americans really don't have to make a choice. The only thing the federal government is required to do on our behalf is defend us from attack and protect our Constitutional rights. One of those rights is our right to privacy, and that's exactly the reason our Founding Fathers put limits on what the federal government is allowed to do.

In a speech before his fellow Virginians, Patrick Henry said, "Is life so dear, or peace so sweet, as to be purchased at the price of chains and slavery? Forbid it, Almighty God! I know not what course others may take; but as for me, give me liberty or give me death!'"

This is the fundamental question this chapter asks. How far will our government, Barack Obama, go under the pretense of protecting us? Will he take away all our liberty to achieve his goal, and the goal of his worshipers, which is the ultimate power to control every aspect of our lives? He now has the wherewithal to do exactly that. Who can stop him?

What is his current capability to control every aspect of our lives? Assuming he will disregard our Constitution, as he has demonstrated he is not hesitant to do, all the elements are in place, or soon will be.

Now, let's digress to the beginning of this chapter. What price must we pay for our security? Will it be only an occasional minor inconvenience as we check through a waiting line to board an aircraft or a bus. Or, will that minor inconvenience bloom into a system of total control to insure that little bit more security? Perhaps the snowball rolling downhill is a good example of what's likely to happen - especially since our government has such unbelievable capability at this time to monitor almost every breath we take. That snowball starts small then grows into a dangerous monster when it gets to the bottom of the hill. A president and his administration could create that monster, especially a president who has little or no respect for our Constitution.

Let's begin with two situations we know to exist, and are growing stronger each day. It's the first two components of power that I mentioned at the beginning of this chapter. Those two are the new healthcare system and the IRS.

Eventually, the healthcare system will be a centralized depository of everyone's health status. One monster machine, or smaller linked systems will know how old you are, how tall you are, how much you weigh, what medicines you are taking and why, any minor or major surgery you have had, your physical limitations - such as can you walk - the status of your vision and hearing, and even what vitamins you are taking that are not necessarily prescribed by a doctor. Keep the vitamins in mind until we reach that part in this discussion. How can they know that?

And, what do we know about the IRS? We know they have a record of all our money transactions, what we earn, what we claim for exemptions, our home address and any other addresses such as post office box numbers. In many cases they also know the names, addresses, and ages of our children and grandchildren - and how many children they have - and their financial status. We also know from recent events that they are not honor-bound to perform their duties in the most honest manner.

For example, their different processing emphasis on tax exempt applications between Conservative and Progressive groups. They used their power in a totally unconstitutional manner. They have set a precedence that has not been censored by Obama's administration. Those who performed, permitted, and directed those actions are still there, lording over every American. Therefore, they have already exhibited they can't be trusted to perform in a manner determined to be just, according to the Constitution. Simply, leaders in the IRS system will do what's in the best interests of themselves.

If they believe their advancement and success are determined by the president or his advisors and supporters,

King Obama

they will do whatever they deem necessary to support that person - at the total disregard for other citizens. History indicates that to believe otherwise is a sign of total ignorance - commonly termed, 'turning a blind eye.'

The third dangerous components are the National Security Agency's (NSA) 'Stellar Wind' and PRISM programs. One would imagine, and American citizens always have, that the security departments of our federal government are designed and chartered by our Constitution to protect American citizens. And, in the past, that's certainly been the case. We Americans have always trusted those designated to protect us to really fulfill that assignment - to the best of their ability and with the highest dedication, honor, and patriotism. New events, however, have challenged our trust in those departments. Prism is one of those NSA programs that now must be questioned.

What is Prism? Often written PRISM, it's a clandestine national security electronic surveillance program operated by the United States National Security Agency (NSA) since 2007. PRISM is a government code name for a data-collection effort known officially by the designation, SIGAD US-984XN.

On September 11, 2007, U.S. President George W. Bush signed the Protect America Act of 2007, allowing the NSA to start a massive domestic surveillance program. The program is operated under the supervision of the U.S. Foreign Intelligence Surveillance Court (FISC) pursuant to the Foreign Intelligence Surveillance Act (FISA).

Its existence was leaked five years later by NSA contractor Edward Snowden, who claimed the extent of mass data collection was far greater than the public knew, and included "dangerous" and "criminal" activities in law. The disclosures were published by The Guardian and The Washington Post on June 6, 2013. Glenn Greenwald and Ewan MacAskill, of The Guardian, published the following information about the program:

"The National Security Agency has obtained direct access

to the systems of Google, Facebook, Apple and other US internet giants, according to a top secret document obtained by the Guardian. The NSA access is part of a previously undisclosed program called Prism, which allows officials to collect material including search history, the content of emails, file transfers and live chats, the document says.

The Guardian has verified the authenticity of the document, a 41-slide PowerPoint presentation – classified as top secret with no distribution to foreign allies – which was apparently used to train intelligence operatives on the capabilities of the program. The document claims "collection directly from the servers" of major US service providers. Although the presentation claims the program is run with the assistance of the companies, all those who responded to a Guardian request for comment on Thursday denied knowledge of any such program.

In a statement, Google said: "Google cares deeply about the security of our users' data. We disclose user data to government in accordance with the law, and we review all such requests carefully. From time to time, people allege that we have created a government 'back door' into our systems, but Google does not have a back door for the government to access private user data."

Several senior tech executives insisted that they had no knowledge of Prism or of any similar scheme. They said they would never have been involved in such a program. "If they are doing this, they are doing it without our knowledge," one said. An Apple spokesman said it had "never heard" of Prism.

The NSA access was enabled by changes to US surveillance law introduced under President Bush and renewed under Obama in December 2012. The program facilitates extensive, in-depth surveillance on live communications and stored information. The law allows for the targeting of any customers of participating firms who live outside the US, or those Americans whose communications include people outside the US. It also opens the possibility of communications made entirely within the US being collected without warrants.

Disclosure of the Prism program follows a leak to the Guardian on Wednesday of a top-secret court order compelling telecoms provider Verizon to turn over the telephone records of millions of US customers. The participation of the internet companies in Prism will add to the debate, ignited by the Verizon revelation, about the scale of surveillance by the intelligence services. Unlike the collection of those call records, this surveillance can include the content of communications and not just the metadata.

Some of the world's largest internet brands are claimed to be part of the information-sharing program since its introduction in 2007. Microsoft – which is currently running an advertising campaign with the slogan "Your privacy is our priority" – was the first, with collection beginning in December 2007. It was followed by Yahoo in 2008; Google, Facebook and PalTalk in 2009; YouTube in 2010; Skype and AOL in 2011; and finally Apple, which joined the program in 2012. The program is continuing to expand, with other providers due to come online.

Collectively, the companies cover the vast majority of online email, search, video and communications networks."

But, healthcare program requirements, IRS program capabilities lacking due regard and respect for the U.S. Constitution, and Prism are only the basic fundamentals of our coming 'Big Brother' control over every citizens of the United States - and eventually of the world. What will soon tie everything together is operation 'Stellar Wind,' that giant NSA mega-computer soon to be completed in Bluffdale, Utah. Reportedly, it will have unlimited capability to collect data from many sources on every human being on earth, including financial transactions. Why would one government agency want that much information?

<u>Why would we as free citizens allow it?</u>

Our basic instincts allow it. We don't protest when our government says we need it for more safety and security.

According to Abraham Maslow, our basic instinct - our basic need - is safety and security. Our government in order to gain more personal power and control is using that concept to destroy our liberties. And, many among us are fools enough to support that erosion of our freedom. Once lost, can we ever regain that freedom? Perhaps we should ask George Orwell and his concept of 'Big Brother.' The answer would be a resounding, "No!"

The fourth component is the government's growing disregard for our U.S. Constitution. Many in power claim it's outdated, and in many purposes for security, should be ignored. Or, they ignore those parts designed to protect our liberty and freedom without discussion or consideration by Congress. Count the times Barack Obama has ignored the Constitution, bypassed Congress on those matters, and instituted his ideas that lack a Constitutional basis by executive fiat. Plus, remember the times he has boldly spoken against the importance or the modern relevance of out 'outdated' Constitution. His unconstitutional processes have prevailed so many times would boldly suggest he would not hesitate to do what he chooses in the future - regardless of the Constitutional application.

To summarize the total takeover of our everyday and individual lives, let's consider the status of these four actions or processes. Provisions under the new healthcare law will require more information from more people. Everyone will eventually be enrolled - even if they can't pay for it. Those who can't pay will get it free. (Update: Just yesterday, July 24, 2013, the government revealed that information from the IRS and healthcare will be consolidated in a central 'Data Hub.')

That information will be expanded to include even more personal, family, and related societal information. For example, some medical questionnaires now ask if you own a gun, or if you feel depressed. (A reason to confiscate your weapon.) The IRS will soon require more information - as shown by example in their harassment of submissions by Conservative groups asking ro tax-exempt status. Obviously, there is no limit to their lines of questions or reasons given for those questions. More personal and detailed information will be gathered by the NSA under their Prism and Stellar Wind programs. That's more information than they could ever use against a normal citizen - so what's left?

<u>Everyday purchases by every citizen.</u>

While there's widespread use of credit and debit cards and checks, many transactions are performed each day with cash. Ordinarily, these cash transactions are carried out without the purchaser's name or other identification being recorded. It becomes simply a matter of a cash register receipt or nothing at all, as in a personal transaction of an item that does not have to be registered or recorded at the county records section. In other words, cash transactions ordinarily become invisible to a system that wants to have a transaction record of everything sold or bought by a person.

Now, one might suggest or argue that a government would never go this far to control its citizens. However, two critical ideas would counter this argument. First, if Stellar Wind has this capability, in your wildest imagination could you believe a government determined to do everything to 'protect you' would avoid using that full technology? If it's there, they must use it. The temptation would be too great.

Second, we are so close to a cashless society now that the transition would not be an unrealistic endeavor. That would be the last component of a system where the government will know everything about everybody. They will know everything you buy or sell. In a cashless society, everything would be saved on a computer and subject to scrutiny by anyone having access - especially our government.

At this point, it's time to consider a Bible reference. It's the reference often referred to as, 'mark of the beast.' This important reference is Revelation, Chapter 13, Verses 16 and 17:

"And he causeth all, both small and great, rich and poor, free and bond, to receive a mark

in their right hand, or in their foreheads.
And, that no man might buy or sell, save he that had the mark, or the name of the beast, or the number of his name."

How would this cashless society be a threat to the average United States citizen? Let's take a simple example of a common purchase. Let's assume you own a family heirloom in the form of a .22 rifle, or an old target pistol. Your weapon is unregistered and not on any document that shows you own a gun. Now, suppose you decide to buy some .22 caliber bullets for target practice or to shoot a pesky rabbit eating all the lettuce in your garden.

In a cashless society, what would happen when you go to the sporting store to buy the ammunition? Your credit card or debit card, or another form of card with a special number, issued by the government, would record that transaction. Immediately the master computer at Stellar Wind would compare that transaction with your foundation data already on the master computer. That transaction would show you own a .22 weapon that has not been reported to the registry. What would happen? At minimum, the master registry would show you own a .22 weapon. At worst, and if certain conditions existed at that time, you would be considered a terrorist with an unregistered weapon. What would happen to you then would be determined by the status and composition of our government at that time.

For another example, consider the simple act of buying boots. Suppose you are a farmer who spends much of your time working outside in bad weather, rounding up cows or other livestock when the ground is covered with either mud or snow. Also, consider that you are a small man who wears a size seven shoe. You like to wear your shoes inside larger boots when you work in those conditions because it keeps you feet warmer, and it's easier to slip out of the boots and keep your shoes on when you come in out of the mud or snow.

So, you buy a pair of size eleven boots for easy on and off.

King Obama

A good pair of camouflage boots fits perfectly. What might happen when you buy those boots?

If that master computer records that you wear size seven shoes, would it be possible the alarm would blink saying you bought boots for someone else if you bought size eleven boots? And, if they were camouflage boots, might that not suggest something even sinister? Would the government consider you a collaborator with someone intending to hide himself in a wooded environment - perhaps a terrorist or a survivalist trying to avoid the purchasing process? Would a despotic government believe your explanations?

A more serious example might be your purchase of gasoline. Imagine you bought twice as much gasoline within a certain period of time that you usually buy. You might ordinarily fill your tank at twenty gallons each week. Then suppose you buy forty gallons a week for four consecutive weeks. The normal assumption would be that you are on a long trip. But, during that time, all your other purchases have been near your home - indicating you have not been on a trip.

If the computer system is, perhaps the modified version of Stellar Wind, working properly, your file would be tagged for an inconsistency. Perhaps the Big Brother government might wonder what you were doing with eighty gallons of gasoline you ordinarily had no need for. It's possible you could get a visit from three armed men in black suits asking where are the eighty gallons of gas - have you stored it in hiding somewhere for a sinister use against the government? Three questions might be: are you providing it to potential terrorists, are you thinking of anti-government action, is it for self-survival to in some way hide from the government?

Let's take this question of the gasoline a little further and assume you bought the extra for your emergency generator, since you live in a hurricane zone and frequently lose electricity during hurricane season. In the 'old days' your emergency generator was a necessity, but in Obama's modern world where certain uses of fossil fuels have been banned. Obama has already banned all coal mining, putting fifty-thousand people out of jobs. And, he has limited the amount of oil that can be taken from domestic oil wells. Several questions pose serious consequences at this time; the noose around your neck gets tighter when questioned by those armed agents.

What are the agents' logical questions? Perhaps: why didn't you have your emergency solar panels in place, why did you violate regulations against society by getting more than you fair share of a controlled product - and where did you get the banned gasoline generator? Gasoline generators had been declared illegal because of the pollution they emit into the atmosphere. How do you answer questions such as these?

The first logical answer is that an old friend who recently passed away gave it to you long ago - you had just ignored getting rid of it - or turning it in to the 'Pollution Control Police Department.' Under this condition this likely would be someone's logical 'cover' answer. I couldn't think of a better one, even as I sit here ten minutes at my keyboard trying to conjecture a better lie. Anyway, that obvious lie probably wouldn't satisfy the inquisitors, so they take their inquiry to the next level - they tell you to go outside while they talk to your wife and 12-year-old daughter.

Threatening your safety if they don't tell the truth, the daughter can't withstand the pressure of the three black suits with holstered 9MM semiautomatics flashing from within as the men move about, so she tells exactly what she's heard. "You traded two men some of your old .22 bullets and two sleeping bags for the generator." The three agents have just discovered two armed terrorists, prepared for evasion, in the wilderness.

Considering current trends in our government of deception, lying, and actions counter to the tenants of our Constitution, what is the likely next action by the government? You and your family will be classified as aiding and abetting terrorists, or as accomplices to terrorism activities.

(This explains how the government will know when and what kind of vitamins, contraceptives, and other personal hygiene products you will buy. This, and similar information, will go into the data bank when government rationing of health care begins.)

So, you don't think our government is capable of, or would do something like that? Think again - remember Eric Holder's charge that James Rosen, of FOX News, was an accomplice to treasonous activities. Then, he even lied in an effort to cover up his dangerous activity. Remember how Barack Obama failed to criticize his chief henchman for that unconstitutional and deceitful activity and says he still has complete confidence and trust in Eric Holder? Does that not clearly suggest - even proclaim from high hilltops - that Barack Obama's administration is dangerous to the survival of the United States as we know it and respect it - and as it was conceived and established under our Constitution?

Now, let's take this plausible scenario a little further, with the understanding that Prism, Stellar Wind, and the merging master assimilation computer are all in full operation. Also, keep in mind as you read this idea that I am not an expert in these topics and ideas. I am only a novice in imagination - an old man of 74 who is assumed to be well past my ability to reason and conceptualize things, especially complex things beyond - "what should I wear today?"

The people in charge of these things obviously have more experience and time in conceptualization and development of these programs. And perhaps Barack Obama is pushing them only in the more sinister direction - and they have no choice. Briefly said, 'If you and I can imagine these things happening - the professional experts have already imagined them and probably already have developed them.' Let's take a military aircraft as a good example - the SR-71.

The Lockheed SR-71 'Blackbird' was an advanced, long-range, Mach 3+ strategic reconnaissance aircraft. That means it can fly more than three times the speed of sound, and take photographs. It was developed as a black project from the Lockheed A-12 reconnaissance aircraft in the 1960s by Lockheed and its Skunk Works division. Clarence "Kelly" Johnson was responsible for many of the design's innovative concepts. During reconnaissance missions, the SR-71 operated at high speeds and altitudes to allow it to outrace threats. If a surface-to-air missile launch was detected, such as the one that shot down the U-2 aircraft Gary Powers was piloting, the standard evasive action was simply to accelerate and outfly the missile.

The SR-71 served with the U.S. Air Force from 1964 to 1998. A total of 32 aircraft were built; 12 were lost in accidents, and none lost to enemy action. The SR-71 has been given several nicknames, including Blackbird and Habu.

What's so special about this aircraft? It was a well-kept secret for at least ten years. Even as a member of the Air Force, from 1957 to 1978, I didn't know of its existence while it was operating after the U-2 flown by Gary Powers was shot down. In the 1960s and early 1970s it was shown in the list of aircraft only as a 'conceptual design' for the future. It was not shown as an active aircraft.

Even as an Air Force officer on the IG (Inspector General) team and as a member of Ninth Air Force Headquarters staff at Shaw Air Force Base, in Sumter S.C., from 1967 to 1972, I had no idea that aircraft existed - although it was still listed as a conceptual aircraft 'of the future.' Since I lived just off base near and parallel to the flight line, I did often wonder what aircraft that was, with a strange and different sound, that would land on the darkest nights at the base. I never asked - I thought it was 'just another aircraft' landing. I wasn't involved directly with aircraft at that time.

The purpose for this little story is to confirm that our government has secrets - some well ahead of the known technology for most citizens at that time. Yes, our government has capabilities and technologies that we haven't even imagined. The serious question is, 'how will they use those technologies?' If recent disclosures and scandals are any indication - they will not be used to favor us or to advance the cause of liberty and democracy.

This unknown territory brings forth the question of drones. Would the Obama administration use drones to kill United States citizens on U.S. soil? Attorney General Eric Holder recently was asked that question. He gave a written reply.

In a March 4, 2013 letter Holder wrote that The Obama administration believes it could technically use military force to kill an American on U.S. soil in an "extraordinary circumstance" but has "no intention of doing so."

Holder's letter was disclosed by Senator Rand Paul (R-Ky.), who had asked whether the Justice Department believed President Barack Obama had the legal authority to order a targeted strike against an American citizen located within the United States.

Holder added, "The Obama administration rejected the use of military force where 'well-established law enforcement authorities in this country provide the best means for incapacitating a terrorist threat.' But in theory, it'd be legal for the president to order such an attack under certain circumstances."

In the letter, Holder wrote, "The question you have posed is therefore entirely hypothetical, unlikely to occur, and one we hope no president will ever have to confront. It is possible, I suppose, to imagine an extraordinary circumstance in which it would be necessary and appropriate under the Constitution and applicable laws of the United States for the president to authorize the military to use lethal force within the territory of the United States," He continued:

"For example, the president could conceivably have no choice but to authorize the military to use such force if necessary to protect the homeland in the circumstances like a catastrophic attack like the ones suffered on December 7, 1941, and September 11, 2001," Holder said he would "examine the particular facts and circumstances" if such an emergency were to arise.

Paul, who had threatened to filibuster the nomination of John Brennan as CIA director over secrecy about the U.S. drone program, said in a statement that Holder's "refusal to rule out the possibility of drone strikes on American citizens and on American soil is more than frightening -- it is an affront to the Constitutional due process rights of all Americans."

Two days later, Holder clarified that President Barack Obama would not have the authority to order a drone to kill an American citizen on U.S. soil who was "not engaged in combat." In a two-sentence letter to Paul, Holder said he had heard Paul wanted to know if the president could use a drone to kill an American outside of an emergency situation. He wrote, "The answer to that question is no."

In relation to our imagined scenario, above, where two people have been charged with terrorism, because giving them bullets in exchange for an emergency generator suggests they have an undisclosed weapon, and other items for primitive survival. In a new Obama total-controlled world, that might be considered terrorism. Notice that Eric Holder left a wide opening with his comment, "not engaged in combat." Even under Holder's qualification, those two men could be considered engaged in combat - and killed with a drone strike. That suggests two more questions: how would the government identify those two men, and would they really kill them without good cause?

Many position cameras are in place now in city locations that leave a track of vehicles and license numbers. Only a minor addition to that would create a starting point to locate that vehicle and identify its owner. The 'eye-in-the-sky' can probably do that now, and if not, certainly it will be developed and improved in the near future. That seeing eye above us could be from satellites that watch over a large area, or by a series of solar-powered drones that remain in place high above with magnification cameras.

Are they there now? Who knows - our secret government certainly will not admit it, even if they are there. If they aren't there, they certainly will be - our government must do it for our own good - to 'protect' us. But would they be reluctant to shoot someone who might be a threat - and not necessarily a proven threat to society? To answer that question, we should ask any of David Koresh's followers, if any were still alive.

David Koresh (Vernon Howell) wasn't a good student in school, suffering from poor study skills and dyslexia, and was assigned to a Special Education class. He was nicknamed 'Mister Retardo' by his classmates. He dropped out of school in his junior year at Garland, Texas High School. He impregnated a 15-year-old girl with whom he had an affair when he was 22.

He later claimed to be a born-again Christian in the Southern Baptist Church. He later joined his mother's Seventh-day Adventist Church where he fell in love with the pastor's young daughter. He tried to convince the pastor that it was God's will that he have his young daughter for his wife. He became so persistent that he was finally expelled from the church.

He moved to Waco, Texas in 1981 where he joined the Branch Davidians, a religious group formed as a separation in the 1950s from the 'Shepard's Rod.' The Shepard's Rod group had separated themselves as a branch of the Seventh-day Adventist Church in the 1930s. Headquarters for this group was located ten miles from Waco, on a ranch they called, The Mount Carmel Center. While there he played guitar and sang at church services. It's also reported that he and his rock band played at clubs in Waco, and that he even tried to form his own record company to produce his own music. That endeavor failed, supposedly for lack of funds.

Vernon Howell (Koresh) petitioned a California court on May 15, 1990 to legally change his name to 'David Koresh.' His petition was granted on August 28, 1990. He chose the name 'David' to show his direct lineage to King David of the Bible. He chose the name 'Koresh' which is a transliteration of the Persian name of King Cyrus. With this name he was professing himself to be the spiritual descendent of King David who was carrying out a biblical quest similar to King Cyrus of Persia.

Koresh and his followers remained at the Mount Carmel location near Waco until the end, which is recent history. His life ended, along with 54 other adults and 28 children on April 19, 1993 when the building in which they had confined themselves in the 51-day standoff ended with the assault by U.S. authorities. The building caught fire, or was set fire, and all those inside perished.

The reason for the Mount Carmel assault remains a mystery, although some authorities claimed illegal gun transaction were somehow involved with the Koresh group. Some conspiracy theorists claim Israel was involved, since Koresh had come to Israel claiming to be Jesus. Questions about the event eventually disappeared without any clear answers from the government. It was never explained why Koresh and his followers were attacked, but they were - by agents of our government - and 83 people died in that attack.

The Mount Carmel assault is not the only example of government agencies and agents creating incidents that resulted in serious harm and death. Ruby Ridge is another.

Ruby Ridge was the site of a deadly confrontation and siege in northern Idaho in 1992 against Randy Weaver, his family, and Weaver's friend Kevin Harris by agents of the United States Marshals Service (USMS) and Federal Bureau of Investigation (FBI). It resulted in the death of Weaver's 14-year-old son, Sammy, his wife Vicki, and Deputy U.S. Marshal William Degan.

Vicki was killed by a sniper - reportedly holding her baby girl in her arms. Although stories differed, the Weaver side claimed Sammy and Harris, alerted by the family dog, armed themselves to shoot wild game the dog had detected. During their outing, they encountered Degan and other agents. That's when shots were exchanged resulting in the deaths of Sammy and Marshall Degan.

Investigations after the fact revealed that as the event unfolded, law officials didn't keep all information current, especially involving dates of scheduled court appearances. The information chain was broken, that resulted in confusion on both sides. Allegedly, some agents reacted to incomplete or erroneous information about a court appearance date - thus the attack on the Weavers, and those deaths at that time.

Public outcry over Ruby Ridge and the subsequent Waco siege involving many of the same agencies and even the same personnel fueled many questions about federal law enforcement. To answer public questions about Ruby Ridge, the Senate Subcommittee on Terrorism, Technology and Government Information held a total of 14 days of hearings between September 6 and October 19, 1995, and subsequently issued a report calling for reforms in federal law enforcement to prevent a repeat of Ruby Ridge and to restore public confidence in federal law enforcement.

What were the final results from Ruby Ridge? The surviving members of the Weaver family filed a wrongful death suit. To avoid trial and a possibly higher settlement, the federal government awarded Randy Weaver a $100,000 settlement and his three daughters $1 million each in August 1995. In the out-of-court settlement, the government did not admit any wrongdoing in the deaths of Sammy and Vicki Weaver.

The attorney for Kevin Harris pressed Harris's civil suit for damages, although federal officials vowed they would never pay someone who had killed a U.S. Marshal. In September 2000, after persistent appeals, Harris was awarded a $380,000 settlement from the government.

Why is the history of these two events important lessons? Because these events demonstrate the scenario I described above is not unreasonable or illogical. Two people could be tracked down and killed for a simple act that might be fact, or might be a misinterpretation of events.

Perhaps those two men who swapped an emergency generator for bullets and sleeping bags just wanted to survive. To do that they needed bullets to shoot wild game, and sleeping bags to be comfortable at night. In a world of total control by a despotic government they would never have the opportunity to explain. They would be annihilated like rabid dogs. And, if technology continues, they would be tracked down by drones that would also fire the fatal bullets - or death rays. In either case, any deviation from orders and expectations of the state would make them enemies of the state who must be destroyed.

In order to gain more power and control, our government is on a course hell-bent to "insure our safety and security."

Once they have enough power, our safety and freedom will be secondary - if considered at all. Those leaders will then focus only on their increasing power and personal survival. Once it's lost, can we ever regain that freedom? Perhaps we should ask George Orwell and his concept of 'Big Brother.' His answer would be a resounding, "No!"

A major question of this impending danger is, "What is guiding this power surge?" Is it for Barack Obama's personal status for autocratic kingship? Is it led by Socialists who want to distribute America's wealth and make everyone 'equal?' Or, is it to pave the way for Islamic law eventually to rule the United States? That answer has not yet shown itself.

King Obama

10

OBAMA'S FOUNDATION

Where did Barack Obama come from, what was his foundation, rushing toward his position of power? Who were his supporters who brought him to prominence and power? Was he chosen by fate and destiny to achiever the position of president of the United States by random luck? Research suggests otherwise.

Research suggests Barack Obama was selected by other forces to be raised to that high level, in order to achieve the goals of those organizations. After they vaulted him to that high achievement, then they praised themselves by actually worshiping him - almost as a god - a deity. The organization at the front, catapulting him to those heights was the Gamaliel Organization. In one event, they actually worshiped him in prayer requests.

Consider the biblically despotic display they made when they worshiped him - on a video - as some kind of redeemer or personal savior. The Gamaliel Organization actually recorded and reported it on Youtube. This video recorded a gathering of the Gamaliel Organization, on December 8, 2008, where some members prayed to Barack Obama, "Hear our cry, Obama," and "Deliver us, Obama."

In response to a press release by the president of the Gamaliel Foundation on October 2, 2009, which refuted that claim and said the members were praying, "Hear our cry, oh God," I listened to the video several more times. Although the audio was rather muffled and distorted, the pleas are clearly aimed at Obama, "Deliver us, Obama," not to God. Below is the video URL.

(http://www.youtube.com/watch?v=JTOZkwrxPao)

In the video, the group chants "Nobody out, everybody in," a reference to health care reform, and delivers a casket symbolizing the death of the current health care system. They then seemingly begin chanting prayers to the president.

What is the Gamaliel Organization/Foundation? It's a group more deeply involved in Obama's rise to power than is commonly known. The Gamaliel Foundation is the group that helped sponsor Obama's initial work in Chicago. And, their history of influencing Obama goes even deeper. As a broad overview, Gamaliel says this about itself:

"Gamaliel is a grassroots network of non-partisan, faith-based organizations in 17 U.S. states, South Africa and the United Kingdom, that organizes to empower ordinary people to effectively participate in the political, environmental, social and economic decisions affecting their lives. Gamaliel's diverse members apply their faith and values to the pursuit of equal opportunity for all, shared abundance, and stronger, more prosperous communities.

Gamaliel provides leadership training, helps build community organizations, and leads local and national social justice campaigns. Gamaliel is the only national community organizing network that marries broad-based grassroots organizing campaigns with state-of-the-art regional opportunity research and policy development."

Although this goal, or purpose, of Gamaliel seems innocuous and harmless, notice the subtle placement of the words, "shared abundance." This is the basic preamble of Socialism - or the announcement of a planned attack on Capitalism and free enterprise. Let's learn more about this "non-partisan" organization.

Discoverthenetworks.org explains further: "Predicated on the notion that America is a land rife with injustice, the Gamaliel Foundation (GF) trains activists in techniques and methodologies for effectively bringing about social change. The Foundation models itself on the principles of Saul Alinsky, who authored the books: 'Reveille for Radicals' (1946), 'The Professional Radical' (1970), and 'Rules for Radicals' (1971).

GF takes a strong stand against current homeland security measures and immigration restrictions. In September of 2003, for example, GF's Director of Civil Rights for Immigrants described the Patriot Act as an "attack on immigrants." Moreover, GF seeks to persuade the U.S. government to "legalize and provide rights to tax-paying [illegal] immigrants in this country." "We support any immigration legislation," adds GF, "that secures the civil rights of all immigrants; leads to the legalization of undocumented persons; provides for full labor protection and labor rights of immigrants; ends the inhumane detention and warehousing of asylum seekers; ends deportation for minor offenses; encourages family unity; provides security of our borders; includes humane border enforcement policies; [and] protects the civil liberties of all people." GF is a sponsoring organization of the Immigrant Workers Freedom Ride Coalition, which seeks to secure ever-expanding rights and civil liberties protections for illegal immigrants, and policy reforms that diminish or eliminate restrictions on immigration."

And, there's much more about this organization. A

Womenofgrace.com article, posted on May 12, 2010 by
Sbrinkman answered a question by a blogger (MS) about the
Gamaliel Foundation. According to this article, the blogger
asks: "Could you do a blog exposing the Gamaliel
Foundation? I'm concerned how it has infiltrated the Catholic
Church - see Voice Buffalo. We are cooperating with churches
that support abortion, gay marriage and worship of false
gods!" Brinkman responds to MS:

"Your concerns are justified, but it's far too late to stop
Gamaliel's infiltration into the Catholic Church. It is already
rampant! First of all, the Gamaliel Foundation is more about
the "Christianization" of socialism than the New Age,
although many of its social ideas dovetail with New Age
ideology.
  For those who don't know, the Gamaliel Foundation is a
community organizing group similar to ACORN with the same
ties to the neo-Marxist Saul Alinsky. Its roots are in the
"Back of the Yards Community Council" started by Alinsky in
1938 which operated in Chicago's stock yards for the purpose
of combating poverty, political corruption, gang warfare, etc.
Many community organizing groups were born out of the
Back of the Yards Council over the years, but most of them
dissolved. In an effort to keep the spirit of community
organizing alive, the Gamaliel Foundation was established in
1968 to support the Contract Buyers League, an African
American organization fighting to protect Chicago
homeowners who had been discriminated against by banks.
  The name "Gamaliel" refers to a wise man who taught
Saint Paul (see Acts 5:38-39; and Acts 22:3) (Paul's original
Roman name was 'Saul' of Tarsus.) whom Saul Alinsky
considered to be the first great congregation-based organizer.
Since that time, Gamaliel has been reorganized into a
community group that funds local leaders in an effort to build
and maintain powerful organizations in low income
communities. The Foundation has grown to more than 45
affiliates in 17 states and three provinces in South Africa.
  The way these groups get into the Church is simple. The

Gamaliel Foundation gets money from an umbrella group named WISDOM, which has many small affiliates throughout the country, many going by biblical names such as JOSHUA, ESTHER, etc. These groups convince local parishes to sign on to their membership by promising to do many of the good works that have traditionally been done by the Church in the community. The groups then use a portion of the money donated by these churches to hire a lobbyist who goes to the seat of government and tells legislators that the congregations of all these churches support their legislative agenda.

A typical legislative agenda for a Gamaliel group includes, but is not limited to: promoting abortion, same-sex marriage, driver's licenses for illegal aliens, promoting ObamaCare, etc. (President Obama was a former Gamaliel Foundation organizer.)

Stephanie Block of CatholicCitizens.org explains what happens once Catholics become involved: "Gamaliel and the Industrial Areas Foundation teach liberationism, a form of 'Christianized' socialism, among their members. This has serious ramifications for Catholics. The Alinskyian networks operate ecumenically and include numerous Catholic parishes. The Catholics involved in the extensive trainings these networks offer are not catechized in Catholic principles of social activism or political analysis but in Marxist analysis and praxis. Their worldview is marred by visions of class struggle and perpetual revolution. They are systematically trained to renounce moral truth in favor of consensus-based 'values.'"

She continues: "Catholics trained in Alinskyian though become confused about the comparative moral weight of the issues they encounter in the public arena. They also become confused about the legitimate authority of the Church, frequently imagining they can apply consensus-building strategies to doctrines and moral truth. They are the same Catholics who people the dissident Call to Action chapters around the country." This could explain the involvement of Catholics in a Gamaliel splinter group known as Voice Buffalo, which MS mentions in her e-mail.

Unfortunately, the infiltration goes much higher. The Rev. Robert J. Vitillo, Executive Director of the embattled Catholic Campaign for Human Development spoke at a Leadership Assembly of the Gamaliel Foundation in 2002. He accepted an award from the group on behalf of the U.S. bishops and gave high praise to the Foundation: "The true "heroes" in the struggle against poverty and other forms of discrimination and injustice are you – the leaders of community-based, self-help organizations with whom CCHD works as a partner to bring about an end to poverty in the United States, not just for a day, but for a lifetime."

Particularly in the last year, the CCHD has come under fire from within the Church for its affiliation with community organizing groups such as Gamaliel and ACORN. The outcry eventually resulted in the U.S. bishops cutting off ACORN funding but only after admitting that they had awarded the organization 320 grants totaling $7.3 million in the last 10 years.

Thankfully, Catholics are fighting back. For instance, Bishop David L. Ricken of Green Bay met with about 60 Catholic core team members of JOSHUA and ESTHER in March of this year and expressed concerns he had regarding the umbrella group WISDOM and Gamaliel. He warned that these groups do not clear their political positions with bishops before involving members in these causes, many of which do not correspond with Catholic teaching.

The extent of the connection between the Catholic Campaign for Human Development and groups such as ACORN and Gamaliel was exposed last fall and made headlines throughout the 2009-2010 winter season. A google search of CCHD and Acorn drew 1450 hits so anyone who is interested in reading more about this topic will have plenty of opportunities!" End of article.

More information about Obama, Gamaliel, and Saul Alinsky continues, from Theobamafile.com in an article titled, The Gamaliel foundation - Obama Meets Alinsky:

King Obama

"Obama first learned Alinsky's rules in the 1980s, when Alinskyite radicals with the Chicago-based Alinsky group Gamaliel Foundation recruited, hired, trained and paid him as a community organizer in South Side Chicago. They also helped him get into Harvard Law School to "learn power's currency in all its intricacy and detail," as Obama put it in his memoir. A Gamaliel board member even wrote a letter of recommendation for him.

Obama took a break from his Harvard studies to travel to Los Angeles for eight days of intense training at Alinsky's Industrial Areas Foundation, a station of the cross for acolytes. In turn, he trained other community organizers in Alinsky agitation tactics. In 1988, he even wrote a chapter for the book: 'After Alinsky: Community Organizing in Illinois,' in which he lamented organizers' "lack of power" in implementing change.

What is the Gamaliel and the Barack Obama connection? Here's an analysis by one inside the organization:

Gregory A. Galluzzo says that president elect Barack Obama has throughout his political career made repeated references to his time as a community organizer on the South Side of Chicago. "It is important that we all understand the connection between Barack and Gamaliel. In 1980 Mary Gonzales and I created the United Neighborhood Organization of Chicago.

In 1982 we decided that we needed some expertise from someone who had done faith based community organizing. A person who had worked as such an organizer in Illinois and in Pennsylvania approached me about joining our organizing team. His name was Jerry Kellman. Jerry helped Mary and myself become better organizers. While he was working for us, he connected with a group called the Calumet Community Religious Conference (CCRC) operating on the South Side in the South Suburbs of Chicago, and in Indiana. CCRC had been formed in response to the massive shut down of major industry and the resulting job loss and all of the concomitant social tragedies.

Jerry and I reached an understanding that we would support his work in the South Suburbs so that he could become director of his own project. It was Jerry Kellman who put an ad in the New York Times about an organizing position in the Chicago area. Barack responded; Jerry interviewed him and offered him a position. Barack accepted. Almost at this very time, Jerry propositioned an old friend of his to return to Chicago from Texas and work with him in this new organizing venture. His friend was Mike Kruglik. Mike and Jerry were the first mentors of Barack in organizing.

CCRC, which spanned communities in Northwest Indiana, the South Suburbs and parts of the City of Chicago proved to be unwieldy. Jerry and I decided to split it into three parts. Barack would work to found a new independent project in the South side of Chicago, Mike Kruglik would be the director of the South Suburban Action Conference and Jerry Kellman would develop organizing in Northwest Indiana. At that point Jerry asked me to become Barack's consultant.

And at this time we were just creating the Gamaliel Foundation. I met with Barack on a regular basis as he incorporated the Developing Communities Project, as he moved the organization into action and as he developed the leadership structure for the organization. He would write beautiful and brilliant weekly reports about his work and the people he was engaging.

When Barack decided to go to Harvard Law School, he approached John McKnight, a professor at Northwestern and a Gamaliel Board member for a letter of recommendation. When Barack was leaving he made sure that Gamaliel was the formal consultant to the organization that he had created and to the staff that he had hired.

Barack has acknowledged publicly that he had been the director of a Gamaliel affiliate. He has supported Gamaliel throughout the years by conducting training both at the National Leadership Training events and at the African American Leadership Commission. He has also attended our public meetings. We are honored and blessed by the connection between Barack and Gamaliel."

King Obama

This article by yidwithlid.blogspot.com, Septeember30, 2009, explains more. It's titled: The Gamaliel Foundation, the Church of Obama, the Savior. It begins, It was the Gamaliel Foundation, not ACORN, where the President got his Alinsky/community organizing training.

"Obama in fact worked for a subsidiary of the radical Gamaliel Foundation, a Chicago-based Alinsky group, and he was paid by the radical Woods Fund, which supports Gamaliel. Gamaliel's web site and history page make plain that it evolved from the Alinsky School of organizing. Its training methods acknowledge an "agitational" style of organizing.

He [Obama] is quick to say that the community organizing he did in Chicago was "the best education I ever had, better than anything I got at Harvard Law School." But he never tells us who educated him, not even in the two memoirs he's written. He also fails to disclose who hired him. Obama claimed in the recent national service forum at Columbia University that he worked for "churches" while organizing on the South Side of Chicago.

The Woods Fund should sound familiar; Obama eventually became the head of the Woods Foundation, where he ran the group along with domestic terrorist, Bill Ayers. But first he had to learn the ways of community organizing from The Gamaliel Foundation.

I would suggest that it was the Gamaliel Foundation that made President Obama what he is today. The Gamaliel Foundation brought the Alinsky community organizing method and Barack Obama to Chicago, taught him all he needs to organize a movement, and sent the future President to Harvard law.

When you read through this overview of the group and its key players, look at the parallels between the group's past and present, with the president's past and present. This is a group that believes in collectivism, social justice, "shared affluence," and blaming dissent on racism, and frighteningly they see using religion as a political movement, which explains the tape of people praying to Obama.

The stated mission of the Gamaliel Foundation (GF) is "to be a powerful network of grassroots, interfaith, interracial, multi-issue organizations working together to create a more just and more democratic society." Predicated on the notion that America is a land rife with injustice, GF agitates for social change by supporting the efforts of a network of organizations (the Gamaliel Network) whose goal is to allow for individuals to "effectively participate" in the political, environmental, social and economic arenas. GF offers, for its network affiliates, programs to teach techniques and methodologies for bringing about social change; ongoing consultations; and organizer recruitment campaigns.

The Gamaliel Foundation is an organizing institute that brings together communities of people living out our faith and values to bring about justice and collectively transform our society. We hold that all people are part of a sacred community, intended by God to realize their own dignity, worth, power, and voice.

We affirm equal opportunity for all and abhor all forms of injustice flowing from racism, poverty, and intolerance. As people with faith in a good and just God, we proclaim the values of shared abundance, sacred community, unrelenting hope, equal opportunity and justice.

Segregation and racism are primary and driving forces inside American politics, culture, and society. Racism fuels the current injustice and the current political reality we experience every day. Racism is masked and concealed inside a system of spatial segregation. Racism ultimately says that not only am I not my brothers' and sisters' keeper, but that they are not my brothers and my sisters. Interestingly, like radical Islam they see themselves as both a religious and political movement. Key people at the organization who influenced Obama include:

Greg Galluzzo Exec Dir, Former Jesuit Priest: When executive director Greg Galluzzo came on board in 1986, he charged the foundation with training new leaders in the style of Saul Alinsky, the famed father of community organizing who emerged a leader in the tough stockyard neighborhoods of Chicago. While Alinsky had worked on a neighborhood scale, empowering residents and workers to demand social reforms such as better housing, safer working conditions, and lower crime, the Foundation has broadened its organizational emphasis to a regional scale lately even tackling policy issues that are national in breadth.

Galluzzo was interview by New Republic's Ryan Lizza and showed him the training manual he uses with new organizers. Galluzzo told Lizza that many new trainees have an aversion to Saul Alinsky's gritty approach because they come to organizing as idealists rather than realists. Galluzzo, along with fellow trainer Mike Kruglik, schooled Obama in Alinsky tactics. The Developing Communities Project, Obama's first employer in Chicago, was part of the Gamaliel network of organizations.

Mike Kruglik: Not long after Obama arrived, he sat down for a cup of coffee in Hyde Park with a fellow organizer named Mike Kruglik. Obama's work focused on helping poor blacks on Chicago's South Side fight the city for things like job banks and asbestos removal. His teachers were schooled in a style of organizing devised by Saul Alinsky, the radical University of Chicagotrained social scientist. At the heart of the Alinsky method is the concept of "agitation"--making someone angry enough about the rotten state of his life that he agrees to take action to change it; or, as Alinsky himself described the job, to "rub raw the sores of discontent."On this particular evening, Kruglik was debriefing Obama about his work when a panhandler approached. Instead of ignoring the man, Obama confronted him. "Now, young man, is that really what you want be about?" Obama demanded. "I mean, come on, don't you want to be better than that? Let's get yourself together."

Kruglik remembers this episode as an example of why, in ten years of training organizers, Obama was the best student he ever had. He was a natural, the undisputed master of agitation, who could engage a room full of recruiting targets in a rapid-fire Socratic dialogue, nudging them to admit that they were not living up to their own standards. As with the panhandler, he could be aggressive and confrontational. With probing, sometimes personal questions, he would pinpoint the source of pain in their lives, tearing down their egos just enough before dangling a carrot of hope that they could make things better

Anne E. Smith President: Smith is the woman leading the Prayers in the video. Smith, in 1985, became the first black female to win a statewide election in Illinois when she was voted onto the Board of Trustees of the University of Illinois. Smith is also on the board of BPI, Business and Professional Leaders for the Public Interest. As a public interest law and policy center, BPI works to create solutions to the Chicago region's most compelling social justice challenges. A tenacious and versatile advocate for the public interest, we work to increase affordable housing, public housing and improve Chicago's public schools. BPI's staff of lawyers and policy specialists uses legal and policy research, advocacy, organizing, litigation and collaboration with non-profit, business, community and governmental organizations to accomplish its mission.

Mary Gonzalez, West Coast Director: Mary began organizing professionally in 1980. Prior to that she was a highly recognized leader in a community organization in Chicago that won many significant campaigns for the immigrant residents of the community.

Prior to assuming her role in California, she was the founding director of the Metropolitan Alliance of Congregations, a regional organization in the Chicago area that has successfully brought together a diversity of faith communities representing many races, income levels and cultures. Mary has led powerful campaigns that are building the political will to end inequity in how public and private resources are distributed in the Chicago metropolitan area.

Mary is a National Staff member of the Gamaliel Foundation and one of its primary trainers. She trains at all the Gamaliel Foundation training events and often travels to Gamaliel affiliated organizations to train. She is Mexican-American, a Chicago native, a resident of the Pilsen community in Chicago, and is the Wife of Greg Galluzzo.

John McKnight, Member of the Board: McKnight also schooled young Obama in the gospel according to Alinsky. He apparently saw much promise in the budding politician, a way to advance Alinsky's radical socialist agenda into the highest levels in government.

Obama had been ready to be radicalized. A revealing profile in 1995 in the Chicago Reader, a far-left free weekly, tells of how the young Obama had fully rejected "the unrealistic politics of integrationist assimilation." According to the profile, Obama said he was "tired of seeing the moral fervor of black folks whipped up — at the speaker's rostrum and from the pulpit — and then allowed to dissipate because there's no agenda, no concrete program for change."

In his 1995 memoir, Obama said he wanted to go to Harvard Law School to "learn power's currency in all its intricacy," with the goal of "making large-scale change" as a national politician. But he needed to get there first. So Obama approached McKnight to write a letter of recommendation, which he did.

Jerry Kellman: "Barack had been very inspired by the civil-rights movement," Jerry Kellman, the organizer who hired Obama, told me recently. "I felt that he wanted to work in the civil-rights movement, but he was ten years too late, and this was the closest he could find to it at the time." Obama, in his memoir, put it more simply when he said he went to Chicago to "organize black folks."

Kellman, a New Yorker who had gotten into organizing in the 1960s, was trying to help laid-off factory workers on the far South Side of Chicago. He led a group, the Calumet

Community Religious Conference, that had been created by several local Catholic churches. The Calumet region — basically the farthest southern reaches of Chicago plus the suburbs in northern Indiana — was an industrial area that had been hard hit by the closings of Wisconsin Steel and other industries. Kellman and the churches hoped to get some of those jobs back.

But there was a problem in the Chicago part of the equation. The area involved, around the Altgeld Gardens housing project and the neighborhood of Roseland, was nearly 100 percent black. Kellman was white, as were others who worked for CCRC. "The people didn't open up to him like they would to somebody who was black and really understood what was going on in their lives," Yvonne Lloyd, one of the key "leaders" — that is, local residents who worked closely with Obama — told me.

"Black people are very leery when you come into their community and they don't know you." Lloyd and another leader, Loretta Augustine-Herron, insisted that Kellman hire a black organizer for a new spinoff from CCRC to be called the Developing Communities Project, which would focus solely on the Chicago part of the area.

So Kellman set out to find a black organizer. He ran an ad in some trade publications, and Obama responded. But at first Kellman wasn't sure Obama was right for the job. "My wife was Japanese-American," Kellman recalled. "I showed her the résumé, with the background in Hawaii. The name's Obama, so I asked, 'Could this be Japanese?' She said, 'Sure, it could be.'" It was only when Kellman talked to Obama on the phone, and Obama "expressed interest in something African-American culturally," that a relieved Kellman offered Obama the job.

Without the Gamaliel Foundation we would have never had a President Obama. They are the source of many of his views and methods."

The following information detailing more of Obama's power base and power sources is from Brad O'Leary's book:

'The Audacity of Deceit.' This information was summarized by World News Daily (WND.com) on October 17, 2008:

"Taken individually, you might brush aside Sen. Barack Obama's association with any single radical, but as you look at all of the people Obama met on the incestuous money trail, you find a pattern of close cohorts who can't be ignored. These are all radicals who work for "social justice" through the redistribution of the wealth.

Obama's plan to solve "global poverty," which would send nearly $1 trillion to the United Nations (a sum equal to the recent bailout) is wealth redistribution on a global scale. His tax program would increase the percentage of Americans who pay no federal income tax from 32 percent to 44 percent, and even give non-taxpayers gravy checks from the government. Nearly half of all Americans, for their entire lifetime, would never pay federal income tax.

That Obama is a product of the radical leftist Chicago machine is nothing new. Though we don't know if he is a "hard-core academic Marxist," which he was accused of being during his 2004 Senate campaign, we do know that he's supported by a socialist activist network. This network includes former members of the Students for a Democratic Society, from which the Weather Underground was born, Communist Party USA, and the Democratic Socialists of America. This axis wants Obama to hold the reins of power in the White House. They have a socialist agenda for America – one that isn't far from Obama's own agenda. In fact, Obama has yet to point out how his agenda differs from theirs.

While Obama might condemn the terrorist acts that communist Bill Ayers committed when Obama was 8 years old, it doesn't explain Obama's continued association with Ayers when Ayers served both as his boss and fellow board member on so many foundations. Nor does it explain why Ayers recruited so many of his friends to help Obama – friends that are still associated with Obama to this day in his presidential campaign.

Since Obama ducks this issue, with the complicity of the

national media, it's worth revisiting not only Bill Ayers, but the entire cast of leftist radicals that surround Obama through his association with Ayers. Obama's cadre of radical leftists can be divided into three categories: "The Mentors," "The Radicals" and "The Enablers." "The Mentors" are people who helped shape Obama's worldview. They are the focus of this fourth installment of "the incestuous money trail."

The mentors

Barack Obama   Sr.: "All of my life, I carried a single image of my father, one that I tried to take as my own," Obama wrote in 'Dreams From My Father.' What was that image? It was "the   father of my dreams, the man in my mother's stories, full of high-blown ideals." Obama adds, "It was into my father's image ... that I'd packed all the attributes I sought in myself."

Though Obama said little about what those "ideals" were, they crystallized in the form of a 1965 paper, written by the senior Obama and published in the East African Journal. In that paper, titled, "Problems Facing Our Socialism," the elder Obama advocated the communal ownership of land and even the forced confiscation of privately controlled land. He also called for the nationalization of "European" and "Asian" owned enterprises, and advocated handing over control of these operations to the "indigenous" black population.

Further, Obama's father wanted to increase taxes on the rich, even up to the 100 percent level, arguing that "there is no limit on taxation if the benefits derived from public services by society measures up to the cost in taxation which they have to pay." Incidentally, this concept is not totally foreign to the younger Obama, whose plan to "spread the wealth around" by raising taxes conceptually mimics his father's plan.

Frank Marshall Davis: As a teen, Obama's mother abandoned him in Hawaii so she could go to Indonesia to seek a Ph.D. At the age of 16, left on his own, Barack Obama developed a relationship with a non-family member – reputed Marxist Frank Marshall Davis. Davis, a former Chicago resident, was a member of the Communist Party USA and an apologist for the Soviet Union. The 1951 report of the Commission on Subversive Activities to the Legislature of the Territory of Hawaii identified him as a CPUSA member. What's more, anti-communist congressional committees, including the House Un-American Activities Committee, accused Davis of involvement in several communist-front organizations. Obama describes "Frank and his old Black Power dashiki self" as advising him before he left for Occidental College in 1979 at the age of 18. Passages from 'Dreams From My Father' suggest that Frank Marshall Davis was something akin to a surrogate dad to Obama in those days. Obama's only contact when he moved to Chicago was Davis.

Alice Palmer: Obama's predecessor in the Illinois State Senate, Alice Palmer introduced Obama to Chicago's radical elite in the living room of Bill Ayers and Bernardine Dohrn's home back in 1995 and endorsed him that year in front of a crowd of 200 supporters. Palmer was an active radical leftist in the decade before she picked Obama for her seat. The FBI notes that she served on the board of the U.S. Peace Council, a front organization and affiliate of the Soviet World Peace Council. Palmer attended the 27th Congress of the Communist Party of the Soviet Union and came away favorably impressed by the Soviet system.

Gregory Galluzzo: A former Jesuit priest and executive director of the Gamaliel Foundation, Galluzzo was interviewed by New Republic's Ryan Lizza and showed him the training manual he uses with new organizers. Galluzzo told Lizza that many new trainees have an aversion to Saul Alinsky's gritty approach because they come to organizing as idealists rather than realists. Galluzzo, along with fellow trainer Mike Kruglik, schooled Obama in Alinsky tactics. The Developing Communities Project, Obama's first employer in Chicago, was part of the Gamaliel network of organizations.

Mike Kruglik: Kruglik was a regional director for the Gamaliel Foundation. Like his boss, Greg Galluzzo, Kruglik also helped train Obama on Alinsky organizing methods. Kruglik was also involved in 2007 with indoctrinating Obama campaign volunteers on Alinsky methods.

Rev. Jeremiah Wright: Rev. Wright was a close friend of the Obamas. He officiated their wedding, baptized their children, and Obama regularly touted his 20-year membership in Chicago's Trinity United Church of Christ as proof of his devotion to Christianity – until remarks by Rev. Wright became an embarrassment to his campaign.

A closer look at Obama's pastor and longtime church reveals that Trinity practices – and preaches – Black Liberation Theology, and Wright sees "his own form of Christianity as profoundly different from Christianity as typically practiced by most American whites and blacks." During one of his more memorable anti-American screeds, Rev. Wright said, "The government gives them the drugs, builds bigger prisons, passes a three-strike law and then wants us to sing 'God Bless America.' No, no, no, God damn America, that's in the Bible for killing innocent people."

Trinity church gave between $5,000 and $10,000 to the Community Renewal Society, which was a pet project of Bill Ayers' father, Tom Ayers.

John L. McKnight: John McKnight is a professor at Northwestern University and sits on the board of the Gamaliel Foundation. McKnight is yet another of the Gamaliel trainers who schooled Obama in Alinsky tactics and methods. In his memoir, Obama said he wanted to go to Harvard Law School with the goal of making large-scale change as a national politician, and McKnight was the individual who wrote him a letter of recommendation. Obama said that being tutored by McKnight, Galluzzo and Kruglik was "the best education I ever had, better than anything I got at Harvard Law School."

11

THE KING RISES

Barack Obama has an unlimited power base. As I described myself, as a young man, I would have been one of his followers, one of the proles, who wanted what he offers and promises. If one offers and promises what those who don't have, enough times, they begin to believe without question - because the thought of having those things they never had blinds their sense of reason. They imagine the end result of 'having,' not the sacrifices of humanity they must trade for that vision of bountiful things that create pleasure. To them the human consequences are irrelevant. It's the having those dreamed-of things and status that's important. To them - 'individual liberty and humanity be damned.'

As a researcher and writer of management and leadership principles, I've delved deeply into the principles of what makes people do certain things, and why they do things at all.

The best theory, or reason, to explain human reactions to things and environments is probably the 'Hierarchy of Needs' theory by Abraham Maslow.

Maslow explains that people react and respond to certain need motivations. He describes needs from the basic to the highest order, beginning with survival and security being the basic and primary needs. Accordingly, when one has satisfied his physical needs of food and water, then he becomes focused on fulfilling the safety need. Once a person feels safe - and has a full stomach, the next motivating need is the urge to belong - to belong to some group to which he or she feels comfortable. Accordingly, once that comfort level is fulfilled, then the need to achieve a feeling of esteem takes over. Not only does one need to 'belong,' he or she then needs to feel some level of importance - or esteem. Finally, the highest level is self-actualization or self-fulfillment. That's when someone needs and wants to accomplish something just for the enjoyment of doing it and being alive - with no other worries or needs.

Maslow's theory also stresses the idea that no level is ever permanent. One who achieves high esteem or self-actualization can always be removed from that status and, once again, feel the need for safety - or to reclaim certain levels of esteem.

Why do I mention Maslow's theory? Because in my view from watching Barack Obama's two campaigns, 2008 and 2012, he used these concepts to gain votes. This strategy is the same Democrats always use, only Obama and his campaign supporters used it on a level never achieved by any other politician.

His common rhetoric was to promise 'poor people' he would give them their fair share (fill their bellies and give them more free televisions and Obamaphones) and give them more status to belong to the middle-class. He used two of the most basic strategies against them - and they never had the slightest idea he was using them as his proles described by George Orwell in his book, '1984' and the concept of 'Big Brother.' In effect, Barack Obama was their Big Brother who was going to take care of them: give them more milk and honey, and more status so they could become part of middle-America.

And, as Orwell described, once elected to a powerful position, he discards them back to their original 'Low' position until he needs them again - then comes those same untruthful promises - that they will believe again. From Obama's position, however, this is a special case where his followers, his proles, might never abandon him, no matter what.

To many, he is a god-like person to whom their total allegiance belongs, no matter what he does. That will be explored further, later. Also, at the end of this chapter I will explain why I feel Barack Obama must hold on to his power base, although he is now serving in his second term as president of the United States. According to the 22nd Amendment, this is his last legitimate term

In summary, Barack Obama has the dedicated following and worship of approximately 15-percent of the population, no matter what happens in other political areas. This is the approximate population who live in poverty in the United States. He owns them, his proles, with his rhetoric. How many of these are registered voters, and how many of them actually vote? Who really knows?

Obama also owns the votes of most black Americans. In the last two elections, approximately 95-percent of black Americans voted for Obama. Although only 13-percent of the population in the Untied States is comprised of black citizens, if they vote in higher percentage numbers than other voters, that number is enough to determine the results of close elections. Although many black voters are included in the poverty rates of all races, with only 13-percent being black, most of the other poverty voters are white or of another ethnicity or race. Black votes are important especially in states with high black percentages, that also have many electoral votes. Electoral votes are not the same as popular votes. It's possible for someone to be elected president without the highest number of popular votes. And, what about Hispanic voters?

A CNN report on November 9, 2012 stated:

"The sleeping giant has awoken: Latinos not only helped Obama win in key battleground states, but they made up 10% of the electorate for the first time ever.

Latinos, the fastest growing minority, making up 16% of the nation's population, made their mark on election night as they voted for President Barack Obama over Republican Mitt Romney 71% to 27%, a lower percentage than Republican candidates have received in in the last three elections.

At 27% this year, Romney's Latino support is dramatically lower than former President George W. Bush's support in 2004, which was 44%, and Arizona Sen. John McCain's 31% in 2008, according to exit polls. The lowest percentage of Latino voters won by a Republican was in 1996, when Bob Dole garnered only 21% of Latinos compared with then-President Bill Clinton's record 72%.

In 2008, Obama received 67% of the Latino vote. Latinos made up 9% of the electorate in 2008 with 19.5 million people eligible to vote. Today, there are nearly 24 million Hispanics eligible to vote. The number of registered Latinos has increased by 26% in the last four years to 12.2 million, according a report by the National Association of Latino Elected and Appointed Officials."

"It's something we saw coming and have seen happen for a numbers of years now. Hispanics are increasing their share of their electorate," said Mark Hugo Lopez, associate director of the Pew Hispanic Center. "That number has been growing for a number of election cycles, and it's going to continue to grow moving forward."

Is there any question why Obama and the Democrats want to see an 'open border' to our south? Is there any wonder why they also want to offer quick 'amnesty' to millions of Hispanics already illegally in our country? Their reason has nothing to do with 'humanity.' It has everything to do with millions of votes - almost all going to Democratic candidates.

My novel, 'America 20XX: The New World Order,' fictionally brings this political take-over situation to life. In the novel, the situation is described where human traffickers, drug smugglers, and Islamic jihadists are cooperating to move their products across the southern borders below Casa Grande, Arizona.

Along the way, inside Arizona, the drug traffickers and the Islamists stash their drugs and weapons in special bunkers for later retrieval. Then, the Hispanics, unaware of contents of the bundles they carry in payment for the guided trip, are processed through a special underground facility that's connected to U.S. agencies that issue permits and social security cards to make them instantly 'American citizens with voting privileges.' Another important concept in the story is that the social security cards are strip-coded to vote for the Democratic president - no matter how the new 'citizen' actually records a vote. According to the 'fictional' story, the voter only has to step inside the voting booth to cast a vote.

Of course, this is only a fictional scenario in my book. Events since I wrote that story two years ago have perhaps inclined me to believe that this scenario is not necessarily fictional. Watching what's happening on our borders, and understanding the lies and deceits from our federal government convinces me that nothing is beyond their zeal to gain more control of our great nation - no matter how they must do it - or what new and inventive tactics they must employ. Just consider the scandals recently discovered by the IRS. How far will they take it? How far can they take it? If I can imagine such a scenario, you can well believe they have already thought of it - and it might be closer that we can even imagine. Perhaps the drive for total power has no restrictions or limitations by those possessed toward that zeal.

There's another voting block the Democrats, especially Barack Obama, has locked tight. That's the homosexual voters. How many are there?

In 2011, The Williams Institute at the UCLA School of

Law, a sexual orientation law and public policy think tank, estimated that 9 million (about 3.8%) of Americans identify as gay, lesbian, bisexual or transgender. The institute also found that bisexuals make up 1.8% of the population, while 1.7% are gay or lesbian. Why is this number an estimate?

"The number of LGBT persons in the U.S. is subjective. Studies pointing to the statistics are estimates at best. The most widely accepted statistic is that 1 in every 10 individuals is LGBT; however some research estimates 1 in 20. Of course, this all depends on one's definition of gay (which may vary by study) and the participants willingness to identify as gay, bisexual, lesbian or transgender. So, why can't the actual number of GLB people be counted? There are many things to consider when trying to count the number of GLBT persons."

Even if you use the lowest percentage number, 1 in 20, this is still a staggering number of approximately 10 million voters. The guess of 1 in 10 is a staggering 20 million voters. Since most of these have a deeply vested interest in the outcomes of most elections - especially today. Not only does Barack Obama support and promote homosexual causes, now other prominent Democrats are jumping on the bandwagon, even those who have opposed homosexual proposals in the past. Perhaps they have counted the votes - and that's all that matters: the higher needs of our country, such as freedom and democracy, be damned!

Any candidate, especially a Republican who references the Bible, especially Leviticus 18:22 and 20:13, that proclaims homosexuality an abomination, who does not openly and strongly support homosexual causes will never get a vote from them. They will vote for the other candidate, regardless of his or her plans for the future of America. Their personal 'needs' are their only concern. What convinces me of this notion? All blogs I have seen by open homosexuals expressly make this point. That is the only reason they say they intend to vote for a particular candidate.

Young voters is another block the Democrats, especially Barack Obama, can count on to support them. Their support was demonstrated in the last election.

King Obama

In a survey by Harvard University's Institute of Politics, likely voters under 30 favored Obama over Romney 55 percent to 36 percent. Exit polls of voters in the 2008 election showed Obama defeating Senator John McCain, Republican of Arizona, among those 18 to 29 years of age, by 34 percentage points, a key to the president's victory. Perhaps young people are more easily persuaded by more rhetorical promises to support their future, than the more realistic and down-to-earth suggestions by most Conservatives. Regardless, it seems to be a locked-in and sure vote for those who promise more.

And, of course we can't forget the issues of gun rights and abortion. Those who oppose individual ownership of weapons for personal defense, and those who want 'no excuses' abortions - especially free abortions on-demand paid for by taxpayers - will always vote for anyone who promises to support these two issues. Conservatives ordinarily support personal gun ownership for protection - and they oppose open and free abortions without some restrictions on abortions to support the right for an unborn, or partially-born, child to live: 'life, liberty, and the pursuit of happiness.'

Obama and his supporters are so desperate to maintain their hold on more voters that they have even abused the 'food stamp' program. In 2008, 34 billion dollars were allocated for food stamp needs. In 2012, that amount rose to 81 billion dollars. Now, the administration even has promotion programs to sign people up for the food stamp program, whether they really need that subsidy support or not. According to a recent report, one in three Americans is now receiving support from one or more food subsidy programs. Although many of these are already 'locked-in' Obama voters, this program means even those who are not totally obligated to Obama and his 'share the wealth' ideology have sold their souls - votes - to support him and his programs even further.

After all, if someone promises you something for doing nothing, why would anyone refuse that opportunity? That's what I wished for when I was a young man staring across that worn-out cotton field before I understood the concepts of 'freedom' and 'democracy.'

During the 2012 presidential campaign, was Mitt Romney's charge that Obama already had 47 percent of the vote locked up erroneous? Not likely, but it was another falsehood Obama and his vitriolic campaign staffers used against him with great success. Obviously, people don't like to be told their votes are taken for granted - even if the statement is true. These 47 percent are proles beyond compare. They have sold their souls and their votes for promises of more 'free stuff.'

But, Obama's plans go even further to create more power for himself. There are also organizations formed to continue that process. There are 41 Barack Obama Meetup Groups. Listed below are the top ten.

Seattle Democracy Group: Seattle Democracy focuses on the wonderful ideas and events of the world and is committed to each person having a breakthrough in their own consciousness. We are dedicated to integrating our shared focus to improve conditions in the world through fun social events and gatherings. Our goal is to keep the vibe of the group 100% positive.

Voterbook NYC (Formerly ObamaNYC.com): Our grassroots group began in January 2007 to support then Senator Barack Obama for President. We are now a group of voters and activists banded together for the common good, concerned with both local and national issues that affect our lives. "The whole is greater than the sum of the parts." Let us know what we can do for you. We want to help.

For Democracy group - Los Angeles: Dear friends and Democrats - welcome to: FOR DEMOCRACY group - Los Angeles. I am your group's organizer, my name is Eric Lafayette. We have decided today March 23, 2008 to support Barack Obama. Why? Because his speeches have shown that he is closer to our principles of true democracy than any other candidate: His last speech on bridging the racial divide is an example. His core message is : from bottom to top and not from top to bottom which is exactly what democracy values should be.

Triangle for Obama Meetup Group - Raleigh, NC: Join up with a diverse community of Obama supporters as we continue the work we began five years ago! Change has happened and can continue, but only if we work together. This election is about you and your community. Please join us to meet other Obama supporters.

Los Angeles Progressive Friends -Los Angeles, CA: Progressive Friends is a political and social club for liberals in the Los Angeles area. Whether you're a Democrat, Green, left-leaning Independent, Progressively Unaffiliated, or unabashedly Socialist, this group's for you! Feel like you can't talk...

Obama London Organizing for America UK - London, United Kingdom: This is the original and longest-active Obama group in the UK. We are the largest Obama group anywhere in the world outside the U.S! We're on BBC, Sky and GMTV! Come to our new Obama events! We did active campaign work for Obama's election. And we have fun! We're in a music video on YouTube! We made a commercial when invited by MoveOn. We invited our sister Hillary Clinton Meetup to our Unite For Change Picnic. We gave a special birthday party for Barack Obama's birthday August 4! And after our huge Obama Election Night Party November 4, we followed it up with our Obama Victory Celebration two weeks later on a beautiful top floor terrace looking out at the Thames River! We're the Obama Group that does work as well as parties! See why other groups try to copy whatever we're doing! You'll find our members warm, welcoming, and very friendly! Our organizer, Carole, has worked 24/7 for two years to make this group the leading and happiest group of Obama supporters! We work with Americans Away From

King Obama

Home to support Barack Obama as President of the United States.

Obama Paris Organizing for America France - Paris, France: This is the original and longest-active Obama group in France. We are among the largest Obama groups anywhere in the world outside the U.S! Come to our new Obama events! Join our discussions! Meet other local supporters of Barack Obama. We did active campaign work for Obama's election. And we have fun!

Dallas Democrats - Dallas, TX: Come and meet fellow Democrats! Interact with people concerned about the issues which excite or worry you. Learn about opportunities to be involved with the party, issues, training or other progressive activities. Meet candidates Bring your ideas and...

Broward 4 Obama! - Fort Lauderdale, FL: Meet fellow Obama supporters and decide the issues you care about most, the work you want to do to make progress on them, and the kind of support you'll need to get it done. Cultivate new leaders and helping train a new generation of volunteers and organizers to help fight for the issues at stake. Get President Obama's back on passing major legislation, like reducing gun violence or immigration reform. And work to help transform Washington from the outside while strengthening our economy and creating jobs. The direction our work takes will be completely in your hands—with the support of this organization behind you every step of the way.

Obama London - London, United Kingdom: This is the Meet Up for Obama Campaign Activity in the UK. This group is for all who want to help register American voters to elect Barack Obama in this election. There are more than 6 million Americans living overseas, but sadly only a small fraction of them voted in the last Presidential election. This time, we must do better! It's easy to register and vote with http://VoteFromAbroad.org/4 Please join us to help spread the word and win back the White House!

Recently there was an announcement that a new group would be formed to support Barack Obama's agenda. It announced: WASHINGTON, January 13, 2013 — President Barack Obama's political organization is forming an outside, nonprofit group to support the president's legislative agenda. The unprecedented move gives Obama a way to promote his agenda outside the confines of the White House and seeks to harness the energy from his re-election campaign into support for legislation. Democratic officials say the group, Organizing for Action, will be announced Friday. The nonprofit will work on key legislative battles, train future leaders and local issues around the country.

According to a report by Justin Sink and Amie Parnes from thehill.com on 3-15-2013 :

"Two months after Organizing for Action was founded to bolster President Obama's agenda, his poll numbers are slipping and the group remains on the defensive.

A link between Obama's declining approval numbers and the group's struggles is tenuous at best, yet questions about how effective the group can be in cajoling Congress to work with Obama were swirling this week at a summit meant to showcase Organizing For Action (OFA.) Watchdog groups have accused OFA of selling access to the White House, while traditional allies like the Democratic National Committee and congressional campaign committees have expressed concern the organization could siphon away important fundraising dollars.

Top campaign donors have been slow to rally around the group. A top Obama donor acknowledged Thursday that OFA has "hit some bumps" at the start and "the money isn't there."

"It's definitely had some turbulence in terms of process," said one former senior administration official. "Has it had the best process start? Probably not. Mostly because I think it's set up against a bunch of negatives and people saying, 'You're never going to raise enough money.' Anytime you do something new, there are going to be some potholes in the road."

Obama acknowledged the problems in a Wednesday address at the "founders summit" intended as a celebratory launch for around 75 top donors and volunteers. He said OFA "has been viewed with some suspicion and people have been puzzled about what it is we're trying to do." But former White House adviser David Plouffe in an earlier address defended the group and said it "should be celebrated, not criticized" for its political efforts.

It's been an inauspicious start for an organization that carries the legacy of two successful presidential campaigns – and has positioned itself as a conduit to break through the gridlock of Washington. Yet the true measure of the group's success will be its effectiveness in winning over lawmakers from key swing districts to back the president's agenda on issues like immigration, gun control, and energy. Obama in his address said for OFA to be effective, it would need to provide political cover to such lawmakers.

"If you have a senator of a congressman in a swing district who is prepared to take a tough vote... I want to make sure they feel supported and they know there are constituencies of theirs that agree with them, even if they may be getting a lot of pushback in that district," Obama said. "If we move aggressively on an issue like climate change, that's not an easy issue for a lot of folks because the benefits may be out in the future, and I want to make sure a congressman, a senator feels as if they have the information and the grassroots network that will support them."

Obama sees the group as having the potential to reverse a pivotal mistake from his first term, when Obama feels he failed to harness the enthusiasm of his campaign to promote his policy agenda.

There's some worry the window for OFA's success might have already begun to close. With slipping popularity and congressional Republicans retrenching for another round of budget fights, Obama's once bountiful post-election political capital is being gradually depleted. But OFA supporters argued that rather than being derailed by the political circumstances, the group was the answer to the problem.

Ben LaBolt, a spokesman for the Obama campaign who led one of the summit's seminars, noted Thursday that "more than one million Americans have already taken action through OFA to urge members of Congress to support comprehensive immigration reform, gun safety measures, and policies that will strengthen the middle class." President Obama told the group that their efforts "may give space here in Washington to do the kind of work — hopefully bipartisan work — that's required."

"This is what inside Washington doesn't get about outside Washington," said the former administration official. "They're thinking about this strictly in terms of process. But it's about how you engage these folks. If you went on and knocked on doors because you're into climate change, you're going to do it on an off year."

A Democratic operative also argued that the group's nonprofit status – which prevents it from explicitly partisan, electoral activity – would actually aid the group in its mission to forward the president's agenda. "Four years ago we tried to construct OFA as an organization with dual missions -- electing Democrats and passing the president's policies -- and we may have bit off more than we could chew," he said. "There's ample need for an organization wholly dedicated to passing this ambitious agenda."

Even donors who acknowledged the group was off to a slow start predicted that just as the campaign heated up, so will OFA. "When the president really starts to push these issues like immigration, that's when you're going to see this operation going at full speed," said one top Obama donor. "This is why people elected the president. It wasn't necessarily about him but what he could do."

On July 12, 2013, Russ Choma at opensecrets.org gave more current information about the group. He wrote:

"Organizing for Action, the politically active nonprofit

closely tied to President Barack Obama, disclosed this afternoon that it raised $8.2 million in the second quarter of 2013, and $13.1 million so far this year. As a nonprofit, the group is under no obligation to disclose donors, but it voluntarily disclosed the names and donations of everyone who gave more than $250.

A large chunk of the group's funding came from a stable of big-dollar Democratic donors who supported Obama's presidential campaign, top Democratic super PACs and his inaugural committee. Two donors each gave $500,000: Fred Eychaner, of Chicago, and David Shaw, of New York City. Eychaner, who owns Newsweb, a publishing company, was the largest individual donor to liberal outside groups in 2012, donating more than $14 million; that included $4.5 million to Priorities USA Action, the super PAC that backed Obama. Shaw, who started hedge fund D.E. Shaw & Co., gave $1.8 million to liberal outside groups.

In total, 13 donors have contributed at least $100,000 to OFA in 2013. After Eychaner and Shaw, the largest donations were $250,000 from prominent Democratic contributors Philip Munger and Amy Goldman. Goldman's brother, John, also gave $125,000. The 12 donors accounted for more than $2.3 million of the $13.1 million raised this year.

One newcomer to the list of top donors was Ryan Smith, of Salt Lake City, Utah. Smith, the founder of Qualtrics, an online survey and data collection software company, has given a total of $100,875. According to OpenSecrets.org data, the largest donation previously made by Smith, 33, was a $12,500 gift to the Democratic National Committee last September."

In a graphic announcing the release, Organizing for Action claimed 237,000 donors this year, with an average donation of $55. According to the data released by OFA, there were 3,697 donors who gave $250 or more so far in 2013. These donors account for $5.6 million of the total $13.1 million, or about 42 percent of the total the group has raised raised this year.

The group inherited the Obama campaign's email list and social media accounts, and has been running ads promoting the health care law Obama signed in 2010. According to OFA, the group has done more than 500 trainings of grassroots organizers.

Nineteen of the five-figures-and-up OFA donors were also bundlers for Obama. Eychaner bundled at least $500,000 in 2012, as did outspoken South Carolina Democratic Party Chairman Dick Harpootlian, who threw in $10,000 for OFA. Barbara Grasseschi, co-owner of Puma Springs Vineyard in Healdsburg, Calif., gave $50,000 to OFA. She was a 2012 Obama bundler credited with bringing in between $200,000 and $500,000. She also contributed $112,000 to various candidates and committees in the 2012 cycle, more than half of it to the DNC.

Another bundler: Orin Kramer, head of the private equity firm Boston Provident. He's sent checks totaling $85,000 to OFA so far, after having bundled more than $500,000 for Obama's re-election. According to news reports, Kramer was being considered for the post of deputy Treasury secretary earlier this year.

Many donors, though they didn't sign on as bundlers for Obama, nevertheless previously contributed to the president, such as Murat Guzel of Bethlehem, PA. Guzel, who owns a company called Natural Food Source Inc., gave to Obama and also sent $22,600 to the DNC in 2012; his contributions in that campaign cycle came to more than $50,000. Guzel gave $25,000 to OFA. (Could Guzel be associated with the new 'school lunch' requirements?)

A report by Anita Kumar from McClatchy Newspapers on April 1, 2013 gives a different view of the new organization. That report said, "President Barack Obama's decision to launch his own political organization has some Democrats wondering: Is he just in it for himself?

Obama's new group, Organizing for Action, will focus on his policy agenda – not on electing Democratic candidates – by raising unlimited amounts of cash and accessing the president's secret list of 20 million supporters, volunteers and donors. The operation won't share money, resources or the priceless Obama email list with the Democratic National Committee or campaign committees that help elect members of Congress, governors and legislators. And it has no plans to coordinate efforts, leading some Democrats to worry that it will take money and manpower away from the party as it heads into the 2014 elections for control of Congress.

"There's only so much money to go around in Democratic circles. There's a limited pool of resources," said Gilda Cobb Hunter, a South Carolina legislator and a member of the Democratic National Committee. "Why can't we strengthen one entity?"

Several DNC members said in interviews that they weren't told about Organizing for Action's formation until it was publicly announced in January. They said that when they'd complained, they were chastised and told by national and state party leaders not to speak publicly. Most spoke to McClatchy only on the condition of anonymity in order to talk candidly about the internal party dispute.

Party Chairwoman Debbie Wasserman Schultz, a congresswoman from Florida, tried to alleviate concerns in a conference call with Democrats in March, stressing that the groups wouldn't compete for money and resources in part because they had different missions. "What I took away was they heard the complaints of the body," said one DNC member who was on the conference call. The DNC declined to comment last week. White House officials have praised the group for helping to promote the president's agenda.

Why have Barack Obama and his extreme supporters and support base separated themselves from the main body of Democrats and the goals of the Democratic Party itself? All indications are that Barack Obama and his closest support groups are reorganizing for something especially designed for Obama. As indicated in the articles above, Obama's new Organizing For Action group is not sharing information and resources with the National Democratic Party, including email lists and names of past donors - especially those donors of larger amounts.

Their claim is that the new organization is to promote the agenda Obama set early in his administration. But, why would a president need a special group to do that? He claims the purpose is to pressure Congress to pass his key projects such as gun control and climate change legislation. Does that sound even close to reasonable? What would seem more logical to an average person - and to one even more skilled in political techniques and agenda? Certainly not to separate from the main body, the Democratic Party, and act in isolation. He would need that group even more.

To pass the legislation he and his close advisors claim they are focusing on does not require new organizations that isolate themselves from the main body whose ideologies are compatible and made from the same mold - in this case, the liberal mold. Why? Because the way to pass more legislation favoring one party, not the country, is to have both houses of Congress comprised of the same party. To do that requires the coalition and same play book of all members of that party, not just a specialized group focusing only on the president. Congress men and women of both houses are elected locally by state - not by a national organization.

What are Obama and his new group, Organizing For Action doing? It's certainly not to support the Democratic Party, and its agenda. Perhaps a clue is given from one of the statements above:

"Several DNC members said in interviews that they weren't told about Organizing for Action's formation until it was publicly announced in January. They said that when they'd complained, they were chastised and told by national and state party leaders not to speak publicly."

This information, in itself, presents a very serious question. Combined with all the secrets and deceptions of the Obama administration, such as 'Fast and Furious,' the 'Benghazi Affair,' the 'IRS Scandal,' the administration's reckless and false charges against innocent people, and more intense scrutiny and invasion of citizens' privacy, perhaps the

King Obama

serious conclusion must be made.

That conclusion must be that Barack Obama and his cohorts do not intend to give up his power at the end of his current term - ending in 2016. Does he plan to be 'President for Life,' 'King of America,' or 'The Great Imam?' But, is this even possible - and how?

First, we must consider Obama's background and training. His background is only that of a 'community organizer' and a college instructor. And, it's not certain of the depth of his college teaching. In the role of community organizer his purpose was to teach people how to get more from the government and government programs. What else would a 'community organizer' do? Obviously, it was not to teach his charges how to get educated, get a job, and contribute something back into society. His task was to guide them in learning how to 'take from' society.

There is little history of Barack Obama before that, while he was in college in the United States. During that time, he made overseas trips and various other explorations. A question that's never been answered is that if he had no real job while in school, who paid for his tuition and all the trips he took to Pakistan and Indonesia. Were the trips free? And, as a side question - what country of origin was listed on his passport for those trips? He will not allow anyone to get that answer.

Who was his sponsor - and for what purpose? Why is he keeping those secrets from a citizenry now entrusted to the leadership of their future? There must be a reason - there's always a reason for every action or lack of responsible action. These secrets and many others suggest honor and honesty might not be his guiding principles. Consequently, can any possible other dishonor be discounted - such as attempting to circumvent our laws to become a powerful and unchallenged leader of America?

Again, is it possible? How could it be done? Of course, no one knows exactly what's on Obama's mind or what he plans to do - or how he plans to do it. Perhaps he doesn't even know the answer to those questions, at this time, himself. But, there are alternatives and possibilities. The most obvious first consideration would to be to eliminate or change the 22nd Amendment to our Constitution - that would allow a president to serve more than two terms, or ten years total. This likely would be the first choice if one could consider alternatives to ascend to that high status. What would be the first actions necessary to make that change?

The plan for that action is already in place. The most likely real purpose for Obama's 'Organizing for Action' is to accomplish just that. That organization has separated itself from the Democratic Party to achieve something other than the goals of the Democratic Party. They claim to help Obama achieve his agenda items, but that could more easily be done with the coordination and cooperation of the party itself. What other reason would Obama and his cohorts separate themselves physically, conceptually, and financially if it weren't for an ulterior purpose - likely that sinister ulterior purpose.

Obama's plan is to have a national Organizing for Action group - plus subordinate groups in every state. What would be the purpose and the goals of state subsidiaries? The answer - to help elect enough state leaders to help pass the repeal of the 22nd Amendment. Is there any other conceivable and logical reason?

The second possible route to an autocratic takeover of America is by simple decree, and a national uprising by his supporters and worshipers. These would be two groups. One is his highly vocal black supporters who would claim "racism," if their great son is not allowed to serve longer. The other group who might demand he stay in power are the proles who have not yet received enough of their promised 'free stuff' from the government. They are still waiting for more. They obviously and statistically must wait even longer.

Recent statistics show that those low wage earners, those who support Barack Obama the most, have seen their wages go down 5-percent since he became president. These are those who actually work and don't wait on the sidelines for those free handouts. Yet, they claim it's not Obama's fault.

They claim it's George Bush's fault their earnings are less, or that it's the evil rich Republican politicians who will not support Obama's policies. They ignore the fact that Obama's policies against fossil fuel production is the greatest cause of their despair. They ignore the idea that their 'God' would do anything that could harm them.

If you think this is irrational and impossible - think again. With another appointment to the Supreme Court, he would have a 'stacked deck' who would do anything the attorney general suggested to keep Obama in power. Is there any doubt the attorney general would find a discrepancy in the wording of the 22nd Amendment that would allow it to be overturned?

Who would stop him? Certainly not our military. The current secretary of defense and chairman of the joint chiefs of staff are clearly ardent supporters and would never do anything to challenge any of his actions - no matter how illegal or disloyal.

The third possible route is by martial law. Obama has already set up that scenario. Perhaps we will never know if this scenario has been planned or is created through ignorance and circumstance, nevertheless a dangerous condition has been permitted to develop - the crossing of our southern borders by many Islamists. Are they radical Islamists; are they Islamic terrorists; are they creating cells waiting for a call to action by a central authority?

Perhaps we will never know how it happened or who guided that action, but it's a serious activity that's been allowed by our government. A report by worldnewsdaily (WND) in May, 2010 explains how serious:

"Almost nine years after terrorists murdered 2,751 people on Sept. 11, 2001, the U.S. is still facing a major threat as hundreds of illegal aliens from countries known to support and sponsor terrorism sneak across the U.S.-Mexico border.

Thousands of illegal aliens apprehended along the 2,000 mile border stretching through California, Arizona, New Mexico, and Texas aren't even from Mexico. The U.S. Border

Patrol calls them "Other Than Mexicans," or OTMs, and many are citizens of countries that are sponsors of terrorism.

A 2006 congressional report on border threats, titled "A Line in the Sand: Confronting the Threat at the Southwest Border" and prepared by the House Committee on Homeland Security Subcommittee on Investigations, indicated that 1.2 million illegal aliens were apprehended in 2005 alone, and 165,000 of those were from countries other than Mexico. Approximately 650 were from "special interest countries," or nations the Border Patrol defines as "designated by the intelligence community as countries that could export individuals that could bring harm to our country in the way of terrorism."

Atlanta's WSB-TV2 aired a segment on U.S. border security after it obtained records from a federal detention center near Phoenix, Ariz., and found current listings for illegal aliens from Afghanistan, Egypt, Iran, Iraq, Pakistan, Sudan and Yemen. "We have left the back door to the United States open," former Rep. J.D. Hayworth told the station. "We have to understand that there are definitely people who mean to do us harm who have crossed that border."

WSB-TV2 published a population breakdown from an Immigration and Customs Enforcement staging facility in Florence, Ariz., dated April 15, 2010, which includes detainees from as far away as Afghanistan, Armenia, Bosnia, Egypt, Ghana, Iraq, Iran, Jordan, Kenya, Morocco, Pakistan, Sudan, Uzbekistan, Yemen, Botswana, Turkey, and many other countries. Based on U.S. Border Patrol statistics, there were 30,147 OTMs apprehended in fiscal year 2003; 44, 614 in fiscal year 2004; 165,178 in fiscal year 2005; and 108,025 in fiscal year 2006. Most were caught along the U.S. Southwest border.

U.S. Immigration and Customs Enforcement investigations have revealed that aliens were smuggled from the Middle East to staging areas in Central and South America, before being smuggled illegally into the United States. Members of Hezbollah have already entered the United States across the Southwest border.

U.S. military and intelligence officials believe that Venezuela is emerging as a potential hub of terrorism in the Western Hemisphere. The Venezuelan government is issuing identity documents that could subsequently be used to obtain a U.S. visa and enter the country."

A more recent report, June 8, 2013 by Kirstin Tate of mrconservative.com confirmed that information and added:

"It is usually assumed that most illegals caught crossing the US/Mexican border are South Americans. You may be surprised to learn, however, that thousands of the illegals caught crossing the borders are classified as "OTMs" (Other Than Mexicans). A substantial number of these OTMs are Muslim terrorists. Records from a detention center near Phoenix, AZ, show illegals from Afghanistan, Egypt, Iran, Iraq, Pakistan, Sudan, and Yemen in custody.

An Arizona rancher, who lives right near the border, found a Muslim prayer rug on his property. He said, "This is a good indicator that there's a whole lot of people other than just Mexicans coming into the United States."

What would happen if these terrorists sneaking into the United States, from southern borders or anywhere else, became active near the end of Obama's current term? Is there any better excuse for a president, especially Barack Obama, to declare martial law - and never let go?

Why does he go out of his way not to criticize Muslim terrorists, but only claim their acts of killing Americans is only a 'bump in the road?' He refused to directly state that the four Americans killed in Benghazi were killed by Islamic terrorists. Finally forced, he made a slightly suggestive remark that terrorism was involved.

Is he so focused on votes that he fears alienating even one vote, by suggesting that Islamists could be associated with terrorism? Perhaps the next chapter will help answer that question.

12

RISE OF ISLAM

Is Barack Obama so intent on protecting votes from his power base: the special interests, the uneducated and uninformed, and deity worshipers, that he refuses to acknowledge there's a real threat from radical Islamist immigration. The Islamic takeover threat in America is not that great at this time, but let's consider what's already happening in Europe, especially Germany:

GERMANY, December 28, 2012 – In an article published December 27th, Soeren Kern, a Senior Fellow at the New York-based Gatestone Institute, wrote a dire message stating that "as a rapidly growing Muslim population makes its presence felt in towns and cities across the continent, Islam is transforming the European way of life in ways unimaginable only a few years ago."

No country was more affected by Islam-related controversies in 2012 than Germany. According to Kern, the

Muslim population in the early 1980s stood at approximately 50,000. Today that number has grown to more than four and a half million.

Much of the anxiety lies in an increasing divide between Germany's political elites, who are determined to build a multicultural society regardless of cost, and ordinary German citizens who are witnessing a progression in the erosion of their freedoms. Several recent studies have arrived at corroborating conclusions. The problem has reached such dynamic proportions that Germans openly discuss the situation with outsiders, tourists, and anyone else who will listen.

In a spate of political correctness where mainstream media is giving credence to the demands of multiculturalism by the power elite, anti-jihadists are being classified as "Islamophobes." It is similar to the manner in which dissenters are called "racists" in the United States for voicing an opinion against another ethnic group.

Among the areas of greatest concern is the refusal of Muslim immigrants to integrate into German society, which inherently brings the institution of Sharia law. Such parallel legal systems will create societal havoc by establishing separate laws for diverging communities within one nation. One estimate claims that more than 400 Roman Catholic churches and over 100 Protestant churches have been closed since 2000, with 700 additional Roman Catholic churches scheduled to shut down over the next several years.

As the number of Christians declines, the number of Muslims is increasing. There currently are more than 200 mosques in Germany, 128 more under construction and 2,600 Muslim prayer halls throughout the country.

In recent months, several reports have surfaced that hard-line Islamic groups, called Salafists, are working feverishly to establish a Sunni Islamic Caliphate throughout the Middle East, North Africa and Europe. Salafists are a radical Islamic sect based in Saudi Arabia. Among the goals of the Caliphate is to establish a world governed by Sharia law, Islamic law, which would apply exclusively to both

Muslims and non-Muslims.

As part of the program, a campaign called "Project Read" was organized in April of 2012 where Salafists set out to distribute 25-million free copies of the Koran, with a German translation. As Kern points out, it was an attempt to place a Koran in every household in the country. In his chronological account of every notable Islamic "event" that occurred in Germany in 2012, Kern writes that German Intelligence Chief, Gerhard Schindler, issued a warning in August that Europe is at high risk of terrorists attacks, especially those of the homegrown variety. Many individuals born and/or raised in Europe have traveled to hotbeds of terrorism for training. As recently as December 10th, authorities in Germany announced that a man linked to al-Qaeda left a bag containing a bomb on a railway station platform in Bonn. Fortunately, the bomb did not detonate even though it had been activated.

As reported in this column in November, Hamburg, Germany's second-largest city, agreed to a "treaty" granting Muslim communities broad new rights and privileges with very little in return. Among the terms of the agreement, Hamburg will now begin teaching Islam in public schools with leaders from the local Muslim community developing the curriculum. By November 30th, the city of Bremen followed suit by creating a similar pact.

Also in November, a 28-page research study, 'Fear of the East in the West,' produced by the Allensbach Institute for Public Opinion Research, showed that a high percentage of Germans do not trust Islam and fear Muslim Immigration. The percentages are telling: 64% of Germans believe Islam is prone to violence; 60% say Islam has a tendency toward revenge and retaliation; 56% state that Muslims are obsessed with proselytizing others; and 56% also say Islam strives for political influence.

Experts have been sounding alarms for decades. The situation is growing worse by the day in Germany. A Salafist Caliphate could be on the horizon if we continue to ignore and to appease."

This article explains what Islamists are doing to Europe. Yet, even as they understand the danger to long freedoms in their societies, they are opening the doors for destruction of those freedoms. Are we in the United States any wiser, or any more determined to protect our freedoms? Obviously not - we continue to let the destroyers of human freedom and dignity in - holding the doors wide open for them. And, what do they plan to contribute to our great nation when they get here? Consider the following example:

"In Afghanistan, a 14-year-old girl was beheaded and killed in an attack by two men, one of whom apparently asked her to marry him. The attack happened Tuesday, a day before new legislation was introduced in Congress calling on the U.S. government to take steps to help protect Afghan women and girls as the U.S. military prepares to exit Afghanistan.

Gasitina, a student, was beheaded in the Imam Sahib district of the Kunduz province. The attack was initially reported by local media, and was confirmed by Amnesty International researcher, Horia Mosadiq, in an email.

The girl was fetching water when she was accosted, according to reports. The men, who have not been identified, were arrested by police. The girl and her parents had refused a marriage proposal by one of the men, according to the Amnesty International report.

This was the 15th deadly attack on a female victim in Kunduz in 2012, the human rights organization said. "Amnesty International is very concerned about the violations against women in Afghanistan," said Cristina Finch, director of the organizations's Women's Human Rights program."

This is just one example of thoughts and reactions by extreme Islamists. And, the most extreme Islamics are identified as Wahhabis. The Wahabbi movement is promoted from Saudi Arabia, and is generally under the guidance of the Muslim Brotherhood. Members of the Muslim Brotherhood are in Barack Obama's administration, and in many cases are strong advisors to Obama's actions pertaining to Muslims and those who are reactionaries to the encroaching Muslim movement into America.

We as individuals have assumed our government would protect us from such insidious jeopardy. We have been deadly wrong - many in our government, even at the highest level, seem involved in that silent encroachment against our country and our freedom. While our government removes major obstacles to that attack, the attack continues - especially in our schools. This is part of a report from a study conducted by 'Freedom House.' highlighting that danger:

'Wahhabism in the United States:' A study conducted by the non-governmental organization, 'Freedom House' found Wahhabi publications in a Mosque in the United States. These publications included statements that Muslims should not only "always oppose infidels "in every way, but "hate them for their religion for Allah's sake", that "democracy" is responsible for all the horrible wars of the 20th century", and that "Shia Islam" and certain Sunni Muslims were "apostasy in Islam."

The Saudi government issued a response to this report, stating: "It has worked diligently during the last five years to overhaul its education system but overhauling an educational system is a massive undertaking."

A review of the study by 'Institute for Social Policy and Understanding' complained the study cited documents from only a few mosques, arguing most mosques in the U.S. are not under Wahhabi influence. Freedom House comments on the study were not entirely negative however, and concluded: American-Muslim leaders must thoroughly scrutinize this study.

Despite its limitations, the study highlights an ugly undercurrent in modern Islamic discourse that American-Muslims must openly confront. However, in the vigor to expose strains of extremism, we must not forget that open discussion is the best tool to debunk the extremist literature rather than a suppression of "First Amendment to the United States Constitution" rights guaranteed by the United States

Constitution

What militant and political Islam connection, if any, there is between Wahhabism and Salafism jihadism is disputed. Natana De Long-Bas, senior research assistant at the Prince Alwaleed Center for Muslim-Christian Understanding argues: "Islamic terrorism - Osama bin Laden did not have its origins in the teachings of Ibn Abd-al-Wahhab and was not representative of Wahhabi Islam as it is practiced in contemporary Saudi Arabia, yet for the media it came to define Wahhabi Islam during the later years of bin Laden's lifetime." However unrepresentative bin Laden's global Jihad was of Islam in general and Wahhabi Islam in particular, its prominence in headline news took Wahhabi Islam across the spectrum from revival and reform to global jihad

Noah Feldman distinguishes between what he calls the deeply conservative Wahhabis and what he calls the followers of political Islam in the 1980s and 1990s, such as Egyptian Islamic Jihad Islamic Jihad and later Al-Qaeda leader Ayman al-Zawahiri. While Saudi Wahhabis were the largest funders of local Muslim Brotherhood chapters and other hard-line Islamists during this time, they opposed jihadi resistance to Muslim governments and assassination of Muslim leaders because of their belief that "the decision to wage jihad lay with the ruler, not the individual believer"

Wahhabis as well as other Islamist fundamentalists also believe in Sharia law. They extol the idea that it's the purest kind of law. Although they try to claim it's not extreme and against humanity, let's consider some of its rules, and what might happen to citizens of the United States if they were to ever rule here.

This is from an article titled, 'Islamic Law in Brief!,' written February 4, 2011, by Syed Kamran Mirza. He states, "These common laws of 'Islamic Sharia' which are regularly practiced in the Islamically ruled (Sharia-based) nations with some minor variations:

1. Jihad defined as "to war against all non-Muslims to

establish the religion" is the duty of every Muslim and Muslim head of state (Caliph). Muslim Caliphs who refuse jihad are in violation of Sharia and unfit to rule.

2. A Caliph can hold office through seizure of power, meaning through force.

3. The head of an Islamic State (Caliph) cannot be charged, let alone be punished for serious crimes such as murder, adultery, robbery, theft, drinking and in some cases of rape.

4. A percentage of Zakat (alms) must go towards jihad.

5. It is obligatory to obey the commands of the Caliph, even if he is unjust.

6. A Caliph must be a Muslim, a non-slave and a male.

7. The Muslim public must remove the Caliph in one case, if he rejects Islam.

8. A Muslim who leaves Islam (apostate) must be killed immediately.

9. A Muslim will be forgiven for murder of : a) an apostasy b) an adulterer c) a highway robber. Making vigilante street justice and honor killing acceptable.

10. A Muslim will not get the death penalty if he kills a non-Muslim.

11. Sharia never abolished slavery and sexual slavery and highly regulates it. A master will not be punished for killing his slave. Slavery still exists amongst Arab Muslims.

12. Sharia dictates death by stoning, beheading, for sins like killing, adultery, prostitutions; and other Quranic

corporal punishments like: amputation of limbs (chopping hands and feet), floggings, beatings and other forms of cruel and unusual punishments even for the sins like: stealing, sexual promiscuity, robbery, burglary, etc.

13. Non-Muslims are not equal to Muslims and must comply to Sharia (pay Zizzya: poll tax) if they are to remain safe. They are forbidden to marry Muslim women, publicly display wine or pork, recite their own religious scriptures, or openly celebrate their religious holidays or funerals. They are forbidden from building new churches or building them higher than mosques. They may not enter a mosque without permission. A non-Muslim is no longer protected if he commits adultery with a Muslim woman or if he leads a Muslim away from Islam.

14. It is a crime for a non-Muslim to sell weapons to someone who will use them against Muslims. Non-Muslims cannot curse a Muslim, say anything derogatory about Allah, the Prophet, or Islam, or expose the weak points of Muslims. However, Muslims can curse, criticize or say anything derogatory they like to the religions of others.

15. A non-Muslim cannot inherit from a Muslim.

16 Banks must be Sharia compliant and interest is not allowed.

17. No testimony in court is acceptable from people of low-level jobs, such as street sweepers or a bathhouse attendant. Women in such low level jobs such as professional funeral mourners cannot keep custody of their children in case of divorce.

18. A non-Muslim cannot rule even over a non-Muslim minority. (Keep this in mind as we discuss Obama's plans further.)

19. Homosexuality is punishable by death.

20. There is no age limit for marriage of girls under Sharia. The marriage contract can take place anytime after birth and consummated at age 8 or 9.

21. Rebelliousness on the part of the wife nullifies the husband's obligation to support her, gives him permission to beat her and keep her from leaving the home.

22. Divorce is only in the hands of the husband and is as easy as saying: "I divorce you" and becomes effective even if the husband did not intend it.

23. There is no common property between husband and wife and the husband's property does not automatically go to the wife after his death.

24. A woman inherits half what a man inherits. Sister gets half of what brother gets.

25. A man has the right to have up to 4 wives and wife has no right to divorce him even if he is polygamous.

26. The dowry is given in exchange for the woman's sexual organs.

27. A man is allowed to have sex with slave women and also with women captured in battle (concubines), and if the enslaved woman is married her marriage is annulled.

28. The testimony of a woman in court is half the value of a man; that is, two women equal to one man.

29. A woman loses custody if she remarries.

30. A rapist may only be required to pay the bride-money (dowry) without marrying the rape victim.

31. A Muslim woman must cover every inch of her body which is considered "Awrah," a sexual organ. Some schools of Sharia allow the face and some don't.

32. A Muslim man is forgiven if he kills his wife caught in the act of adultery. However, the opposite is not true for women since he "could be married to the woman he was caught with."

33. It is obligatory for a Muslim to lie if the purpose is obligatory and is known as Taqiyya (Islamic Deception). That means that for the sake of abiding with Islam's commandments, such as jihad, a Muslim is obliged to lie and should not have any feelings of guilt or shame associated with this kind of lying.

34. The perpetrators of genocide, mass rape and plunder will not be punished if they repent.

35. To prove rape, a woman must have 4 male witnesses. Women's testimony is not accepted - Pakistan's Hudood ordnance 7 of 1979 amended by 8B of 1980. Thousands of raped women and girls in many countries have been charged with Zena (physical relations outside marriage) and punished by Sharia courts for want of witnesses.

36. All modern music including sexually explicit music of any kind is strictly prohibited and punishable by Islamic Sharia code of justice. Only Islamic songs are allowed.

So, with all these rules in Sharia Law, what does Islam say about truth and honesty? It's required that Muslims defend Islam, even if they must be dishonest. In Mirza's article he emphasizes, "Caution! Islam permits devout Muslims to lie, cheat, and deliberately bluff non-Muslims to protect or promote his religion of Islam, anytime, anywhere. And this tactic is known as "Islamic Taqiyya" and was originally used by the Prophet of Islam to fool, and later subjugate and destroy enemies of Islam. As Prophet of Islam repeatedly asserted: "War is a deception" and with this holy-tactic, Prophet of Islam established his most intolerant religion of violence (by 80 plus bloody battles) which he later named as: 'religion of peace'!" (Updated: see page 296.)

He continues, "Therefore, today's Islamists will follow the holy path of their Prophet and will deny that—Sharia is really Islamic law! They will try to cheat by saying that, all these Sharia laws that are practiced in Saudi Arabia, Iran, Sudan, and elsewhere are not true Islamic, and they have been distorted. They also will try to fool people by saying: Saudi Arabia is ruled by King (Monarch) and Islam does not permit Kingship, etc. But, their dishonest assertion is furthest from the truth. Ancient Caliphs of Islam were nothing but the kings of ancient Islamic nations having supreme despotic and dictatorial authoritative rulers. In fact, ancient Islamic Caliphs were more despotic and brutal rulers than the present day Saudi king.

No one should be fooled into believing that these harsh and draconian laws were invented out of any wishful imagination of the so called "Islamic radicals/extremists" who came long after Muhammad. Actually, these harsh and barbarically cruelest laws came directly from the founder of Islam in his Quran and in his example in the Hadith. Almost 98% of the above samples of Sharia justice can be traced-backed to Quran and Sunnah positively.

In fact, Prophet Muhammad himself actually practiced them and deliberately laid down these corporal punishments and policies to rule the ancient Islamic Caliphate. Modern kings and presidents of today's Islamic nations are doing exactly the same to emulate Islamic Prophet and those ancient rightly guided Caliphs."

Is there a direct connection between Barack Obama and his commitment to Islamic forces? Consider the following information that not only gives more direct connections. It also suggests the level of Obama's trust, honor and ethics.

This is an article from whiteoutpress.com, published on September 21, 2012. It's titled: 'Barack Obama and the Muslim Brotherhood.' It begins:

"Washington, September 21, 2012. With President Obama's re-election less than two months away, his critics are mounting an aggressive effort to link him with Islamic extremists, specifically the Muslim Brotherhood. Below, we outline the argument of two separate, widely-referenced sources claiming the American people should be alarmed. Should we be? Investigators detail Barack Obama's ties to Chicago's Arab and Muslim activist community.

The Obama You Don't Know

In a 10-part series published by the Washington Examiner two days ago titled, 'The Obama You Don't Know', the news outlet attempts to correct a number of public misconceptions about President Obama.

The first chapter details an Obama childhood based on privilege, not hardship. Another section reminds readers of how Barack Obama made a fortune in a seemingly rigged real estate deal with a convicted Chicago mobster that netted the future President an all but free house and a number of new friends with high-level political connections.

Yet another section of the 10-part series details the plight of Barack Obama's neighbors on Chicago's war-torn south side. Suggesting the President left the poor behind with little care about them, the poverty-stricken city has seen the homicide rate skyrocket, while the foreclosure and unemployment rates are still some of the worst in the nation. Another chapter in the report argues that contrary to popular media sentiment, Illinois State Senator Obama was not the reformer he portrays himself as.

The Arab-American network behind Obama

The most controversial section of the special report however, is Chapter IX, 'The Arab-American Network Behind

Obama'. The account begins with President Obama's past links to Columbia University professor Rashid Khalidi and ends with an FBI raid on a Middle East charity patronized by Barack Obama and accused of being tied to Palestinian terrorist groups.

Prior to becoming a university professor, Rashid Khalidi worked for Yasser Arafat and his Palestinian Liberation Organization, before the PLO became a legitimate government calling itself the Palestinian Authority and while it was still fighting as an underground insurgent army.

The account then jumps to Tony Rezko, who was repeatedly referenced by Hillary Clinton during the 2008 Democratic primary. Rezko is a convicted 'political fixer' from Chicago who finagled a nearly free house for the Obamas in a controversial real estate deal. Tony Rezko isn't the typical Chicago Democratic Party operative and fundraiser, controlled by Chicago's Irish Mafia. He's also a native of Aleppo, Syria – home to Syrian dictator Bashar al-Assad.

Currently serving a 10-year federal prison sentence for corruption and bribery, Tony Rezko has given more than $100,000 to various Obama election efforts over the years. In addition to the controversial $1.6 million home purchased by the still mysterious Obama-Rezko partnership, investigators have documented as much as $168,308 in monetary donations from Rezko to Obama. The Obama campaign has gone so far as donating $85,000 of those donations to charity in an attempt to distance themselves from the convicted Democratic Party operative.

The Chicago Arab-American network

That's how the small, tight-knit group of wealthy, powerful and politically-connected Arab-American businessmen in Chicago is referred to by some of its own members. Ray Hanania is another figure, with the report describing his group of Arab-Americans as being 'at the heart of Obama's political apparatus'. Hanania is a journalist and activist who in 2007 called the small, unofficial group, "a small cluster of activists".

As is so often the case in Chicago and Illinois government, once a special interest group gains control of an agency or government body, it's a gluttony of financial feasting like pigs at a trough. Once IL State Senator Barack Obama became Chairman of the Illinois Senate health committee that oversaw appointments to the state medical board, he filled the panel with Tony Rezko's foot soldiers.

First, to insure control of the medical board that outsourced construction projects, building maintenance and improvement jobs, one of Barack Obama's first acts was to reduce the size of the board from 15 to 9 members, making it easier to control with 5 loyal patrons instead of the previous 8. One by one, Obama and Rezko filled the state medical board with Arab-American political operatives and Obama financial contributors.

Dr. Imad Almanaseer, a Rezko ally, was appointed to the health board after giving Obama $3,000. After his appointment, Almanaseer and his family members paid $10,000 more to Obama. Fortunee Massuda is identified as another Tony Rezko crew member. Massuda gave Obama $2,000 shortly after being appointed to the same medical board.

Follow the money...to Barack Obama

The Illinois health board wasn't the only secret partnership the Obama team had with Rezko's "cluster" of Islamic activists in Chicago. The Washington Examiner special report goes on to list others.

Investigators report, 'Elie Maloof was granted immunity by federal prosecutors after he told U.S. attorneys he funneled two $10,000 contributions to Obama through Rezko.' Abdelhamid Chaib is another activist at the center of the scandal. Chaib was convicted in 2010 of federal corruption charges after giving $10,000 to the Obama team.

Another tainted figure is Ali Ata. The report writes, 'Ali Ata was a key witness during Rezko's 2008 federal corruption trial. He donated $5,000 to Obama's campaign and claimed to have given an additional $10,000 in "straw donations".'

Ali Ata and Nadhmi Auchi

The connection between Barack Obama and global Islamists takes a mysterious, underground turn when it comes to Ali Ata and Nadhmi Auchi. At the time, Ata was the President of the Chicago office of the Arab-American Anti-Discrimination Committee.

Ata was an investment partner of Tony Rezko and a third man, Nadhmi Auchi. Auchi is well-known to the US Department of Homeland Security. He is an assumed Islamic terrorist and known member of Iraq's Baath Party, the party of Saddam Hussein. Being on the US government's Terror Watch List, Auchi is banned from entering the US. But that didn't stop him from taking part in the funding of Barack Obama's political ambitions. It also didn't stop him from coming to Chicago and meeting Obama personally.

In 2004, Tony Rezko petitioned the federal government to allow Auchi into the country to attend a business meeting in Chicago. Stewart Levine, Rezko's business partner and a key witness in the corruption trials, testified that it was there that accused terrorist Nadhmi Auchi met with future President Barack Obama at Chicago's Four Seasons Hotel.

When Rezko was indicted in 2008 for bribery and corruption, Auchi wired him $3.5 million to help with his defense and legal fees. Another Rezko and Obama associate - Mustafa Abdalla - gave $1,000 to Obama and then generously put up his property as collateral to pay for Tony Rezko's criminal defense.

AADC and AAAN

The special report continues by detailing parallel connections between Tony Rezko and Barack Obama on one side, and Arab-American political organizations on the other. Two such Chicago groups that benefitted from their associations with Obama and Rezko were the Arab American Democratic Club (AADC) and the Arab American Action Network (AAAN).

The account details one documented link between the Obama-Rezko crew and AADC when it reports, 'Rezko was involved in the AADC with Khalil Shalabi. Shalabi was fired from a state government job in 2007 after the Illinois inspector general reported he had been fundraising at work for Rezko and Blagojevich.' Blagojevich of course refers to former Illinois Governor Rod Blagojevich, also currently imprisoned for corruption

Detailing Barack Obama's ties to the AAAN, investigators reveal that Barack and Michelle Obama have attended numerous AAAN dinners, including one honoring Khalidi. In April 2010, AAAN executive director Hatem Abudayyeh even attended a White House policy briefing. Just five months later in September 2010, the FBI raided Abudayyeh's Chicago home, accusing him of being 'a conduit for funding to the Popular Front for the Liberation of Palestine and other Middle Eastern terrorist groups.'

Hillary Clinton and Huma Abedin

Barack Obama isn't the only high-level member of the Obama administration with links to Islamic organizations. The most well documented case is that of Secretary of State Clinton's personal aide Huma Abedin. Who is Huma Abedin? Aside from being one of Hillary Clinton's most trusted assistants, she is also the wife of former NY Congressman Anthony Weiner.

Sun News also answered that question recently with a video being redistributed by a number of activists including the Tea Party Patriots.

"Huma Abedin is the daughter of two American-Islamist academics," says Muslim Canadian Congress founder Tarek Fatah in the interview, "who as soon as they got American passports and she was born, took the daughter, went where? Saudi Arabia. They were not Saudis. One was a Pakistani, the other was Indian.''

For his part, Tarek Fatah is also the author of the book, 'The Jew is Not my Enemy'. He goes on to describe Huma Abedin's family and their connection to the Muslim Brotherhood. "Deeply involved with the Muslim Brotherhood, they kept their daughter and subjected her to a childhood of education in that segregated, fascist society, until she was old enough to go to American universities," Fatah recounts, "Then, they brought her here."

"As soon as they brought her here, she became an intern in the White House when President Clinton was there," Tarek Fatah details, "Later on, served Senator Clinton." He describes Huma Abedin as, "a bright young woman" and "a roll model for many Muslim young women because she defies every stereotype of what a Muslim woman is." The Muslim Brotherhood connection:

Fatah slowly builds to the connection explaining, "When she was in Georgetown University, she was on the executive board of the Muslim Students Association. The MSA is a Muslim Brotherhood front organization, that in various universities take different forms. But at the core of it is a radical Islamist group that does not go far from the goals established by the Muslim Brotherhood in Egypt and Pakistan."

"While she was there, she was also a member of the editorial board. She was assistant editor to this Muslim Brotherhood magazine called, 'The Journal of Muslim Minority Affairs'," Tarek Fatah continues describing Huma Abedin.

Reading from the magazine's masthead, Fatah explains, "Her mum's the editor...Then she's got her brother as associate editor. Then, Huma Abedin is the assistant editor. Her younger sister, who has changed her name, is the other assistant editor." Explaining the significance of the Journal, Tarek Fatah reveals, "It was a Saudi publication, funded by a radical, terrorist-supporting individual."

King Obama

Oath of Allegiance

Going back to Huma Abedin's college days, the interview with Tarek Fatah goes on to scrutinize the Muslim Students Association and its Oath of Allegiance. "MSA, Muslim Students Association, has an Oath of Allegiance," Fatah explains, "It's not what I'm alleging. This is what they proudly put on the YouTube and you can listen. It is an exact reflection of what is asked or demanded by the Muslim Brotherhood in Egypt."

The video report from Sun News and the Tea Party Patriots inserts a clip of what they say is the MSA's Oath of Allegiance, and the oath it suggests Huma Abedin once took:

"Allah is my Lord.
Islam is my life.
The Koran is my guide.
The Sunna is my practice.
Jihad is my spirit.
Righteousness is my character.
Paradise is my goal.
I enjoin what is right.
I forbid what is wrong.
I will fight against oppression.
And I will die to establish Islam."

In summary, the Muslim Brotherhood is a consortium to destroy everything non-Muslim on the face of the earth. It's in their doctrine. The Saudi king, who pretends to be a bystander to the Islamic revolution, is actually one of the main players to clandestinely overthrow Western ideology and civilization. That includes American citizens.

Barack Obama, who has taken an oath to protect and defend the Constitution of the United States; and whose first and primary function as commander-in-chief is to protect American citizens is failing to fulfill that responsibility. Are his actions intentional; is he part of the conspiracy? He could easily demonstrate his patriotism to the United States of

America by promoting our domestic resources, by allowing more fossil fuel development in the United States and its surrounding waters. As already described earlier in this book, he and his administration have a direct plan to penalize and execute anyone who tries.

Instead, he continues to buy that same fossil fuel from Saudi Arabia, and other countries that vow to destroy us. He bows to their Saudi king then funds their plan to help them destroy us. Obviously, he was well trained in 'Islamic Taqiyya' while he was in Kenya and Indonesia.

And, how is our government - led by Barack Obama - protecting American citizens? On March 21, 2013 as I was writing, I heard a report on TV that was shocking - it matched exactly what I was typing. It was further information about the 'evil alliance' between the United States and Saudi Arabia. I researched the information online after I heard it on a the news report. This is what I found:

"Saudi Arabia, the nation which produced 15 of the 19 hijackers in the 9/11 attacks, is about to become one of a handful of countries whose travelers can bypass normal passport controls at major U.S. airports. Sources tell the Investigative Project on Terrorism that this will mark the first time that the Saudi government will have a direct role in vetting who is eligible for getting fast-tracked for entry into the United States.

Homeland Security Secretary Janet Napolitano announced the agreement in January after meeting with Saudi Interior Minister Prince Mohammed bin Nayef. It "marks another major step forward in our partnership," Napolitano said at the time. "By enhancing collaboration with the Government of Saudi Arabia, we reaffirm our commitment to more effectively secure our two countries against evolving threats while facilitating legitimate trade and travel."

What are Barack Obama's plans for our future? Is it for us to survive and persevere as free people our Founding Fathers intended when they sacrificed and died for us? Or is it that he plans to go his own way - whatever that destination might be?

Finally, regarding Obama's support and encouragement of the 'Rise of Islam' in America, and his refusal to criticize them and what they do, a very serious question must be asked. That question is:

> Why do women who won their freedoms and rights in the last generation want to destroy those things in this generation?

They fought for and won their rights to own property, to vote, to have an equal say in most things in their lives, the right to say 'no' and the right to be their own persons to determine their own destiny. Why would they voluntarily throw these hard-earned rights away just to support Barack Obama? If he remains in power, he will certainly continue to support Islam in our great nation - and will eventually allow those Islamists to enforce many of their Sharia laws in a nation that should be more concerned about human principles and freedom for everyone - including all women.

Page 239 gives a list of these activities and atrocities allowed to be perpetrated against women in the Muslim world. Can any normal human being imagine the fear and pain a young Muslim girl, 8 or 9 years old, must feel when her arranged marriage is consummated by a grown man? And they call their religion a religion of 'peace.'

Women of America, continue to support Barack Obama at you own peril - and that of your daughters. Never forget - Barack Obama has a Muslim background, and he will support their ideology.

13

THE ANTICHRIST

Recognizing that many who read this book, and countless others throughout the world, despise the Bible and everything for which it stands and represents, this chapter will have no meaning to them, only continued disdain. Mainly for that reason I choose to add this chapter after the conclusion of the main part of the book. This chapter is for those who still believe in God, and the word He presented for others to write in the Bible. Having no interest in the Bible the information in this chapter will have no meaning to them. However, on the possibility that some of those non-believers might be the least bit curious, I will explain many of the readings as the chapter progresses - and in an order of possible events as they might occur.

There are three references, however, that might help some unbelieving souls take a different look at the meaning of God, prophesy, and the Bible. It's about things said two thousand years ago that could not have been understood until our modern age. John wrote these things in the Book of Revelation. How did John know today's possibilities two thousand years ago? Those references are in Chapter 13, Verses 13-15. They are explained at the end of this chapter. That's why I put this information in Chapter 13 of this book. It's that significant.

But for those among us who still worship God, there are a few things John wrote in the Book of Revelation that we will understand and respect. It's foretold there's nothing we can do to affect the outcome of events written therein; the option left to us is personal salvation. We must recognize the signs of the end times and be prepared. The Bible gives this warning at the beginning of Revelation, the very first chapter:

> "The Revelation of Jesus Christ which God gave unto him, to shew unto his servants things which must shortly come to pass; and he sent and signified it by his angel unto his servant John;
>
> 2 Who bare record of the word or God, and of the testimony of Jesus Christ, and of all things that he saw.
>
> 3 Blessed is he that readeth, and they that hear the words of this prophecy, and keep those things which are written therein; for the time is at hand."

Will there be any doubt when He comes? Will He be confused with one of the other Antichrists? There's some confusion here so let's review the meaning of 'Antichrist.' It's not just one. According to Apostle John there will be many deceivers, and obviously for many purposes. In modern times the reference is generally 'the Antichrist.' Since this idea that the Antichrist is only one, many have not been identified as one of the Antichrists, in the past. This is what First John 2:18 in the Bible says:

"Little children, it is the last time; and as ye have

heard that Antichrist shall come, even now are there many Antichrists; whereby we know that it is the last time."

Here John says there are many Antichrists, then he asks the question, do we know if the current one is the last one? Throughout history, we have asked the question if someone of that time is the Antichrist. After they pass and Armageddon doesn't occur, then we say, "That must not have been the Antichrist." Adolph Hitler probably is the best modern example of this concept.   Was Hitler 'the' Antichrist? No. Was Hitler 'an' Antichrist? Yes.

There have been many other 'Antichrists' in recent years, people who have followers who believe their leader has certain special powers to, in some way, save them. That's the general description of an 'Antichrist,' not someone 'against Christ,' but someone 'in the place of Christ.' Several others include: Jim Jones - 1978, William M. Branham - 1965, David Koresh - 1993, Haile Selassie - 1975, and Sun Myung Moon - 2012.

How will we know the difference? How will we know when Christ, himself, returns to earth? Verses 7 and 8 continue and make that answer very clear:

> "7 Behold, he cometh with clouds; and every eye shall see him, and they also which pierced him; and all kindreds of the earth shall wail because of him. Even so, Amen.
> 8 I am Alpha and Omega, the beginning and the ending, saith the Lord, which is, and which was, and which is to come, the Almighty."

The question now is: when will the ending begin to happen? Of course, that definite date does not exist and one would likely be considered a false prophet if he or she pretended to know that exact date or time, such as boarding a space ship following the Halle-Bopp Comet, as did Marshall Applewhite, another Antichrist. In March, 1997 in an event known as 'Heaven's Gate' Applewhite led a group of followers to a new life. Most of the dead had been with him about 20 years. There were 21 women and 18 men who committed suicide with Applewhite.

However, there are many signs which signal the quick decline of humanity prophesied to grow larger before the ending. Most of those signs include man's growing immorality, sin, and turning away from God's word. Today, who is the one leader most visible in that decline. He is also the one actually worshiped in words and thought by many of his followers.

At this time, Barack Obama is at the forefront of much of that immorality and social decline. His leadership in this process is another indicator that the serpent he so proudly wears on his ring (the ring he has worn for years and the one he gave Michelle to place on his finger when they were married) represents Satan, that old dragon often identified in the Bible.

Many sins encouraged by Satan, 'that old serpent,' are stated in the Bible, but some are more clearly emphasized than others. Consider these and look around to see how often many of these are coming more commonplace in everyday life. These are many of those things John wrote about as transgressions and fornication. These things will also be magnified in the end times supporting the arrival of the Antichrist. Many of these abominations are also encouraged and promoted by Barack Hussein Obama:

Leviticus 18:22, "You shall not lie with a male as with a woman; it is an abomination."

Leviticus 20:13, "If a man lies with a male as with a woman, both of them have committed an abomination."

Proverbs 6:6-19, "There are six things that the Lord hates, seven that are an abomination to him: haughty eyes, a lying tongue, and hands that shed innocent blood, a heart that devises wicked plans, feet that make haste to run to evil, a false witness who breathes out lies, and one who sows discord among brothers."

Galations 5:19-21, "Now the works of the flesh are evident: sexual immorality, impurity, sensuality, idolatry, sorcery, enmity, strife, jealousy, fits of anger, rivalries, dissensions, divisions, envy, drunkenness, orgies, and things like these. I warn you, as I warned you before, that those who do such things will not inherit the kingdom of God."

Romans 1:26-27, "For this reason God gave them up to dishonorable passions. For their women exchanged natural relations for those that are contrary to nature; and the men likewise gave up natural relations with women and were consumed with passion for one another, men committing shameless acts with men and receiving in themselves the due penalty for their error."

Proverbs 12:22, "Lying lips are an abomination to the Lord, but those who act faithfully are his delight."

Isaiah 49:1 "Listen to me, you islands; hear this, you distant nations: Before I was born the LORD called me; from my mother's womb he has spoken my name."

Most of those sins or abominations identified above are clear and easy to understand. There are two, however, that can specifically be identified to Obama, 'one who sows discord among brothers' and 'a false witness who breathes out lies.'

Since the beginning of his first campaign for president, in 2008, he has sown discord among brothers - pitting the poor in our society against the more successful. He intentionally turned citizen against citizen in his zeal for power - claiming the rich and powerful kept the poor and less successful from having their fair share. Also, he is not hesitant to play the race card, for example the young police officer and the man who appeared to be breaking into a house, although it turned out to be his own house.

Another example of using racial comments or implications to alienate and separate American citizens was his comment relating to the George Zimmerman and Trayvon Martin case in Florida. Even before he knew all the facts of the case, he publicly stated his racial prejudice - in attempt to influence judgement. A man in such a position would resort to attacking a citizen without first waiting for an investigation?

This is what Abigail Thernstron from CNN wrote on 7-15-2013:

"Every American can make their own judgment about whether justice was served by the verdict in the George Zimmerman murder trial but one thing we should all recognize: President Obama's interference in a local law enforcement matter was unprecedented and inappropriate, and he comes away from the case looking badly tarnished by his poor judgment.

'If I had a son, he'd look like Trayvon,' the president said when asked about the case in the Rose Garden on March 23, 2012, after many had called for Zimmerman's arrest but several weeks before he was charged. "When I think about this boy, I think about my own kids."

In fact, if the president had a son, he would have been born to extraordinary privilege and raised with all the advantages of two very affluent and highly educated parents. He would have gone to private schools. His path in life would have been almost as dissimilar from Trayvon's as one could imagine."

And, as to those who "breathe out lies and have lying lips," two quickly come to mind. First, regarding the healthcare law - he said you could keep you own doctor and the cost would not be increased. He lied. Regarding the Benghazi event - he said it was caused by a spontaneous reaction to a youtube video. That was a lie. These are only two quick examples of one who 'breathes out lies.'

Obama is also a strong supporter of abortion - even killing unborn babies in late term. This is another of those transgressions he actively supports and promotes in many ways, including medications and abortion - after a fetus has matured well past the human identification stage.

How do these abominations and transgressions affect a nation and not just the individual who commits them? Leviticus 18: 24,27-28 explains:

> "Defile not yourselves in any of these things; for in all these the nations are defiled which I cast out before you." "(For all these abominations have the men of the land done, which were before you, and the land is defiled;)" "That the land spue not you out also, when ye defile it, as it spued out the nations that were before you."

In effect, this reference says a sinner's transgressions not only affect that sinner. It adds that any nation who condones those transgressors will also be spued from God's favor. It's not unreasonable to believe that God's wrath against a nation might be even worse (if that's possible) if the nation chooses a leader who demonstrates, supports, and promotes these abominations.

Finally, after reading this first part of Revelation many times it became clear why John's message to the seven churches in Asia Minor is so important and so relevant today, and to the end times described later in Revelation. It associates those transgressions and those abominations with the other events announcing the pending arrival of the Antichrist, the beast, and his mark that requires absolute obedience and total turning away from the real God. It's a final reminder in the last book of the Bible that God will allow mankind to determine his own destiny - individually, and as a nation, and as a world. It's a choice, not a demand. But, the consequences will be to the land of the people as well as to the individual transgressor.

The greatest question is: is Obama seeking this power as a personal quest to be ruler of one nation, or is he trying to position himself for a greater cause such as the leader of a one-world system? Perhaps at this time he doesn't even know that answer himself. He is merely on a quest he doesn't understand that drives him to that time when there becomes one united world. A united world would require a one-world leader. Perhaps his destiny moves closer. Perhaps the serpents in his ring, that icon of the 'old dragon' will guide him to that destiny.

If his desire or natural urge is for more power, as is natural within most of mankind, that urge can be commonly understood. That's the natural urge of greed the Bible warns against. It's something most people understand and control within their own sense of right and wrong, or in their honesty to conform to God's word. That part could be inborn within his deep personality. It could also be guided by his Muslim faith that he claims 'not' that demands certain things must be followed as dictated by those in position to do the dictating.

It's most likely that this drive for personal power is his natural inclination. However, the other possibility can't be totally discounted. Perhaps he could be following a plan by puppet-masters to create that 'New World Order.' We know what an autocratic government or a dictatorial government looks like. We've seen those come and go throughout history. The extremes go from much loss of life to total elimination of personal aspirations. Ordinarily, over time, those collapse.

But what might a New World Order look like? At the moment, that could consider three different scenarios. When either of these occur, it could represent the 'end of times' mentioned in the Bible.

The first could be a simple autocratic world government with a figurehead, or with a group acting as a figurehead. This is the organizational structure ordinarily envisioned when the concept of a one-world government is discussed. Under this form, countries would still exist as separate entities, socially and religiously, but with all political decisions made by the central government. Likely, religious differences would be tolerated so long as nothing in that religion interfered with the concepts and dictates of the central government.

Of course, all military functions would be under the single authority and organization of the world leader. This would be to enforce dictates, and to prevent or discourage wars between assigned boundaries. Perhaps titles of those within assigned borders would be such as they were during the old Roman Empire; governor or proconsul.

Biblically, this could be the worst time for Israel. The leaders of Israel would have to make a serious decision; would they become a member of the new order? Or, would they have that option? According to Bible prophesy, this could be the time Israel is forced to agree to something they know might sign their death warrant. Perhaps Daniel 18: 23 and 25 gives a clue:

> "And in the latter time of their kingdom, when the transgressors are come to full, a king of fierce countenance, and understanding dark sentences, shall stand up."

> "And through his policy also he shall cause craft to prosper in his hand; and he shall magnify himself in his heart, and by peace shall

destroy many -"

"And by peace shall destroy many." Perhaps that danger would begin slowly, such as signing a peace agreement to become a member of the world body to have access to world trade. Can you imagine a country completely cut off from imports or exports? Could a small country such as Israel provide itself with enough food, chemicals, mechanical devices and other raw materials to survive? They would have no choice if the world body made the decision to cut them off. This would be similar to the condition individuals would face in having to choose the 'mark of the beast' described in Chapter 13, Verses 16 and 17:

> "And he causeth all, both small and great, rich and poor, free and bond, to receive a mark in their right hand, or in their foreheads: And that no man might buy or sell, save he that had the mark, or the name of the beast, or the number of his name."

Then, once Israel signs that agreement to become part of the world order and accepts the policies therein, what if the world order demands Israel give up its defensive weaponry? Would Israel do that if that were one of the requirements for the world governing body to maintain peace between borders? If this were the case, and if Israel refused to abandon or destroy their protective weaponry we can only guess what might happen then. The Book of Revelation describes that possibility in gory detail.

Would the United States come to the aid of Israel at that time of its greatest need? Absolutely not. If Obama has his way, the United States will be no stronger than any other country at that time. As the Bible says, that's when the 'restrainer' that protects Israel will be lifted. This event is identified in Thessalonians 2:6-7, which reads:

> "And now ye know what withholdeth that he
> might be revealed in his time. For the mystery
> of iniquity doth already work: only he who now
> letteth will let, until he be taken out of the way.
> (This is the verse that many believe identifies
> the 'Rapture.' The word 'Rapture' does not exist
> in the Bible. This event means when the
> 'protection' of Israel is lifted Israel could be
> attacked.)

The 'beast,' the world leader at that time will be the first to lead the attack against Israel. It will be on the Plain of Jezreel, near the ancient site of Megiddo - the word that's forms the concept of 'Armageddon.'

Already one of Obama's great supporters and chief advisors has issued statements condemning Israel. Samantha Power even recently sat on Obama's National Security Council. She is extremely anti-Israel and suggests that Israel is the source of most problems in the Middle East. In an interview in 2002 she said Israel should be invaded to force them to allow Palestine to set up a separate state. She also scoffs at the idea that Iran is planning to build a nuclear bomb to use against its neighbors, especially Israel.

In a 2007 interview, Power said that America's relationship with Israel "has often led foreign policy decision-makers to defer reflexively to Israeli security assessments, and to replicate Israeli tactics..." The United States, she explained, had brought terrorist attacks upon itself by aping Israel's violations of human rights. She claimed America should be blamed for the terrorist attacks against our country.

Samantha Power is the wife of Cass Sunstein, the recently departed Regulatory Czar in Obama's administration. He resigned reportedly because the administration was not moving fast enough toward policies of Socialism. At this moment, Samantha Power has been picked by Obama to be the U.S. Ambassador to the United Nations to replace Susan Rice. This is more danger that moves us ever closer to that Biblical time prophesied in Revelation.

It certainly wouldn't be in Israel's best interest to sign an agreement with a world governing body, if this person is sitting on a council there that could make a decision to invade Israel for lack of compliance with one of their rules. Certainly the leaders of Israel are aware that to sign any agreement with a world government would be to sign Israel's death warrant.

The next one-world option to consider is that which the Islamic world has threatened - or promised. Those who are most boastful claim they will convert everyone to Islam throughout the world or kill (behead) those who refuse to convert. They are not subtle about their plans. They openly shout it from the greatest halls of government. A strong clue to this possible scenario is given in Revelation, Chapter 20, Verse 4:

> "And I saw the souls of them that were beheaded for the witness of Jesus, and for the word of God, and which had not worshiped the beast, neither had received his mark upon their foreheads, or in their hands; and they lived and reigned with Christ a thousand years."

Radical Muslims seem to delight in beheading people who don't agree with them. In our modern culture the word 'beheading' is not commonly associated with any other cult, religion, or organization. Therefore, this reference would suggest that the beast and his followers would likely be Muslims. Otherwise, why wasn't the word 'killed' used in this reference?

Now, considering from a practical point of view, what known Muslim exists today that has the world stature to occupy the highest position on the planet? Not one. In fact, isn't it ironic that Muslims spend too much time fighting and killing each other to allow one known Muslim to ascend to a higher position? Much of their dislike of each other is power politics, but the fundamental internal hate is from their basic religious ideologies.

They are ideologically separated by a similar difference that separates Christians and Jews. One part, the Shiites, believe their Messiah, the Mahdi, has already arrived on earth and is just waiting for the right time to start leading them to create purity in all the world - thus the beheadings. The other part of Islam, the Sunnis, don't believe the Mahdi has arrived yet. Since this divisive concept was developed hundreds of years after Christianity appeared, it's likely it's a concept copied directly from the differences in beliefs between Christians and Jews. And, as with Christianity, there are even further divisions in each of the two major parts of Islam.

Although some die-hard Christians still hate Jews because they believe the Jews crucified the Messiah, generally Christians and Jews have a cooperative respect for each other. Regardless of their differences, Christians still respect the Jewish nation for being the fountainspring of Jesus. The Islamic world exhibits less tolerance to one another - or to anyone else who disagrees with them. If they don't have a good excuse to kill each other, they seem to be capable of inventing one.

At the moment, no self-proclaimed Muslim is in a position to be recognized for consideration as a world leader. If as the Book of Revelation proposes, as suggested by the act of 'beheading,' then that leader, that beast, would likely be a Muslim-in-waiting, or a Muslim-in-disguise. There's only one Muslim supporter today, who claims not to be a Muslim, who occupies a position to fill that role, and who is exhibiting extreme ambition to do so. He has also been trained as a Muslim to be a Muslim. According to their doctrine, once he is a Muslim, he is not permitted to turn to another religion and abandon his belief in Islam. That person is Barack Hussein Obama. But who is this man? Does anyone really know - for sure?

Many in America are uncomfortable with his position as their leader - with the full power and influence of the position he occupies. They are aware that he has the power to fundamentally change their lives as he promised to do when he said he would "fundamentally change" America. Yet, many do not trust his origin, his development, or his goals.

What is the goal and purpose of someone who would fundamentally change the great qualities of the United States? For almost 250 years America has had great struggles and has had many good things and bad things happen to its economy, culture, and society. But, America has maintained the one great fundamental; freedom and democracy guided by our United States Constitution. To 'fundamentally change' something means to change the constitution of the foundation. To fundamentally change America is to destroy the Constitution that guides us, thereby meaning to destroy America.

That's what he promised when he first campaigned for president of the United States. Many people followed him, trusted him, believed him, and agreed with him. That means his followers also wanted 'fundamental change' in America. In effect, they wanted to destroy America as it was established and still existed.

Certainly those followers didn't purposefully and willfully intend to destroy America and the idealism it represented with the change they envisioned. Obviously, most love America as much as those who looked at Obama and realized the danger he presented to our Constitution. Those who respect our Constitution, but followed Obama to the cliff of despair were mesmerized by his voice and his great words; they looked no further than the great presentation. They imagined only great things for themselves in the future. His great words were forecast in Revelation 13:5 and 6:

> "And there was given unto him a mouth speaking great things and blasphemies. And he opened his mouth in blasphemy against God, to blaspheme his name, and his tabernacle, and

264

them that dwell in heaven."

His worshipers saw not the future of the country. They saw only the imaginary utopia he promised them. He promised them their illusive 'fair share.' He failed to explain that a fair share includes the fair share of economic and cultural despair that often accompanies illusive dreams. They didn't question his promises. Instead, they were swept away by his rhetoric, believing he had all the right answers. But, did he? What are his principles and character?

Now, we come to the important question many people ask: is Barack Hussein Obama the Antichrist - that last one? Many people already believe he is. Is he? At the moment, the answer is NO. He is not the Antichrist identified as the 'beast' in the Book of Revelation. At the moment that status does not exist, but perhaps the person who will occupy that status does exist. And, there are many references that suggest it could be Barack Obama.

That status will begin when the world, the seven continents, are under one rule, or one ruler. That likely will begin in the United Nations. That body will select their leader and give him a title. Who knows what the title will be - perhaps president, chairman, or czar. In either case he is the one likely to emerge into the 'beast.' Revelation describes him as the 'beast.' Other parts in the Bible describe him as the 'Antichrist' or the 'little horn.' What Biblical verse announces this transitional event? This is indicated by Revelation 13:1-2:

> "And I stood upon the sand of the sea, and saw a beast rise up out of the sea, having seven heads and ten horns, and upon his horns ten crowns, and upon his heads the name of blasphemy.
>
> 2 And the beast which I saw was like unto a leopard, and his feet were as the feet of a bear, and his mouth as the mouth of a lion: and the dragon gave him his power, and his seat, and

great authority."

The sea is mentioned many places in the Bible, however it doesn't actually mean a sea as in an ocean or a body of water. Many references incorporate another part that describes that sea as a large body of people. The significant part of the first verse is that John includes the word 'sand' to indicate an actual body of water - in this case the water of the earth from which the seven continents - the seven heads - rise. The ten horns and crowns are described as powerful countries and leaders by most interpreters. Each of those ten leaders will (blaspheme) deny or mock God.

Verse 2 is the one that actually creates the 'beast' or the 'Antichrist.' That's when " the dragon gave him his power, and his seat, and great authority." Until this time, the person who will become the Antichrist is not actually the Antichrist. But what about the other descriptions of the leopard, bear and lion?

Since no other references or descriptions are given, the likely suggestion is to consider the strengths of each and compare to the newly-created beast. What are the strengths of each?

The leopard is a cat. All cats are stealthy - which perhaps could be considered 'deception.' The bear has great strength. Another reference describes the beast as 'stout.' The lion is known not only for its strength, but also for its great roar. Perhaps this analogy indicates the beast will have a great mouth and can speak well - with great persuasion.

Who is the only person known in the entire world today who has all three of these qualities? No one other than Barack Obama.

Although Satan gives the Antichrist his power when the one-world government is formed, when those 'seven heads rise from the sea,' clearly many people must be fooled, deceived, to follow him and worship him. This is the job of the false prophet, to promote the Antichrist, and prove he is worthy of worship. He will promote the Antichrist as Christ on earth. Let's analyze his function first.

According to the Book of Revelation another person will appear toward the end time who will support and promote the Antichrist, the first beast. He will be known as the second beast, or the false prophet. He will be part of what's termed the 'unholy trinity.' GotQuestions.org gives a description of this person:

"The apostle John describes this person and gives us clues to identifying him when he shows up. First, he comes out of the earth. This could mean he comes up from the pit of hell with all the demonic powers of hell at his command. It could also mean he comes from lowly circumstances, secret and unknown until he bursts on the world stage at the right hand of the Antichrist. He is depicted as having horns like a lamb, while speaking like a dragon. The horns on lambs are merely small bumps on their heads until the lamb grows into a ram. Rather than having the Antichrist's multiplicity of heads and horns, showing his power and might and fierceness, the false prophet comes like a lamb, winsomely, with persuasive words that elicit sympathy and good will from others. He may be an extraordinary preacher or orator whose demonically empowered words will deceive the multitudes.

Verse 12 gives us the false prophet's mission on earth, which is to force humanity to worship the Antichrist. He has all the authority of the Antichrist because, like him, the false prophet is empowered by Satan. It is not clear whether people are forced to worship the Antichrist or whether they are so enamored of these powerful beings that they fall for the deception and worship him willingly. The fact that the second beast uses miraculous signs and wonders, including fire from heaven, to establish the credibility of both of them would seem to indicate that people will fall before them in adoration of their power and message. Verse 14 goes on to say the deception will be so great that the people will set up an idol to the Antichrist and worship it."

Ever wonder why John's vision that produced the Book of Revelation has been so difficult to understand in the past? As we get closer to the basis for his vision, many things are becoming more clear, and make more sense if taken in context of modern times. Two verses in particular are more relative to today's happenings than they were when they were first written. In these verses, John is speaking of this second beast, that false prophet, who is the supporter and promoter of the first beast, the Antichrist. This second beast is believed to be a religious man. At one time in the past, many even believed it was the Pope. Let's look at that ancient information in terms of our modern times. This is the information I referenced at the beginning of the chapter that perhaps even non-believers might want to consider. It begins:

> Chapter 13, Verse 13, "And he doeth great wonders, so that he maketh fire come down from heaven on the earth in the sight of men."

This was to prove to people that he was a messenger from God and was endowed with great powers. Therefore, people should believe him when he proclaimed how great that god, the Antichrist, was and they must worship him.

Two thousand years ago when John had that vision from Christ he had no idea what to call missiles and rockets. He saw streaks of fire trailing missiles and rockets and didn't know how to precisely describe what he saw. And, during John's vision of the Apocolypse, there's no mention of Jesus explaining the vision, only showing it. John had to explain it the best way he saw it.

John probably knew that to call it bolts of lightening would not be accurate, so he simply called it fire. If he had described it as bolts of lightening he was probably aware that description could have referred to other Roman and Greek gods of that time, such as Zeus and Thor. Zeus was still a great recognized god of that time.

Logically, fire was a generic description. In our modern world, we know that many rockets and missiles leave a trail of fire. Now, we even have the beginning of laser weapons that could be called fire coming from the sky. This description fits more with our modern times than during the time of John.

And, even more recently we hear of drones that already have amazing capabilities. Isn't it conceivable that very soon a small camouflaged drone could hover overhead, unseen, and send fire down to earth, even aimed at targeted people who refuse to worship the beast? That aerial platform, drone, could be so small and unseen that it would appear fire was falling from heaven. And, considering even further; couldn't a laser beam or a missile be targeted to a specific RFID chip implanted in someone's hand - that 666 mark of the beast so often mentioned? These end times could be danger beyond our wildest imaginations. Perhaps John interpreted this fire as miracles rather than a forceful military action.

> Chapter 13, Verse 14, "And he deceiveth them that dwell on the earth by means of those miracles which he had power to do in the sight of the beast; saying to them that dwell on the earth, that they should make an image to the beast, which had the wound by the sword, and did live." (According to both Christian and Muslim writings, the first beast (the Antichrist) and the Mahdi had been injured.)

> Chapter 13, Verse 15, "And he had power to give life unto the image of the beast, that the image of the beast should both speak, and cause that as many as would not worship the image of the beast should be killed."

Two thousand years ago, John likely had never seen a keyboard, a computer, or a hologram. Even if he saw those things in his vision, how would he have explained them at that time - other than the way he did? The image was a computer that could speak. So what? Many computers and their little wired or wireless friends speak to us now, everyday. We also have the internet, a world-wide system that can speak to anyone in the world. This is likely the way the

King Obama

'mark of the beast' will be applied, enforced, and controlled. Verses 16 and 17 explain the use of that master computer, the image of the beast:

> "And he causeth all, both small and great, rich and poor, free and bond, to receive a mark in their right hand, or in their foreheads: And that no man might buy or sell, save he that had the mark, or the name of the beast, or the number of his name."

This information would have been a cryptic puzzle to John, and to those of that time who read his writing. Anyone today can easily see how these applications can be applied. Most are already active, even today in our everyday lives. We have social security numbers, driver's license numbers, credit card numbers and many other ways to be identified. According to the verses above, we will accept another central world number saying we worship the beast - or we will be killed.

The mark in their foreheads might have a different meaning than as it's simply stated. In other places in the Bible a mention of a mark in their foreheads of Christians, simply means that they have accepted Christ. There's not necessarily a physical mark present.

Finally, in Revelation, the apostle John gave us a clue to help identify the beast or the Antichrist. Although he didn't specify a name of a person, he left a number to represent that name in the next Bible reference: Revelation 13:18. This is the most identified and quoted verse in the Book of Revelation, The Apocalypse. John wrote:

> "Here is wisdom. Let him that hath understanding count the number of the beast: for it is the number of a man; and his number is Six hundred threescore and six." (666)

Scholars have long tried to interpret those numbers by

association with the Greek alphabet. Would someone trying to tell us something that important create a cryptic puzzle too complicated to understand? Let's simplify John's information: "count the number of the beast for it is the number of a man;" John said count; he didn't say interpret. If we count 6+6+6, the answer is 18. Now, let's say the beast's name will have 18 letters. That's counting; it's what John said to do. Now, use your imagination to picture a possible candidate of our time who has 18 letters in his full name. Surprised? One name fits perfectly. Another interesting fact, perhaps designed by John for the purpose of confirming that number relationship - this information is given in Verse 18.

BARACKHUSSEINOBAMA

King Obama

CONCLUSION

Wouldn't it be great if our president would respect and praise the United States of America for its achievements and contribution to the greatness of humanity - and not apologize to all corners of the world for our shame and disgrace for being unfair and impudent to the rest of the world? Wouldn't that be great for our future! Shouldn't that be the goal and a guiding torch to light the way to higher aspirations of our great nation?

Every president before Obama struggled to show America as a shining example to the rest of the world, even during times when the country struggled for mere existence and survival. Perhaps all were not totally successful, but the welfare and progress of the United States were the ideals that guided their path and their decisions. Obama's torch seems to light his path to a different direction for the future of America. His doesn't seem to be focused in the same direction as all other American presidents before him. Shouldn't the safety of citizens and the freedom to develop to their highest and best be the highest concerns for any president or leader?

He divides the country by rhetoric and deeds, criticizing those who have been blessed by our great nation to achieve higher levels of prosperity and success. That's the success necessary to offer ladders to others to achieve even more success for themselves. Without successful people with enough to invest in opportunities for others America would not be the shining star of the world. Obama's actions have been to extinguish that opportunity ladder by penalizing those who reach those success levels. He uses magnificent rhetoric to extol his virtues as an economic genius and leader who will help those at the bottom rise to middle-class, while at the same time he kicks the ladder of success from beneath them so they can remain at the bottom. They remain at the bottom with no place to go except to the government to beg for more welfare and direct assistance. He is clearly a great deceiver. Who else has that gifted ability to smile into one's face while stabbing that same person in the back.

One of his first acts against Americans and their values was his emphasis on racism - suggesting that white people targeted black people for discrimination. He, as well as other race-baiters fail to acknowledge an important fact. White people, racists or otherwise, don't spend their time thinking about how to put down or harm black people. There's not enough time in one's life to do that, and still accomplish something for yourself or for society. Most white people spend their time and energy the same as black people - trying to do something for themselves - trying to find an avenue to making a living, and perhaps a little beyond that.

White people as well as black people have their own economic and social problems to worry about. It's been my life experience to recognize that people are people. Some black people don't like white people and some white people don't like black people. If there were any purple people, some of us would dislike purple people, and some of those purple people would dislike some of us. Regardless, the president, any president, any leader has the responsibility to bring all people together in a common cause for a country. Barack Obama has failed miserably in accomplishing this task. He hasn't even tried. In fact, he has contributed to the racial divide.

To bring the racial divide together two things are key - and he has failed at both. First is education. To get a job, ordinarily one must be educated to the level of a job requirement.

When he became president, the first thing he did was to

appoint the least qualified education leader in America to be the secretary of education. Was Obama's destruction of the education system intentional, or was he doing a favor to one of his Chicago buddies? At least 50-percent of black children never graduate effectively from high school. Many who do are not 'educated.' Are Obama and Arne Duncan not astute enough to realize that those who can't compete in a classroom must still be educated to qualify for a job - other than selling drugs on street corners, and committing burglary? Can't they understand that many kids who do these things want a job - and would do well in realistic job-training programs. Job training programs must replace many of our standard high school academic programs - or this generation will be lost forever. But, even if they are trained they still need job opportunities.

Obama has also effectively killed millions of jobs with his attitude and attack on many industries - especially energy resources. His war on coal and oil has devastated those industries - as well as the thousands of industries that support them. One industry does not function by itself - it must have supplies, maintenance, and many other auxiliary products to function effectively. Without jobs available, where does a trained person go to find well-being and success?

Obama has destroyed their route to freedom and prosperity. Their only resort is to the streets, or to the corner waiting for a government handout. And, to be successful one must have a foundation. Historically, America's foundation has been based on Christianity and the traditional family unit He has also attacked that foundation by casting aside Christianity and by promoting non-traditional marriage.

The list of Obama's anti-Christian actions, rhetoric, and blasphemies is too long to identify each individually. A casual review of his actions and comments against churches, especially the Catholic Church, Defense of Marriage Act, cabinet appointments, and exclusion of Christian leaders from religious events are clear proof that he has no respect for God, Christian values, or any reference to the value foundation that allowed the formation of our great country -

The United States of America.

John Griffing, from World News Daily, perhaps explained this best. On October 14, 2012, he wrote:

"On a deeper level, Obama is the consequence of a nation without God. And America, to a great degree, is a nation without God. America has many "gods," but to determine whether a nation has a dominant faith, it is necessary to look at where it spends the most of its time. America spends less time in pews than at any other time in history, and it spends more time in arenas and theaters. America worships entertainment. Where to turn when the money funding the entertainment cult dries up?

When people are without material security, and the walls of the house that is a nation-state seem structurally unsound, two directions are possible: a march into the sanctuary, or a march into the halls of government. America has opted for the latter, choosing to place its faith in man, specifically in a man and not in the saving power of its past God. The results of such a trajectory are never pleasant for the subject populace. Assuming, for a moment, that no true unitary deity exists, and that worship of a Judeo-Christian God is of little value, consider that when America has worshiped said deity, it has been the most free and most prosperous. Could it perhaps be that the values engendered by such Judeo-Christian socialization are the most conducive for and consistent with the principles of freedom and liberty that undergird the American way of life?

Without assuming solely a Judeo-Christian consumption of this column, it is useful to examine some key Bible passages of unique modern-day relevance to Americans. The following scene is a description of Israel, circa B.C.

In the days of the Bible, Israel was ruled by "Elders" who represented the people but had no concrete power – in other words, democracy. The Book of Samuel tells us that during this period, the Israelites faced a powerful invader and envied the other nations for their efficiency and apparent lack of turmoil. Israel demanded the Elders "appoint a king" to "judge us like all the nations." Samuel warned the Israelites that a king would take everything from them, their land, the fruits of their labor, and send them to die in war. He concluded his warning with a powerful admonition:

> "Then you will cry out in that day because of your king whom you have chosen for yourselves, but the LORD will not answer you. ..."

The Israelites chose to have a king, against all wisdom to the contrary. That much is clear.

But how has America chosen to appoint Obama its king? Haven't most Americans fought and resisted the actions of the president? In word, maybe, but not in deed. At the subconscious level, America's plight grows more complex, especially when the generational element is factored in.

America chose to have a king, "like the other nations," when it placed individual and personal pursuits above civic duty to politically engage. Voter turnout amongst Republicans and traditionally minded Americans has steadily declined over the last few decades. As the "me" generation has assumed the dominant position in society and the "greatest generation" has slowly but surely died off, the communal "we" has become less and less visible.

America's psyche has undergone a vast makeover at the subterranean level. No longer do Americans by and large rush to God amidst a crisis. Rather, those products of the FDR generation and their descendants have been reprogrammed subconsciously to rush to government as the cure for their ills, especially during periods of crisis. A Pew Forum study done in October of 2008 found that a sizable majority of Americans believe government can "solve" our nation's problems.

The American Dream evolved substantially from earlier surveys. Earlier surveys registered majorities aligning strongly with the view that "there are no limits to growth in this country." The October 2008 study saw a shift from this view to a large percentage embracing the notion that "people should learn to live with less." When Obama was elected, he obliged, chillingly uttering the words, "Only government can provide the short-term boost necessary to lift us from a recession this deep and severe. Only government can break the cycle that are [sic] crippling our economy. That's why we need to act boldly and act now. ..."

America has voted with its soul. We traded financial security later for food stamps and government housing now.

We no longer value freedom, its risks and its benefits. We no longer want to, as Patrick Henry did, live free, even if it means our death. We would rather be molested at airports and have our emails reviewed by government analysts for our "protection."

We no longer see economic hardship as a growth opportunity and chance for ingenuity; we would rather trade the potential for prosperity for a full tank of gas and a charismatic face on our television sets telling us he "feels our pain."

We no longer see business as a path to individual success and the realization of dreams, but as an evil entity that prizes greed above the individual.

We no longer see government as our servants, but as our employers.

We do not want independence, but dependence.

We no longer mistrust government, but trust government with our lives and fortunes.

We, Americans, are the reason for Obama.

We will not unseat this king unless we first unseat ourselves. As long as we use our careers, our families, our hobbies, our pastimes and our vices as excuses for inaction, those whose careers, pastimes, hobbies and vices consist of the orchestrated and total transformation of the United States from free nation to despotic and destitute wasteland will continue their "forward" march." End of article.

Increased surveillance of innocent citizens, political correctness gone wild, restriction of free speech - especially against a 'strange god,' that's allowed to push itself upon our citizens, declining aspirations and loss of hope by average citizens, and a burgeoning federal government that must take more power to justify its existence will soon destroy the nation that our forefathers dreamed would last forever. Our children, grandchildren and all those who come after them might never know the country we loved and respected.

Can this tyranny and despotism destroying our nation be halted or reversed? Is it too late? Maybe not, but it will take positive planned action and boldness by the most patriotic elected officials.

Presently, elected officials who oppose Obama's despotism are attacked by a vicious and dedicated group who will not allow their 'God' to be challenged. These challengers must walk a very thin and specific line. Any comments or allegations pointing to Barack Obama, personally, will earn a wild and loud cry of 'racism' by this guardian group. The attack against their leader will be great; it will be widespread; and it will be non-ending. One who would rise to seriously attack Obama's kingly rise will certainly risk the end of his or her political career - and possibly even his or her good reputation.

Instead, a leader for democracy who wants to save our nation must directly attack the czars and other policy-makers who are directing the actions alien to democracy, good government, job creation and aspirations. And these attacks must be as pointed, direct and vicious as those who would attack them if he offended their 'God' leader. As usual, Obama will not be directly involved with these policies - so he can stand back with 'clean hands.'

The exception to this possibility of recovering our democracy and freedom is if an occasion arises for Obama to declare martial law - as in multiple terrorist attacks explained earlier in another chapter. If direct pressure on his control grows too heavy, this is the most likely scenario for him to maintain his power. If that happens we might all soon be required to say, "Your Highness."

King Obama

This might be the last book I'm allowed to write critically analyzing Obama and his plans for our future. Hopefully, my interpretations have been totally in error. Whatever happens to me, nevertheless, it's been a great ride in a to-now great country.

Although Barack Obama is against this prayer:

God bless America.

Things We Must Never Forget
Until We Know All the Answers

Benghazi
Why were four Americans killed?
Where was Hillary Clinton while it was happening?
Where was Barack Obama while it was happening?
Why did they lie and blame the event on a video?
Why were rescuers on 'stand by' told to 'stand down?'

Fast and Furious
Who authorized the operation?
Why did the operation continue after weapons were lost?
Why did the procedure have no procedure?
Why weren't tracking devices used?

The IRS Scandal
What was the highest level involved?
Who initiated it?
Why hasn't anyone been fired or reprimanded?

Greatest Quotes
of
Our Time

————————————

Michelle Obama
February 18, 2008
"For the first time in my adult life I am proud of my country."
(Age 44)

Barack Obama
March 9, 2008
"We are no longer a Christian nation - at least not just."

Nancy Pelosi
March 9, 2010
"We have to pass the bill so that you can find out what is in it."

Hillary Clinton
January 23, 2013
"What difference, at this point, does it make?"

King Obama

Saul Alinsky's
12 Rules for Radicals

Beginning in the 2008 presidential campaign, I noticed something different in Democratic campaigning style and rhetoric. It was subtle, at first, and seemed a bit strange. I wondered why Obama and his supporters were becoming so harsh and 'pushy' in their commentaries, debates, and conversations with talk-show hosts. And, I wondered why they were never 'called out' for all their harshness.

Then, beginning in the 2012 campaign season, everything was clear and predictable. Obama and his supporters, even people not directly connected to the campaign, such as editorial writers and 'letter to the editor' writers, were using the same tactics: attack and disregard the important issues being discussed or questioned. I also wondered why those on the conservative side were not responding in kind. Only since I've been researching for this book do I understand why.

It's been well-known that Barack Obama and his close allies have been well-versed and indoctrinated in the 'Saul Alinsky' method. Obviously, his supporters have taken a cue from their activities and responses - or they have been introduced to the Saul Alinsky techniques themselves. On recently learning this information, I realized I should share it with as many people as possible - so everyone on both sides of these political issues would understand what the overly-aggressive Democrats are doing. They are following the guidelines of Saul Alinsky. It's a concept of: attack, distract, surprise, and confuse the other party.

King Obama

Bestofluck.com describes Saul Alinsky's '12 Rules for Radicals.' They are:

RULE 1: "Power is not only what you have, but what the enemy thinks you have." Power is derived from 2 main sources – money and people. Have-Nots must build power from flesh and blood. (These are two things of which there is a plentiful supply. Government and corporations always have a difficult time appealing to people, and usually do so almost exclusively with economic arguments.)

RULE 2: "Never go outside the expertise of your people." It results in confusion, fear and retreat. Feeling secure adds to the backbone of anyone. (Organizations under attack wonder why radicals don't address the "real" issues. This is why. They avoid things with which they have no knowledge.)

RULE 3: "Whenever possible, go outside the expertise of the enemy." Look for ways to increase insecurity, anxiety and uncertainty. (This happens all the time. Watch how many organizations under attack are blind-sided by seemingly irrelevant arguments that they are then forced to address.)

RULE 4: "Make the enemy live up to its own book of rules." If the rule is that every letter gets a reply, send 30,000 letters. You can kill them with this because no one can possibly obey all of their own rules. (This is a serious rule. The besieged entity's very credibility and reputation is at stake, because if activists catch it lying or not living up to its commitments, they can continue to chip away at the damage.)

RULE 5: "Ridicule is man's most potent weapon." There is no defense. It's irrational. It's infuriating. It also works as a key pressure point to force the enemy into concessions. (Pretty crude, rude and mean, huh? They want to create anger and fear.)

RULE 6: "A good tactic is one your people enjoy." They'll keep doing it without urging and come back to do more. They're doing their thing, and will even suggest better ones. (Radical activists, in this sense, are no different than any other human being. We all avoid "un-fun" activities, and but we revel at and enjoy the ones that work and bring results.)

RULE 7: "A tactic that drags on too long becomes a drag." Don't become old news. (Even radical activists get bored. So to keep them excited and involved, organizers are constantly coming up with new tactics.)

RULE 8: "Keep the pressure on. Never let up." Keep trying new things to keep the opposition off balance. As the opposition masters one approach, hit them from the flank with something new. (Attack, attack, attack from all sides, never giving the reeling organization a chance to rest, regroup, recover and re-strategize.)

RULE 9: "The threat is usually more terrifying than the thing itself." Imagination and ego can dream up many more consequences than any activist. (Perception is reality. Large organizations always prepare a worst-case scenario, something that may be furthest from the activists' minds. The upshot is that the organization will expend enormous time and energy, creating in its own collective mind the direst of conclusions. The possibilities can easily poison the mind and result in demoralization.)

RULE 10: "If you push a negative hard enough, it will push through and become a positive." Violence from the other side can win the public to your side because the public sympathizes with the underdog. (Unions used this tactic. Peaceful [albeit loud] demonstrations during the heyday of unions in the early to mid-20th Century incurred management's wrath, often in the form of violence that eventually brought public sympathy to their side.)

RULE 11: "The price of a successful attack is a constructive alternative." Never let the enemy score points because you're caught without a solution to the problem. (Old saw: If you're not part of the solution, you're part of the problem. Activist organizations have an agenda, and their strategy is to hold a place at the table, to be given a forum to wield their power. So, they have to have a compromise solution.)

RULE 12: Pick the target, freeze it, personalize it, and polarize it." Cut off the support network and isolate the target from sympathy. Go after people and not institutions; people hurt faster than institutions. (This is cruel, but very effective. Direct, personalized criticism and ridicule works.)

On April 13, 2012, John Hawkins from Townhall.com submitted an article designed to rebuff the Alinsky tactics used by radicals. It's titled: '12 Ways to Use Saul Alinsky's Rules for Radicals Against Liberals.'

"Saul Alinsky was a brilliant man. Evil, but brilliant. Unfortunately, whether we like it or not, everyone on the Left from the President on down is playing by his rules in the political arena. Not all liberals have read his book or know his name, but his tactics have become universal. Sadly for conservatives, when two evenly matched forces go head-to-head outside of a fairy tale, the side that tries to play nice usually ends up with its head in a box. So, don't lie or become an evil person like Alinsky, but learn from what he wrote and give the Left a taste of its own medicine. He gives a summary of the rules (omitted) then explains:

1. Power is not only what you have but what the enemy thinks you have. Boycotts have fallen out of favor on the Right because the Left has used that tactic to target

conservative radio. This is a mistake. That's because there are a lot more conservatives than there are liberals and we're much more capable of using the tactic effectively. There are roughly 120 million people who identify with conservatism in this country and almost twice as many Christians. When there are threats that Christians and conservatives will refuse to go see movies, stop buying products, or cancel subscriptions, it will scare some people straight. That threat should be used and carried out much more often.

2. Never go outside the experience of your people. Want to know why Republicans are so terrible at reaching out to minorities? Because identity politics works really, really well and conservatives tend to oppose it on principle. So, white Republicans are constantly trying to go outside of their experience and reach out to minorities who are generally disinclined to listen to them because they have the wrong skin color. When the GOP accepts reality, adopts the tactics of the Democratic Party, and starts paying off our own Sharptons and Jesse Jacksons to reach out to minority groups and call Democrats racists, we'll start making inroads with minorities for the first time in decades.

3. Wherever possible go outside the experience of the enemy. The GOP often foolishly retreats from social issues. This is a huge mistake in an era when 76% of the country is Christian and most liberals find sincere Christian beliefs to be repellent. We don't have to preach at anyone, wag our fingers, or turn into legions of Ned Flanders, but we shouldn't be afraid to talk about our Christian beliefs, stick up for Christians who are under attack, and hammer the Left for its anti-Christian bigotry. Conservatism is a pro-Christian ideology and Liberalism is an anti-Christian ideology. We should never be afraid to drive that point home.

4. Make the enemy live up to their own book of rules. This is something conservatives have gotten much better at in the last few years, but we seldom take it far enough. If we did, a tax cheat who advocates higher taxes could certainly never be our Treasury Secretary, Barack Obama would be

afraid to associate with race hustlers like Al Sharpton or one percenters like Warren Buffet, and Al Gore would have either given up his mansion or his status as the leader of the cult of global warming.

5. Ridicule is man's most potent weapon. Conservatives have a tendency to try to win every debate with logic and recitations of facts which, all too often, fail to get the job done because emotions and mockery are often just as effective as reason. The good news is that liberals almost never have logic on their side; so they're incapable of rationally making the case for their policies while conservatives can become considerably more effective debaters by simply adding some emotion-based arguments and sheer scorn to their discourse. This has certainly worked on Twitter, where conservatives keep making the Obama campaign look like buffoons by taking over its hashtags.

6. A good tactic is one that your people enjoy. Sometimes Republicans get too serious about politics. Why not hold a fund raiser at the gun range? What's wrong with having Kid Rock or a bunch of popular country musicians play at a massive voter registration drive? How about building some giant puppet heads of our own, featuring Nancy Pelosi injecting botox into her face or Barack Obama punching the Pope in the stomach? A little controversy and fun draw in the eyeballs and gets people excited.

7. A tactic that drags on too long becomes a drag. This one seems self-explanatory, but in practice, it can be tough to keep things on a timeline. This is what happened to the Occupy Movement, the wars in Iraq and Afghanistan, and the Republican race for the presidency, too. If it goes on too long, people sour on it whether it's a war, an election, or a tactic.

8. Keep the pressure on. Conservatives fall down on this one all the time. Just when Obama's SuperPac was starting to feel real pressure over taking a million dollar donationfrom Bill Maher, conservatives eased up. This is also why liberal film stars feel so comfortable trashing conservatives,

Christians, and Americans -- even right before their film comes out. It's because we get offended, shrug our shoulders, and then almost immediately let it go. Sometimes, an apology doesn't fix everything. How often do liberals accept an apology at face value and let an issue go?

9. The threat is usually more terrifying than the thing itself. How about we treat the Left to some of its own medicine? Libs throw a pie at a conservative author on campus; then we promise to shower every liberal speaker on the same campus with garbage. They post a conservative address online; we post two liberal addresses online. They hold a protest at someone's house; then we hold a protest at someone's house. They hit one of our politicians with glitter; we hit one of their politicians with coal dust. Liberals have a mentality that says, "Everything we do is harmless, but everything conservatives do is potentially dangerous." Yet, we're usually too well behaved to copy their tactics. Mimic those tactics once or twice and the Libs will freak out so hard that they'll start declaring it to be off limits for everyone, including their own activists.

10. The major premise for tactics is the development of operations that will maintain a constant pressure upon the opposition. When you launch an attack, tie it in as part of a theme and never stop hammering the theme as long as it's true and it works. John Kerry is a flip-flopper, Bill Clinton is a liar, Barack Obama is bankrupting the country and wrecking the economy -- tie your attacks into themes that can be picked up on social media, talk radio, cable TV, and in the blogosphere over the long haul. Why does McDonald's keep running ads? Because it may be that 50th ad or 100th ad you see that gets you to go buy a Big Mac, just as it may be the 50th or 100th time someone hears that Obama is bankrupting the country and wrecking the economy before it sticks.

11. If you push a negative hard and deep enough it will break through into its counterside. The winner in politics is almost always whoever is on offense. Liberals understand this

in an intuitive way that most conservatives don't. We think because we have this wonderful, honest, logical response to a charge that we're scoring major points -- but, except in rare cases, it's not true. If you're spending all of your time refuting the charges that you're extreme, racist, hate women, and despise the poor -- you're losing. That's because some people will assume where there's smoke, there's fire, and disbelieve you no matter how good your explanation may be. Additionally, if you're busy defending yourself, you can't go after the other side. Defend when you absolutely have to, but make sure most of your time is spent attacking, relentlessly attacking.

12. The price of a successful attack is a constructive alternative. Honestly, this is more of a liberal problem than a conservative one, since liberals always seem to be clamoring to rip out some functional necessity of American society so they can replace it with an ill-defined hodgepodge of ideas that they think will shift power their way or be less "mean." Our ideas work; so coming up with a constructive alternative is seldom a problem.

13. Pick the target, freeze it, personalize it, and polarize it. Conservatives tend to do well with this one until they get to the last part. Polarization is at the core of the Left's strategy. According to liberals, if you're conservative, you hate blacks, Hispanics, gays, Jews, Muslims, women, the poor, the middle class, the environment, and probably a half dozen other groups I've forgotten. Even when something is in front of our face, conservatives shy away from polarization. What's wrong with pointing out how hostile the Democratic Party has become to Christianity? Why not point out the truth: that most white liberals are racists who think black Americas are too stupid and incompetent to compete with white Americans, which is why they push Affirmative Action and racial set asides? Why not note that liberals want poor Americans to stay poor and dependent, because as long as they do, they'll keep voting for the Democrat Party? There's a reason Barack Obama bows to foreign leaders, is constantly apologizing for

America, attended an anti-white, anti-American church for 20 years, and it's why his wife was proud of the country for the FIRST TIME because she thought it was going to elect her husband. The sad truth is that these are people who hate and despise this country. Why do you think "hope and change" appealed so much to Obama that he made it his theme? When you look at America as an evil, racist, unfair, horrible place to live inhabited by ignorant trash and "bitter clingers," what else would you do other than hope for change? If you love this country and the values it represents, the people in the White House not only don't share your values, they hold people like you in utter contempt."

I was going to add several more suggestions (rules) to John Hawkins list, but as I typed these and evaluated them, I found everything was here. He has obviously given much time and thought to this article. I will add one additional comment to emphasize what Hawkins wrote.

Do you remember the 2012 presidential candidate debates? The only debate Mitt Romney clearly won was the debate in which he attacked Barack Obama and his policies boldly and without hesitation. Obama was rocked back on his heels and had no answers to rebut Romney's comments and questions. Mitt Romney's rating shot sky-high the next day. Then, during the next debate, Romney backed-off and returned to Conservative complacency of being 'nice guy.' His rating immediately plummeted - and he lost the race. What does that say about campaign and persuasion tactics?

In addition to John Hawkins ideas, I have two others to offer. First - Barack Obama can never be personally attacked. He is black. Black people will interpret that as an attack against his 'blackness.' Instead, his policies should be clearly identified and viciously attacked - one by one - as policies that will destroy our nation and poor people - especially black people. Those policies are identified within this book.

Second, many of the Liberals' pointed attacks should be

answered with a Biblical question. Don't explain the Bible reference, but let it fester in the mind of the attacker. For example: "Do you have any idea what Leviticus, in the Bible, says about that?" (Leviticus 18:22, is a reference to homosexuality.) Many blacks relate to Christianity and the Bible - perhaps they might wonder about the Liberal attacker's response.

Why is this special information important, now? Because I don't believe Barack Obama will go peacefully from his powerful position as president of the United States. The longer he maintains clear and unquestioned leadership power, the stronger that threat becomes. He must be discredited - where truthful, and appropriate - as strongly and as often as feasible. And, it must begin before his devious plan goes too far to turn back.

If, perchance, Barack Obama does not succeed in maintaining power as president after his legally elected term, his successor-in-waiting is likely Hillary Clinton. Obviously, she will use the same tactics as Obama, since they succeeded for him. If that happens, a day should not go by without the statement splattered all over the airwaves - "What difference does it make?"

About the Author

Will Clark's author experiences began by writing inspection and evaluation reports in the U.S. Air Force. He is a retired Air Force officer and a Vietnam veteran, serving in Saigon from 1966 to 1967. His other overseas assignments include Misawa, Japan and Ankara, Turkey.

In 1995, he authored a book, 'How to Learn,' as a county-wide study skills project to encourage students to improve their grades in DeSoto County, Mississippi. Education supporters printed and distributed four thousand copies. He also wrote a weekly education column for a local newspaper, The Desoto County Tribune.

His next published book was 'School Bells and Broken Tales,' a parody of nursery rhyme characters, also a motivation and education book for children. His other books include 'Shades of Retribution,' a historical novel, and 'Simply Success,' a motivation guide for students and employees.

His action novels include a trilogy based on Atlantis and crystals. The first book is titled: 'The Atlantis Crystal.' The second book is titled: 'She Waits In Atlantis.' The third is: 'Return to Atlantis.' This trilogy is based on his travels while assigned to Turkey, site of the ancient city of Troy. While in Turkey, he visited the ruins of Troy and the seven biblical churches described in the Bible Book of Revelation.

His last novel, '666: Mark of the Beast,' is a sequel to his previous book, 'America 20XX: The New World Order.'

Clark and his wife, Marie, live in Diamondhead, Mississippi, where they play golf with many friends.

King Obama

Update Added

An article by Todd Starnes of Foxnews.com, July 29, 2013, gives even more information of Islamic bias in our schools - as a religion of 'peace.' In his article, Starnes writes:

"A world history book used in an Advanced Placement class is under review by a Florida school board over allegations it favors Islam at the expense of Christianity and Judaism. State Rep. Ritch Workman told Fox News the Prentice World History textbook rewrites Islamic history and presents a biased version of the Muslim faith. "The book has a 36-page chapter on Islam but no chapters on Christianity or Judaism," Workman said. "It's remarkably one-sided."

The textbook is being used in an Advanced Placement class in Brevard County schools. The book is on a state-approved list and has been used in the school system for the past three years without any complaints. Workman said he received a copy of the book and he said it's clear the authors "make a very obvious attempt not to insult Islam by reshaping history." "If you don't see it from the eyes of a parent, kids are going to take this book as gospel and believe that Christians and Jews were murderous barbarians and thank God the Muslims came along and the world is great," he said.

For example, Workman said a reference to Mohammed and his armies taking over Medina states, "people happily accepted Islam as their way of life. It leaves out that tens of thousands of Jews and non-believers were massacred by Mohammed's armies," he said. "It's a blatant deception."

"The book indicates that Jesus proclaimed himself to be the Messiah while stating as fact that Mohammed is a prophet,"` Workman said. Students are also given lessons on the Koran and the five pillars of Islam. They don't do that for Christianity,"

Related Books by the Author

AMERICA 20XX:
THE NEW WORLD ORDER
Synopsis

Vision is the new federal constabulary force established by U.S. President Arabar when funding is not available for states and municipalities to fund their own police and security forces. This major funding crisis results from the continuing rise in oil prices. Oil prices are controlled by an Islamic king, King Rayeed, determined to execute a successful jihad in America. He knows he must destroy America's strength before he can attack his final target, Israel.

President Arabar, conspiring with King Rayeed, refuses to use American resources to avert the crisis. Pretending to increase development of ethanol to counter that crisis, Arabar creates a food shortage crisis.

Vision increases its numbers by using jihadists smuggled into the United States through the porous Texas and Arizona borders. Their first act is to confiscate registered weapons from gun owners. Then they plan to rush in more Vision troops by ship to expand control. They are free to act as security forces because President Arabar has ordered our military forces to stand down and be prepared to guard against a foreign aerial attack.

The Texas governor, cooperating with Arizona Governor Ann Melody, enlists the help of his good friend, a retired Marine named Carl Brannan, to slow the invasion. Brannan forms a network of old friends throughout America to defeat the invasion. Their first goal is to thwart Vision's efforts to confiscate personal weapons. They do this by giving receipts for the weapons using Vision's receipt documents. Brannan and his three partners continue to harass Vision departments and installations, giving hope to others that someone is resisting the jihad.

Eventually, Brannan and his group are captured. To quell all resistance, President Arabar plans their public hanging in the National Mall. He is pleased when a million citizens show up to witness the event. Just before the levers are pulled, a million citizens point their weapons at Arabar and the hundred jihadists guarding the event.

Given the option of facing charges of treason or exiling himself to another country, Arabar chooses exile to King Rayeed's country. When he arrives, he gets the same homecoming as Saddam Hussein's sons-in-law. Before he left the United States he signed documents contrary to Islamic principles and beliefs.

Governor Ann Melody is elected president to reestablish a government based on the U.S. Constitution. John Marker, the Texas Governor, returns to Texas, to his favorite fishing hole.

666: MARK OF THE BEAST
Synopsis

This story depicts a scenario of how and why the Battle of Armageddon might evolve in the near future. Although fictional, it incorporates current events and international relationships to show this evil and evolving situation. It begins with the question: Who is most likely to initiate that apocalyptic battle against Israel? That answer is simple, by considering who wants to destroy Israel at this very moment. It's the radical Islamic nations. They will stop at nothing to destroy Israel.

The leader of that battle will be the one-world leader at that time. This means the one-world leader must be a Muslim or a Muslim supporter. Muslims might even consider him their Messiah, while he pretends to be the other Messiah. That leader is described in the Bible as the 'Deceiver.'

When his reign begins he will be lauded as a 'man of peace' and will be respected and revered by all nations. His power will begin by becoming leader of the ten European nations (the countries of the north) that once were part of the Roman Empire.

Through treaties, sanctions, and threats, he will disarm countries and make them vulnerable to his real plans of destruction. He will also initiate his 'mark' to allow people to transact business. Without his mark, people will not be allowed to buy or sell items. The mark will be an interactive computer chip that will identify each person as a follower of the one-world leader. Once he has computer control over every person, he will evolve into the 'Beast' and begin his inhuman acts against humanity.

This book considers three situations. First, citizens must decide if they want to accept the Beast's mark so they can continue to live normally. They ask how can they live like humans if they can't buy or sell anything. Second, if they refuse the mark how can they survive, especially when the Beast's enforcers are trying to track them down and kill them. The Beast is enforcing his condition of 'homogeneity' whereby the population must be controlled within acceptable environmental factors. Third, the Beast must destroy America's strength to allow his final attack on Israel. What will happen to Israel? What will happen to America? The deadly Battle of Armageddon is the final scene in the book.

Other Books by the Author

Novels:
Shades of Retribution
The Atlantis Crystal
She Waits in Atlantis
Return to Atlantis

Childrens' Books
Forest Trails and Fairy Tales
Wishing Wells and Broken Tales
Student Study Skills
American Heroes: Students Who Learn

Non-Fiction:
Simply Success
The Education Jungle
How to Learn
The Day America Died
Obama's Ring: The Seat of Satan
Managing Without Conflict
The Peer Pressure Monster

King Obama

10 Blogs by the Author

Go to
Authorsden.com
to see more.

1. Very strange — I just saw a news report that some terrorists were foiled in their plot to spread nerve gas and mustard gas in the United States and Europe. That was only two minutes ago as I type this message. At the same time, I was thinking of how to incorporate my fictional account of how terrorists moved canisters of gas across our southern borders to use in attacks against Americans. That fictional account is in my novel, 'America 20XX: The New World Order.'

In my new writing (fictional) I'm going to show how a leader who wants to be 'President for life' could allow or create a terrorist incident that would allow him to reasonably declare 'martial law' and eliminate voting until the crisis was over. Of course, in reality, we know that could never happen in America?

In this current news report, the really strange coincidence is that the mode of delivery is eerily similar. In my book, the gas canisters were dropped by parachute from ultra-lite aircraft onto the desert in a designated area seen only in a black light mode from above. Those gas canisters were to be used by terrorists waiting on the ground with their black light detectors. The news report I just heard said that in the foiled attempt, terrorists planned to release gas from toy airplanes. The purpose for the story in my book is to demonstrate that there is no limit to the possibilities terrorists will use to attack us.

Another example in my book, is that toy remote controlled boats can also be used in devious and cunning terrorists activities. This example in the book demonstrates how a toy boat could deliver a leader-line to the opposite side of the Rio Grande near El Paso to transfer weapons underwater during the dead of night. Does this seem far-fetched? Look into the mind of a dedicated and desperate terrorist and realize that nothing is impossible or inconceivable. That reality is the purpose for that book.

2. Recently, I posted a blog reporting information about the new NSA spy center being built in Utah. That blog includes this quote:

"A new story in Wired Magazine reveals details about how the National Security Agency is quietly building the largest spy center in the country in Bluffdale, Utah, as part of a secret surveillance program codenamed "Stellar Wind." According to investigative reporter James Bamford, the NSA has established listening posts throughout the nation to collect and sift through billions of email messages and phone calls, whether they originate within the country or overseas.

The Utah spy center will contain near-bottomless databases to store all forms of communication collected by the agency. This includes the complete contents of private emails, cell phone calls and Google searches, as well as all sorts of personal data trails including: parking receipts, travel itineraries, bookstore purchases and other digital "pocket litter."

According to this report, this center will have almost endless ability to collect data. Built under the Obama administration, this is a highly dangerous endeavor that will curtail our liberty and freedom - in the name of safety and security. This concept is based on Maslow's 'Hierarch of Needs' motivation theory: survival, safety, belonging, esteem, self-actualization. Accordingly, the safety need must be fulfilled before the higher-order needs can affect one's motivations. 'Stellar Wind' is to focus our thoughts only on safety and security, disregarding liberty and freedom. In observing Obama's actions and words - he knows exactly what he's doing to destroy our once great nation. What could be planned?

When IRS data and health care data are merged into this system, the government will know - INSTANTLY - when you sneeze or buy a roll of toilet paper. For women, they will know the ovulation period by their purchases. They will know who is incontinent and who is buying birth control items. Although at the moment they haven't banned firearms, they will know the instant you buy a hunting rifle, shotgun, or pistol - including air rifles; and they will know the serial numbers and the amount of ammunition: instantly! The next step will be universal firearm registration, so there will be no secret threats to the pending total government autocratic takeover.

Then, what's the next step? A cashless society - so every transaction must be recorded. And, what's the next step? Read Revelation, Chapter 13, Verses 16-18.

3. Many who read my blogs that are usually highly-charged against Barack Obama's leadership and actions might wonder if I've lost my mind - if I'm off my rocker. I often wonder that, even myself, until another event pops up that slams the same questions in my face: Is he telling the truth? Is that in the best interest of America?

If there weren't so many of his followers who worship him as their God, I wouldn't spend so much of my time researching and writing about his deviations and the danger I feel he presents to our country. But, with nearly half our population instinctively believing that their Obama God can do no wrong, there must be someone who questions that religious devoutness. There must be some balance to reason. He can remain in control of our wonderful country, forever, with only a gentle support from an undecided few. Hillary Clinton and Joe Biden are looking forward to their opportunity for 2016. There's a strong possibility they will never get that chance. Obama's worshipers will demand his presence. And, don't be fooled - there are ways he can do it.

Who could stop him? Our Constitution has no definition of how to stop one who would assume total power - even if the Supreme Court condemns it. Our military is not allowed to act!

Obama's whole time in office has been one long deception, beginning with his birth certificate. Why did it take him over a year to finally present one that he claims is his. Why did he send a special courier to Hawaii to retrieve it? He doesn't allow information to be presented to Congress about 'Operation Fast and Furious.' What happened to 2500 high-powered weapons. Then there's the Benghazi question: who ordered the military stand down? Obama is stifling that information - only the president has the authority to do that. What was he doing while four patriots were being slaughtered valiantly serving their country? Does anyone really believe he was not involved with the IRS targeting of his opponents? Why did his IRS chief visit his office 157 times during that activity? These are enough examples - there are too many to list during the next eight hours.

With all my posts about Obama, some might wonder if I'm concerned about my welfare and safety. I'm human - of course I'm concerned, but not to the point of being paralyzed by fear. At 74, I've lived almost one-third the life of our great nation. It's been a wonderful life of ups and downs, fear and delight, and wins and losses. With that experience, the thing I see now for our country is danger that it's never faced before. A younger person ordinarily doesn't have the freedom to express some things, even if he or she understands. The family and making a living must take priority. The worst Obama can do to me is make me disappear. Could he also make FOX news disappear? Interesting.

4. I had one of the greatest experiences of my life this morning. Of course, just living life with a lovely family and with many good friends is a fantastic journey, but this was very different on an even more personal level. If you read my blog posts you know most are very serious. That's because I'm

a retired military officer who still respects the oath to defend my country against all enemies - foreign and domestic. Now, I feel the most serious threats to our freedom is from within. However, ordinarily in my day-to-day life I have a much softer side. I can find happiness in just exploring the feeling of taking in a full breath of air. I am aware God put the air there for me to breath.

For some reason, this morning was special. I did my usual: got up at five, had my cereal, put a cup of water in the microwave to make coffee, then went outside to get the paper so it would be on the table for my wife when she got up.

Before I leaned over to pick up the paper, I stopped in total awe. There were at least five different types of birds chirping and singing all around me - the world was totally alive with majestic sounds. Instinctively, I looked up and said, "Thank you, God." (Even sitting inside, now, at my computer, I still hear the mocking birds loud mouths chirping.)

Before I picked up the paper, I listened to all the individual songs and tried to imagine - Why? Then my inner voice answered that it was to help start the day with beauty - to begin on the positive side with a feeling that all life is precious. Then I tried to imagine what it would be like if there were no precious sounds to begin the day. There would be only a weird silence of our globe whirling through space - if that makes a sound. The other would be the sound of blood swishing its way through our arteries and veins. Can you imagine the distraction of only hearing blood pulsate past your ear sensors?

Then, I imagined further and considered that every space of our earth is filled with life: germs filling the air; and worms, mold, germs, and many other large and small creatures occupying the dirt. The last thing I murmured to myself before I picked up the paper was, "Can you imagine anyone not believing God exists - and His existence is to make life wonderful for his followers here on earth."

5. I keep trying to work on my new novel, 'From Troy to

Ephesus,' but I keep getting distracted with more revelations about Obama's intentions for our great country. I just recalled that not a single cabinet member, advisor, or supporter of Obama has ever had anything positive to say about America. Then I remembered something about Samantha Power that I had reviewed before. She is Obama's new choice to be the Ambassador to the United Nations, replacing Susan Rice. I'll report on anti-American stances of Susan Rice and John Kerry later. But now for Samantha Power:

Philip Klein of the Washington Examiner reported that in a 2003 op-ed attacking the Bush administration in the liberal 'New Republic,' Samantha Power proposed a "doctrine of the mea culpa" that would supposedly raise America's stature in the eyes of the world, likening it to the historic example of German Chancellor Willy Brandt kneeling at a Warsaw ghetto memorial. She wrote:

"We need a historical reckoning with crimes committed, sponsored, or permitted by the United States. This would entail restoring FOIA to its pre-Bush stature, opening the files, and acknowledging the force of a mantra we have spent the last decade promoting in Guatemala, South Africa, and Yugoslavia. A country has to look back before it can move forward. Instituting a doctrine of the mea culpa would enhance our credibility by showing that American decision-makers do not endorse the sins of their predecessors. When Willie Brandt went down on one knee in the Warsaw ghetto, his gesture was gratifying to World War II survivors, but it was also ennobling and cathartic for Germany. Would such an approach be futile for the United States?"

Klein's report continues, "Contrary to Democrat accusations that Romney made up the apology tour scenario out of thin air, Power is on record pushing for U.S. foreign policy to be completely re-worked so as to tell the world we are sorry. Power even implied that the kinds of horrors Nazis committed toward Jews have been carried out by the U.S. against other people around the world. In that context, Obama's visit to Allied-bombed Dresden, on a tour that included the Buchenwald concentration camp, may seem to make sense after all."

Clearly, Samantha Power is a real danger to the security of the United States by any exercise of power or influence in or near the White House. Since she was also involved in the Benghazi event, clearly her promotion to a higher level and more visible position is her reward for being a 'good soldier' for Obama's plans for America. His plans, certainly most devious, cannot be for the betterment of freedom and democracy. If that's not the case, then why is he keeping so many secrets? Why is everyone in his administration refusing to tell the truth, or anything, about their activities? They are hiding everything. Why? Does Samantha Power need to be representing the United States in a United Nations forum?

6. While I was having my first cup of coffee this morning and watching Fox News to catch up on overnight events my mind wandered off a little into 'What If' land. Then one of the TV hosts said, "And, if you have an ADT security camera in your home, the government can even be watching everything you do." This was referencing the NSA security question. Since I was an ADT distribution manager for several years, that caught my attention and sent my thoughts into overdrive. It reminded me of Winston in George Orwells' book about Big Brother. Winston was the main character, trying to find peace within the system. The telescreen was always watching him. He finally found a hideaway to make love with a woman, but that was also a trap.

Written in 1949, Orwell's idea of an all-intrusive telescreen was somewhat futuristic, but it's an idea that exploded beyond imagination. Now, that telescreen that could be seen and somewhat avoided at that time has taken on a different character. Now that 'telescreen' can be the size of a pinhead, placed anywhere, and transmitting a wireless signal. As a fiction writer, can you imagine the implications of that? In the name of 'safety and security' our not-too-transparent government is moving further away from individual liberty and freedom. The scrutiny gets tighter.

What are these implications for a fiction writer? Suppose your writing sees a few years into the future, such as a scene I used a few years ago with a cell phone thrown on a garbage truck to escape pursuers. The bad guys tracked the cell phone to the garbage dump, instead of following the good guys. Now, that wouldn't be an unusual scenario.

Now, the bad guys can watch you from the sky and fire a bullet from a drone right through your heart. But, suppose in your writing, you included an imagined event known only to the secret intelligence world as reality. What might happen to you? Where would the telescreen be watching you; how many telescreens; and could they see you in the dark? Could Big Brother analyze the document section of your computer? If you tried to write a novel by hand, instead of typing on the computer, would that be considered a dangerous activity by a Big Brother government?

These are similar questions Winston faced. He didn't know who was watching, where they were watching or how often they were watching. Although Winston never did anything wrong he didn't escape. He didn't even know what he didn't escape from. Big Brother needed too much security.

7. I've been somewhat criticized recently by two of my Authorsden friends about my over-zealous criticism of Barack Obama, especially pertaining to my interpretation of his actions regarding Muslims, socialism, etc. I also learned that my observations were 'nonsense.' I was also informed that Obama is a 'good man' and a 'true American.' So, taking those comments to heart, I will present a blog about Obama without those criticisms and 'nonsense.' In this blog, I will only ask questions.

1. If Obama is a 'good man' why did he cast aside and abandon his long-time 'good friend' and mentor, Jeremiah Wright, when Wright became a burden to him?

2. If he is a 'true American' why did he not criticize the Black Panther members who intimidated white voters at a voting place in Philadelphia during the 2008 campaign? Why

did he allow Eric Holder to dismiss that case?

3. If Obama is a 'true American' why did he label a young white police officer a racist for questioning a black man who appeared to be breaking into a house - although it was his house? Wouldn't a 'good man' have asked for the facts before condemning someone - and calling him a racist?

4. Why did Barack Obama refuse to allow Eric Holder to give Congress information about operation 'Fast and Furious?' Operation Fast and Furious resulted in the loss of over 2000 weapons, the deaths of hundreds of Mexicans, and the death of a Border Patrol agent. Doesn't Congress and citizens have a right to know why one of our own was murdered? What happened to most of the 2000 weapons? Why did his administration order 1.6 billion rounds of ammunition for similar weapons?

5. During the 2012 campaign, although Obama didn't personally criticize the TEA party, his staff were totally vitriolic against them. As a result, obviously to support Obama, did the IRS intimidate TEA party groups who submitted for tax-exempt status? If Obama wasn't involved, why did the IRS head visit the White House at least 51 times that year?

6. Why did Barack Obama not censure, reprimand, or ask for Eric Holder's resignation when Holder falsely accused a news reporter of being a participant in a criminal activity? Does that sound like a good man or a true American?

7. To me, the Benghazi event raises the most serious questions for a Commander-in-Chief. Where was Barack Obama during the Benghazi activity? He has never said. Where was Hillary Clinton during the massacre of four brave Americans fighting for their lives? She has never said. Military units were on stand-by to intervene - to try to offer aid to those four people who knew they were going to die if they didn't get help. Stand-by units were told to stand down. Who gave that order? Where was Barack Obama? He refuses to say where he was or what he was doing. Is that the response of a 'true American?' Is that not the responsibility of a real Commander-in-Chief?

8. What's Obama's real purpose for the secret program "Stellar Wind" being built in Bluffdale, Utah? It can review phone calls and emails of every person on earth. What are his plans for it?

9. How does Barack Obama keep his hands clean from all the negative activity and scandals in his administration? Why doesn't he say where he is when all these things are happening? Is he perpetrating these activities - then hiding from scrutiny?

10. Finally, why does every discussion of Barack Obama's weaknesses always involve a comparison with George W. Bush? Should Obama be compared to other presidents, forever, or should he be evaluated on fulfilling his own responsibilities as the current president of the United States? George Bush is not the president - and he is prohibited by the Constitution from ever being president again!

8. Is he a radical Conservative who's lost control of all logic and self-control? Asking this question of myself, of course, as I'm sure many readers of this blog often ask - or shake their heads in confusion and frustration with some of my comments. Actually, the answer is - no. I consider myself a Constitutionalist with individual opinions about certain political matters.

For example, I think it's a dangerous situation when both houses of Congress and the president are all controlled by the same party - be that Democrat or Republican. One of the three must be of the other party to keep the checks and balances as planned by our Constitution.

Did I support George W. Bush's rush to declare war on Iraq? Absolutely not! Sadam Hussein was no threat to the United States. Furthermore, Sadam Hussein's regime was the only power keeping Iran under control. They would not have allowed Iran to develop nuclear weapons! Their hatred of each other was too deep. Removing Hussein opened 'Pandora's Box.' The U.S. cannot be the police for every action throughout the world. Our first defense must be for our own citizens. Let the Islamists focus on themselves, as they have for hundreds of years, not on us. They likely will never find peace among themselves.

And, a question that many must ask is why I criticize Barack Obama so often. Actually, I don't think he directly means harm to our country. My own belief is that he is inexperienced and incompetent, and allows so much confusion that others are taking advantage. For example, on one side the Socialists are trying to slip in their charter. While, at the same time, the radical Islamists are trying to slip in the back door. In the confusion, Obama allows both to gain further advantage. In the meantime, he's only concerned about votes - for himself, and for the 2014 campaigns so he can gain both houses of Congress.

My Conservative biases appear more on the subjects of personal development, fair share, spread the wealth, and criticizing 'evil rich people.' Obama promises too much to too many people - just for their votes. Certainly, everybody should have enough to live comfortably and decently, but there should be some personal effort by individuals to achieve those conditions. My bias on this topic comes from my own family life.

My mom was born in 1921 to a sharecroppers' family. Her mother died when she was the oldest of seven siblings, at ten-years-old. She had to quit school to become the family 'mother' caregiver. She went no further than the third grade. When I was six, she started working at a shirt factory, the only industry in town. When she got off work, she then worked until dark in our cotton field, corn field, and garden. Then she spent weekends canning food and washing clothes - before running water and electricity - which we didn't have until I was twelve. She loved America, her children and her grandchildren - and she made sure I graduated high school by helping the best she could with my lessons each night. She was always there. I was the first of my extended family to graduate from high school. Her last thoughts when she left us, at eighty, was what would happen to her great-grandchildren. She was the perfect example of one who cared and one who never gave up.

Why do I criticize Obama's 'fair share' and 'spread the wealth around' comments and ideas so vehemently? He is telling people to wait and he will take care of them. That's an insult to every American - and my mom. That's denying people, who need it most, the right to work for pride and a feeling of a 'job well done.' It's also an insult to the idealisms of the American way of life. I'm not sure, but I don't think God put us here on earth to 'wait for free stuff.' Obama should encourage people to work for pride and success - not wait for it.

9. An article reported by Clash Daily.com on March 4, 2013 reminded me of George Orwell's description of actions by the 'Thought Police.' The Thought Police (thinkpol in Newspeak) are the secret police of Oceania in George Orwell's dystopian novel '1984.' This is the article:

"Yet another student has been suspended for having something that represents a gun, but isn't actually anything like a real gun. This time, it was a breakfast pastry.

Josh Welch, a second-grader at Park Elementary School in Baltimore, Maryland, was suspended for two days because his teacher thought he shaped the strawberry, pre-baked toaster pastry into something resembling a gun. WBFF, the FOX affiliate in Baltimore, broke the story.

Welch, an arty kid who has reportedly been diagnosed with attention deficit hyperactivity disorder, said his goal was to turn it into a mountain, but that didn't really materialize, reports Fox News.

"It was already a rectangle. I just kept on biting it and biting it and tore off the top of it and kind of looked like a gun," he said. "But it wasn't," the seven-year-old astutely added.

The boy's teacher was not happy with his creation. "She was pretty mad, and I think I was in big trouble," Welch told the FOX affiliate."

This story is only one example of what's happening to

innocent Americans every day. Even countless young children have been harassed and abused for things done ordinarily and naturally without a thought of hurting anyone. Just wait until it reaches the adult level - perhaps it already has?

In Orwell's book it's the job of the Thought Police to uncover and punish thought-crime and thought-criminals. They use psychology and omnipresent surveillance (such as telescreens) to search, find, monitor and arrest members of society who could potentially challenge authority and status quo, even only by thought, hence the name Thought Police.

10. Before I became focused on the dangerous threat Barack Obama is to our great nation, I was more focused on researching and writing about the education dilemma in America and what we could do to improve it. Improving education effectiveness is not only helping students, individually, to become successful and productive, it's another link in the important chain to protect America.

A more educated society is certainly a society that can more easily recognize and interpret the dangers from within - such as exist today. With 30 percent of our students becoming disillusioned and dropping out of school, how can we expect to continue our great country at the level which it has existed all these years?

Last month I wrote a 'letter to the editor,' locally, expressing my concern about the waste of taxpayer money on the new rush to 'Pre-K' education. Two educators responded saying that my reference to justify my position was 'outdated.' This is a copy of the letter I just submitted in reply to that letter:

"In a previous letter, I wrote that Pre-K education is a futile endeavor that wastes taxpayer money. Two educators disagreed, and said the study I referenced was outdated. Strange - because it's the same study that's still the basis for current school integration, busing, and 'social capital' concepts and programs.

That study is the 'Equality of Educational Opportunity

Survey,' called the 'Coleman Report,' named for Professor James Coleman. His survey was the largest ever conducted, over a two-year period beginning in 1964. It included over 4000 schools, 60,000 teachers, and 570,000 students. In 1966, the research team concluded, "the social class of the student body was the determining factor in education - not school curriculum or school quality." Coleman said, "Families make the difference, not schools." Their conclusion did not support the purpose for the survey, which was to prove that schools getting more funding were more successful.

Coleman's survey is the only objective major national education survey ever done. Current studies and surveys are now designed to prove a conclusion made before the survey. They are most often conducted by those with something to sell, such as curriculum developers or training programs - or those who want to create more jobs to get more taxpayers money.

From objective research, Pre-K education does help students to the third grade. After that, the family influence becomes the overbearing factor to education success. Dropouts are our greatest education and social dilemma - 30 percent - not standardized test scores. Yet, society ignores this greater tragedy."

End

www.ingramcontent.com/pod-product-compliance
Lightning Source LLC
Chambersburg PA
CBHW070848290526
45795CB00001B/29